17 Days and
17 Miles Apart

Also by Donald J. Porter

*A Jet Powered Life: Allen E. Paulson,
Aviation Entrepreneur* (McFarland, 2019)

17 Days and 17 Miles Apart

The Crashes of TWA Flight 529 and Northwest Flight 706

Donald J. Porter

McFarland & Company, Inc., Publishers
Jefferson, North Carolina

ISBN (print) 978-1-4766-9606-5
ISBN (ebook) 978-1-4766-5499-7

Library of Congress cataloging data are available

Library of Congress Control Number 2025000329

© 2025 Donald J. Porter. All rights reserved

No part of this book may be reproduced or transmitted in any form or by any means, electronic or mechanical, including photocopying or recording, or by any information storage and retrieval system, without permission in writing from the publisher.

Front cover image: crash of TWA Flight 529, taken in the early morning hours the day of the crash (courtesy of Clarendon Hills Historical Society).

Printed in the United States of America

*McFarland & Company, Inc., Publishers
Box 611, Jefferson, North Carolina 28640
www.mcfarlandpub.com*

To my late mother, Elsie,
who inspired me to pursue writing,
and to my wife, Rita, for nurturing that career.

Table of Contents

Preface   1
Introduction   5

1. California Bound   9
2. The Crash   22
3. Nightmare   39
4. Smoking Gun   51
5. Who Did It?   69
6. Howard Hughes   79
7. Scary Flights   93
8. Difficult Day   113
9. Coincidence?   126
10. Aftermath   148

Chapter Notes   167
Bibliography   177
Index   181

Preface

It's likely that some of the stories revealed in this book might never have been told. It is also amazing that what happened at two major airlines more than a half century ago is now influencing the safety of jetliners designed and built by Boeing.

In questioning teenagers or young adults about how many airline crashes happen each year in the United States, the responses are often predictable. Many of them falsely assume that modern airliners never crash.

During marginal weather conditions on February 12, 2009, while enroute from Newark, New Jersey, to Buffalo, New York, a fatal accident involved a twin-engine Bombardier DHC-8-400 turboprop. Colgan Air, Inc. (now a defunct regional air carrier) employed its pilots. Designated Flight 3407, it was being flown under a codeshare agreement called Continental Connection for the benefit of mainline carrier Continental Airlines.

Flying blind through foggy and icing conditions, its pilots lost control while preparing to land at the airport in Buffalo. Descending in poor visibility, the airliner stalled, slamming into a house in a neighborhood known as Clarence Center. Carrying a heavy load of ice, the Q400 exploded in flames on impact. The crash killed all 49 passengers and crewmembers aboard, along with an occupant of the house. The distracted captain had not responded properly to an audible stall warning. Far worse, the crew failed to monitor the plane's airspeed and activate its deicing system during the severe icing conditions.[1]

The Colgan accident brought about nationwide concern over airline safety. It also resulted in the implementation of additional training for flight crews at all of the nation's air carriers.

Throughout this country on any given day, well over 100,000 airline

Preface

flights are thought to be as safe (or safer) than riding in a car, bus or taxicab. Unlike a half century ago, today's well-trained pilots, automated flight control systems, increased radar coverage, redundant instrumentation, reliable jet engines, and sophisticated maintenance practices provide those safeguards. They prevent the kinds of fatal mistakes that had been common in the past.

So-called "near misses" involving airliners flying in and out of the nation's major airports still occur, mostly due to air traffic controllers having insufficient training. The excellent safety record for airline maintenance is well documented. But in the past, for passengers who were forced to travel aboard fleets of older airliners, they weren't nearly as fortunate.

You are about to learn about the crash of Flight 529, a piston-powered Model 049 Lockheed Constellation operated by Trans World Airlines. The crash resulted in the deaths of all 78 passengers and crewmembers aboard. A front-page story on newspapers throughout the Labor Day weekend in 1961, the loss was the worst accident of a single airliner in United States history. It held that record until American Airlines Flight 191, a McDonnell Douglas DC-10, crashed immediately after takeoff from O'Hare International Airport in Chicago on May 25, 1979. The crash killed all 273 people aboard, the worst air tragedy for years to come. Ironically, the crash occurred due to poor aircraft design and the failure of an engine mount resulting in the loss of all hydraulic system control.[2]

TWA Flight 529 crashed about nine miles west of Chicago's Midway Airport, adjacent to a suburban community in Illinois known as Clarendon Hills. A bolt was said to have fallen out from the Constellation's tail assembly onto a farm field or maybe a homeowner's backyard. Over the course of a yearlong Civil Aeronautics Board investigation, it was never found. This meant that an exact cause of the crash would be impossible for the investigators to determine. The missing bolt, along with its companion cotter pin, created endless controversy with anyone having a connection to the accident or working in the aviation industry.

Seventeen days after this crash, Flight 706, a Northwest Airlines Lockheed L-188 turboprop Electra, crashed at O'Hare International Airport and killed the 37 people aboard. It was a shocking coincidence.

None of the people having a connection to either crash admitted guilt and the government closed out its investigations shortly after they

Preface

were finished. But a nagging question remained unanswered: Did an intentional act cause both of the planes to crash or were they due to pilot error or maintenance oversight?

Following the Constellation crash, TWA officials sent the next of kin of its dead passengers a brief letter acknowledging the loss of their loved ones. Some had lost children in the crash. The compensation they later received was little more than payment for funeral services. Even today, the next of kin remember their loved ones—and have little respect for what was once known as Trans World Airlines.

The 78 passengers and crewmembers were killed because their plane had climbed at a sharp nose-high angle, completely out of control, followed by a rapid descent, then smashed into a cornfield, and burst into flames. After the government investigators concluded that a missing bolt had caused the crash, other concerns surfaced regarding the design of not only the ill-fated plane but also every other Constellation built by Lockheed. Many accidents and incidents involving its planes resulted from malfunctions or failures of their flight control systems.

The government said one thing and the airline something else. Because TWA never assumed responsibility, few lawsuits were filed. Throughout the investigation, TWA appeared to call all the shots. Meanwhile, its lawyers made sure that the airline didn't get blamed for mistakes that Lockheed could have made.

The final unanswered question had to do with what actually caused the crash. Howard Hughes, the airline's billionaire owner, was a principal suspect. It's possible his interference could have derailed the government's investigative work. Owning 78 percent of all TWA stock could have had something to do with it. He or someone else at his airline had made a decision to ignore what the investigators uncovered, with its findings being pushed aside.

After more than six decades from the time of these crashes, the losses of both TWA 529 and Northwest 706 are largely forgotten. Their airlines are no longer in business, and Lockheed stopped manufacturing commercial airliners after producing hundreds of Constellations and Electras. Industrialist Howard Robard Hughes, Jr., TWA's sole owner for decades, died at age 70 from natural causes on April 5, 1976. If his close executives were alive today, it's likely they would disagree with the conclusions offered by the government.

Although the cause remains a mystery, for anyone who was fortunate to have not boarded Flight 529, but who lost family members in the

Preface

crash, September 1, 1961, will always be remembered as though it happened yesterday.

On a final note, remember that today's airline pilots depend on a myriad of technical advances in their cockpits. It means that many of them rely on automation rather than actual hand-flying skills, this according to a recent Civil Aviation Organization study. Many of those pilots don't maintain these basic skills due to a lack of adequate practice.[3]

In today's world of air transportation, airliner flight decks require only a bare minimum of basic flying skills. Some of the training requires that a pilot only know what button to push during an emergency—assuming that the cockpit lights don't fail. Consider this possibility the next time you board an airliner. In many ways, today's cockpit automation is causing air travel to be as dangerous as it was a half century ago.

Introduction

In addition to studying English and math during my high school years, I decided to pursue another consuming interest: learning how to fly a small airplane. During the winter months of the 1960s, I began taking flying lessons at a local airport in Santa Monica, California, about five miles from my parents' home in Los Angeles. Without an automobile or even a driver's license, I regularly left the house in the early morning, boarded a city bus, and arrived at the peaceful airport in time to practice flying a Cessna 150 with a flight instructor at my side.

On one of those days, before leaving for the airport, I noticed the front page of a newspaper. The headline read: "78 People Die in Worst Air Crash." It involved TWA Flight 529, a Lockheed Constellation. Running late for a lesson to practice landings, I finally arrived at the airport and continued to think about the crash.

Seventeen days after Flight 529 crashed, a Northwest Airlines Flight 706 Electra repeated the tragedy, less than an hour's drive from where the TWA plane ended up. In common with the Constellation, everyone aboard the Electra died on impact. A lengthy investigation later revealed that a hydraulic boost system to control the plane's ailerons had malfunctioned. Apparently, a mechanic had forgotten to install a tiny piece of safety wire. More shocking, a similar mistake brought down the Constellation. It became clear to the accident investigators that mechanics at both airlines had been negligent in performing their duties.

A Constellation crashes, kills everyone aboard, but nobody seems to have an interest in pinpointing its cause. Howard Hughes, owner of TWA, with Lockheed and the FAA refused to step up and take responsibility for improving the safety of the Constellations at TWA and other airlines throughout the world.

Introduction

Toward the final months of 1969, a struggling aircraft manufacturer in Culver City, California, became one of my first employers. I had noticed that "Aircraft Division, Hughes Tool Company" was printed on my business cards.[1] Howard Hughes owned 100 percent of that company. Actually, the aircraft division in California was nothing more than an unprofitable subsidiary of his family's highly profitable Hughes Tool Company in Texas, a world-renowned manufacturer of metal bits used for oil drilling.

Months after joining the aircraft division, I discovered something I had not been aware of: the company had posted a financial deficit for more than 30 years.

During the 1970s, two new employees worked for me at the Hughes company on an aircraft project for the U.S. Army called the Advanced Attack Helicopter.[2]

A unique aircraft, it was powered by two large gas turbine engines, complex control systems, and an array of frightening ordnance capable of bringing any enemy of the United States to its knees. Both of these men had earlier been employed at TWA's maintenance hangar at Los Angeles International Airport. One of them was an expert on anything to do with Lockheed Constellations. The airline had trained him to start the planes' engines, conduct functional checks, and even taxi the planes around airports following maintenance work. He sometimes even went along on local test flights.[3] On one occasion, he told me that he accompanied several other mechanics in the cockpit to start and run up a Constellation's engines following oil changes. A different mechanic was responsible for replacing the oil in each engine. Shortly after the engines were started, their power was increased to conduct a series of routine tests.

Without warning, each engine began smoking heavily, while their oil pressures dropped significantly. Soon overheating, one of the engines caught fire. All four of the engines had just been overhauled but would need to be replaced with four new ones, an unplanned and expensive error.

The mechanic who forgot to replace the oil was later fired. A mechanic who worked with him told me he had made a fatal mistake in past years. During 1961, the Constellation that crashed near Clarendon Hills in Illinois was a frequent visitor at the Los Angeles maintenance hangar. The fired mechanic was the same person who forgot to install a bolt in the elevator mechanism of Flight 529. He had worked on that

Introduction

plane in Kansas City, Missouri. It happened while the plane was undergoing an inspection at TWA's expansive maintenance facility there. For unknown reasons, his first mistake had been forgiven—but certainly not his last.

Today, the crash of Flight 529 continues to trouble the people who helped remove dozens of mangled bodies from its crash site. Most of them are now senior citizens. Over their entire adult lives, they had been forced to live with the horror they witnessed during those unforgettable early morning hours. Even now, after decades of silence, facts concerning many details of the crash are difficult to discuss.

Over the years, the loss of both Flight 529 and Flight 706 remained in my mind. Decades later, as a longtime aviation author, I decided to write this book and reveal exactly what occurred following government investigations of the crashes. To describe many of these situations, there was no one still living to interview. To compile the stories, I was forced to rely on whatever was written by other people during careers at TWA, Lockheed, or the federal government. Assisting this effort, descriptions of victims, family members, and related people from long ago was researched by examining public documents, newspaper clippings, and in a very few cases, interviews with related figures. In conclusion, I've taken whatever facts are publicly available, combined with my decades of experience working in the aviation industry under Howard Hughes, and woven the story into a narrative that I hope you'll find both suspenseful and informative.

1

California Bound

As the 1960s began to unfold, the first years were filled with a mix of tension and excitement. What became known as the Space Race took center stage throughout the United States and much of the world. At the same time, major political conflicts were beginning to erupt on several continents. One of them was construction of the Berlin Wall, which restricted freedom of movement for millions of German citizens. And in the Soviet Union, leader Nikita Khrushchev threatened to begin a nuclear war with America.

On January 20, 1961, John F. Kennedy was inaugurated as the 35th president of the United States. Among many other tasks, he was forced to confront Khrushchev about the nuclear threat. As the relationship between the men neared a boiling point, Kennedy warned his fellow Americans to consider installing bomb shelters in the back yards of their homes. Fortunately, the threat eventually cooled off and the president's shelter precaution idea was abandoned.

On April 5, 1961, astronaut Alan Shepard, Jr., was launched into space aboard *Freedom 7*, becoming the first American to orbit the earth and complete the journey safely. A week later on April 12, cosmonaut Yuri Gagarin from the Soviet Union also completed an orbit around the earth. President Kennedy promised that America would land a man on the moon during the decade. After Kennedy's assassination on November 22, 1963, the nation went forward with the space program and delivered to every citizen in America what he had promised.

On the home front, the average price of a new automobile was about $2,850. Popular entertainment on TV at home included *The Dick Van Dyke Show*, while a top movie showing in the nation's theaters was *West Side Story*. The year 1963 also witnessed the births of future president Barack Obama and actor George Clooney.

17 Days and 17 Miles Apart

Although major changes were taking place in other countries during the 1960s, the airlines in America were also changing. Prior to World War II, Trans World Airlines, later known as TWA, had operated flights only in the United States. On July 5, 1945, the airline was granted permission by the Civil Aeronautics Board to operate two newly approved international routes. Its passengers were now able to fly from Boston, Chicago, Detroit, New York, Philadelphia, or Washington, D.C., to several cities in Europe and beyond.

High-speed, jet-powered airliners could now be seen at the nation's airports, transporting people to cities in Europe and to both coasts of the United States. Those airports had become increasingly crowded with passengers, causing the cities owning their facilities to renovate the well-worn boarding areas and expand their overflowing parking garages. The major changes were needed to accommodate a massive glut of people arriving to board flights.

For travelers having little or no interest in flying aboard the latest jets, some domestic airlines continued to operate older Lockheed Constellations and Douglas DC-7 propeller-driven airliners on routes throughout the United States. One airline providing inexpensive air travel was TWA, owned by industrialist Howard Hughes. For occasional travelers, many of those flights had rock bottom fares, compared to the prices being charged by a multitude of competitors. For many passengers planning domestic coast-to-coast trips, there was only one drawback: the airline required its ticket holders to schedule trips during nighttime hours. TWA labeled this service the "Sky Club Coach." One of those popular coast-to-coast flights was designated as Flight 529.

In order to fly across the United States to California from the East Coast, passengers purchasing tickets at TWA could board a Sky Club Coach flight at the Logan airport in Boston. Or if they wanted, they could also board at other stops like Idlewild in New York, Pittsburgh in Pennsylvania, or Midway in Chicago. Some of its well-worn Constellations could be seen traveling two thousand miles from Chicago to Las Vegas, Los Angeles, and a final destination in San Francisco.

Compared to other far faster jets, the slower piston-powered Constellations needed to stop for refueling in order to fly coast-to-coast. As an example, Flight 529 was regularly scheduled to leave Boston during the early evening hours on a Thursday and land at Los Angeles International Airport early Friday morning. It was not considered to be a

1. California Bound

nonstop flight. Passengers with a need to travel on a tight budget welcomed this Sky Club Coach service.

Those tourist-class flights were flown using older model Constellations on an exclusive basis. The planes had been refurbished with bright new fabrics fitted to all its headrests, with green, beige, and orange selected as colors. Curtains surrounding the cabin windows featured distinctive pastel shades. Center aisles of the cabins were carpeted in dark blue. Altogether, the changes were successful in transforming an earlier mundane cabin environment into a bright and cheerful one.

Howard Hughes and his executives transformed the interiors of an entire fleet of Constellations in this manner and at great cost. The process could be compared to brightening the décor of an older home by doing nothing more than painting its walls and upgrading the floors. At the airline, a goal of the major upgrade was to attract a younger generation of passengers, many never having flown before. For people living on a limited budget, a specific marketing campaign was developed to attract married couples and their children. It was the first time that TWA had moved away from serving only affluent business travelers. By doing this, it was thought that the airline might bring in anyone wishing to fly inexpensively, particularly if they wanted coast-to-coast transportation. TWA owner Hughes made sure that his airline ran advertisements in every major newspaper throughout the United States, as well as in many other newspapers overseas; they continued to publicize the airline's Sky Club Coast service.[1]

A display advertisement published in newspapers throughout the country during 1958 was used to profile the flights:

> Fly in world-proven TWA Constellations with sparkling, new décor. Enjoy complete comfort. Stretch out in deep-cushioned reclining chairs that lean far back. Cocktails, refreshing fruit, tempting snacks and hot soup are served at budget prices by attentive hostesses. Next trip, give yourself a treat. Fly Sky Club Coach ... it's the most wonderful low-fare service yet.

The advertisement went on to discuss the airline's payment plans: "Fly now ... pay later with TWA's liberal Time-Pay Plan. Only 10% down ... up to 20 months to pay the balance."[2]

The passenger terminal at Logan International Airport was built on hundreds of acres of undeveloped land, only feet away from the shoreline of the Atlantic Ocean in East Boston. Flights departing Logan could offer their passengers a stunning view of the bay passing below them on takeoff. The facility handled dozens of TWA flights each week. Throughout most of the 1960s, the airport was expanded on a continuous basis to serve countless additional travelers arriving from cities across the country. Some of the flights departed Logan for cities along the West Coast. Others were headed across the Atlantic with their passengers going to business meetings or vacations in Europe.

Four women in their early 20s, friends since childhood, had also attended high school together. They planned to fly together, relocate to California aboard Flight 529, and find jobs in the Golden State. During the late afternoon, they left their homes in Suncook, a picturesque town located in Merrimack County in New Hampshire.[3]

The only downside connected with a low airfare was a need for its planes to make several landings and takeoffs at airports in states other than Massachusetts. It also meant that passengers would have to fly all the way to California during nighttime hours.

Traveling over 2,000 miles to reach the West Coast would consume an entire evening and the early morning hours of Friday, September 1. Strapped in five-abreast passenger seats, having no middle armrests during the entire flight, meant it would become extremely tiring. Even worse, the expected boarding of additional passengers at other stops along the way would require rearranging dozens of neatly stowed suitcases and bags pushed into the overhead storage compartments. It meant that the passengers flying out of Boston would need to remain seated and not crowd the narrow center aisle while newer passengers were boarding.

Robert Aiken, a passenger boarding in Boston, was serving as a petty officer third class in the U.S. Navy. Before flying to Las Vegas aboard Flight 529, the 21-year-old lived in Silver Spring, Maryland. He had flown to Boston during a military leave to visit his younger brother, a student at the Berklee School of Music (now Berklee College of Music). A 1958 graduate of Montgomery Blair High School in Silver Spring, Aiken had earned a four-year scholarship to attend George Washington University. However, he decided to leave college after a year and join the Navy; his longtime interest was the study of atomic physics. Now in military uniform, he was assigned to serve as an instructor at an atomic support agency near Mercury, an isolated military facility in the Nevada desert north of Las Vegas.[4]

Not connected to the military was a 17-year-old passenger living in Milford, another smaller town in New Hampshire. Timothy Hubley was

1. California Bound

about to travel alone from Boston after receiving permission from his parents to board the flight. He paid for the trip with the money he had earned doing odd jobs around town during the summer months. He was planning to visit his aunt and uncle in Sun Valley, the couple living outside of metropolitan Los Angeles.[5]

In common with other infrequent air travelers, the type of airliner TWA had assigned to Sky Club Coach service made little or no difference to its passengers. Their only interest was to arrive at an eastern city, and then Las Vegas or California as fast and as cheaply as possible.

The cabin inside older Lockheed Constellations could be described as having extremely tight seating, offering only a narrow aisle for reaching seats along each side. The width of its cabin wasn't wide enough to stuff in another aisle or an additional row of seats. The plane had been modified by TWA to transport a maximum of 81 passengers. The airline's owner, Howard Hughes, bought three early model Constellations and had them flown to the Lockheed plant in California to install the latest passenger configuration. The galley was moved to the rear cabin area. The so-called "new look" consisted of nothing more than changes to the coach seats: five seats in each row with the single narrow aisle between them extending all the way to a door entering the cockpit. The result looked like a truncated narrow tube with seats pushed against doors in the front and aft ends of the cabin.

This latest design came about because a principal goal of the airline's marketing department was to sell as many tickets as possible for its coast-to-coast service. Within a few years, the entire fleet of early model Constellations would be modified this same way.

The executives at TWA were well aware that an untapped air travel market had been ignored by other airlines for years: selling economical tickets or free fares to parents to take their young children along with them. Some passengers boarding Flight 529 brought their kids with them to save whatever money they could in the process. In still another advertisement appearing in the nation's newspapers that same year, the inexpensive Sky Club Coach service was pitched to that longtime untapped market: "Low fares mean great savings for Sky Club Coach family travelers! TWA's superior new service is really designed for them, too. Children are kept delighted and busy with intriguing new color games and comic books. Bring your family along and enjoy the fun."[6]

Scheduled to board Flight 529 in Boston, Francis Gilliam, a mother from California, was likely to have seen the TWA advertisement and did exactly what it asked. Similar to what many thousands of other young women did during World War II, she had joined the U.S. Navy to serve as a member of a U.S. Navy program called Women Accepted for Volunteer Emergency Service. It was more widely known as the WAVES program. Once the war ended, she settled down and moved to a quiet neighborhood in the seaside community of Eureka in northern California, not far from the Oregon border. Employed for several years in an administrative office, she and her husband had three children, who accompanied her on this trip. Her husband planned to meet them upon their arrival at San Francisco International Airport on Friday and drive them back to Eureka.[7]

Flight 529 began its nationwide journey early Thursday evening from the airport in Boston. It was the last day of August, and the long Labor Day weekend was quickly coming up. Actually, only a dozen passengers would board the Constellation in Boston. Although many of its seats remained unoccupied, they would be snapped up quickly during the next stop in New York. The flight to Idlewild Airport on Long Island would be brief and not expected to take more than half an hour.

With the advent of jet transports, much of the traveling public had grown weary of making long, tiring flights. To fly coast-to-coast, older propeller-driven airliners took up to ten hours between first boarding and deplaning at their destinations. Constellations such as the one used for Flight 529 took even longer. Jets flown by major airlines such as TWA could double the older Constellation's speed. But the cost of tickets to fly aboard a new jetliner proved prohibitive for many customers, other than a limited number of seasoned corporate executives on their way to business meetings. Their employers generally paid for those tickets. In addition, if a passenger wanted to fly during only daylight hours, the cost of a ticket would skyrocket.

In spite of expensive tickets, the jets had a major impact on the nation's air transportation system. The newer planes were able to shrink the time spent flying over continents and oceans. They reduced coast-to-coast flight times to five hours, even with another hour spent for arrival and departure at each end of the flight. When it involved international travel, the difference was even more dramatic. London was now only seven hours from New York City via a jet. But for passengers stuck in the crowded cabin of an older Constellation, the trip could easily turn into a 12-hour ordeal.

After considering all of these issues, there was seldom a shortage of

1. California Bound

passengers willing to book cross-country flights. Many of their tickets specified California as a destination. In spite of the advantages offered by jet travel, the Constellation's relatively slow speed and "above weather" flying capability was appreciated by much of the traveling public. Its pressurized cabins were especially popular. The competitive piston-powered airliners of that era were forced to slog through exceedingly rough air thousands of feet below the cruising altitude of a Constellation. Commercial over-the-weather flight operations were made possible because of cabin pressurization systems built into the planes; those systems were previously designed for use only in military aircraft.

The elderly Constellation the passengers boarded had flown almost every day after joining TWA shortly after World War II. The streamlined, four-engine transport was one of the first airliners Lockheed delivered to the airline in December 1945. It was unique in an important way. The first scheduled international service operated by TWA was inaugurated on February 5, 1946, when the same Constellation that later crashed near Clarendon Hills, Illinois, took off from LaGuardia airport for Paris. It carried 36 passengers, a crew of eight and a load of cargo. Making refueling stops in Gander, Newfoundland, and Shannon, Ireland, the flight took almost twenty hours to reach Paris. Operating this schedule throughout the 1940s, the plane was nicknamed the Star of Paris for its many trips abroad. Compared to other airlines, it had earned this distinction by flying the largest number of passengers aboard any airliner from the United States to Europe.[8]

A day before TWA's inaugural flight to Paris, another Constellation was under the command of TWA's president, Jack Frye. He flew from Burbank to LaGuardia in the record time of just over seven hours.[9] Actually, only ten days after the European service began, the airline also began offering New York to Los Angeles flights. Not unexpected for some TWA employees: on February 15, 1946, owner Howard Hughes made a flight from Los Angeles to New York as its captain, covering the route in less than twelve hours. The flight represented a beginning of the airline's coveted coast-to-coast service with Constellations.

A TWA flight engineer assigned to Flight 529 in Boston kept busy walking around the Constellation he was about to board for Chicago. He was looking for damage to its airframe or anything else needing repair. After making sure the amount of fuel in the wing tanks was correct, he wrote up several items in his logbook that required attention. One of

17 Days and 17 Miles Apart

Form ACA 331
(2-46)

UNITED STATES OF AMERICA
DEPARTMENT OF COMMERCE
CIVIL AERONAUTICS ADMINISTRATION
WASHINGTON

AIRCRAFT

TYPE CERTIFICATE No. 763

This certificate, issued to LOCKHEED AIRCRAFT CORPORATION, certifies that the following is of proper design, material, specifications, construction, and performance for safe operation, and meets the pertinent minimum standards, rules, and regulations prescribed by the Civil Aeronautics Board:

AIRCRAFT MODELS 49-46, 49-51, 649-79 AND 749-79.

This certificate is of indefinite duration unless canceled, suspended, or revoked.

Date December 29, 1945
49-46 approved October 14, 1946
649-79 and 749-79 approved March 14, 1947

By direction of the Administrator:

(Signature) ......Charles F. Dyour......
Director, Aircraft and Components Service.

This certificate may be transferred if endorsed as provided on the back hereof.

Any alteration of this certificate is punishable by a fine of not exceeding $1,000, or imprisonment not exceeding 3 years, or both.

On December 29, 1945, the U.S. government issued type certificate number 763 approving the use of Lockheed Constellations (courtesy American Aviation Historical Society [AAHS-11522]).

1. California Bound

them was an inoperative light bulb in the plane's tail cone. He called on a TWA flight line mechanic to replace it.[10] Another item needing attention was a system used to direct refrigerated air throughout the passenger cabin. Its purpose was to make sure the passengers remained as comfortable as possible throughout the plane's longer flights. The cabins of all early Constellations were known to be stuffy, especially during hot summer days while parked on the ramp, and most of the time while in the air. Distributing cool and fresh air throughout the passenger cabin was also an important marketing consideration.[11]

To provide enough heat or cooling temperatures throughout the cabin, the output from a ground-based cooling and heating unit (its choice depending on the temperature) would be rolled across the ramp next to the plane. The device was used to pump the proper temperature airflow into the plane's circulation system. A longtime Constellation flight engineer offered his opinion why this was not always popular: "If this was not available, the passengers had the idea they were being placed in either an oven or a refrigerator."[12]

Lockheed, the plane's manufacturer, had never corrected the troublesome ventilation systems in 049 Constellations. After handling hundreds of complaints from TWA passengers over the years, the airline's mechanics installed a large blower on a bulkhead below the ceiling at the front of the passenger cabin. It was considered better than nothing and circulated an increased amount of air throughout the cabin.

During 1956, the engineers at TWA, with Lockheed's inattention to the longstanding ventilation issue, designed an improved cabin cooling system. It was similar in concept to the older system that seldom worked properly. TWA went on to develop and certify the updated system. Ten years after the airline first introduced Constellations, it also installed air conditioning systems with individual "eyeball" outlets to direct cold air onto passengers and crewmembers occupying each seat. The system was installed at considerable expense in all Model 049 Constellations. Unfortunately, once again, its reliability never met expectations. Not surprisingly, Lockheed refused to pay for any of those expensive modifications.

There wasn't enough time in Boston before Flight 529's departure to troubleshoot and repair the ventilating system. Instead, a decision was made to instruct each flight engineer assigned to a given flight to manually adjust the Constellation's cabin altitude to correspond with the altitude of various airports where the plane was intending to land.[13]

17 Days and 17 Miles Apart

While departing, the cabin was unpressurized until reaching 6,000 feet, when the plane was then pressurized to the field elevation of its next stop. The procedure was repeated after each route stop to cool down the cabin for passenger comfort.

After making several interim stops, the crew would take Flight 529 all the way to Chicago. Meanwhile, TWA workers stationed around the ramp kept busy loading suitcases, shipping boxes, heavy sacks of mail, and even a large quantity of U.S. currency. The latter was being moved by government officials and placed in the forward baggage compartment. Meanwhile, the flight crew prepared for its first leg to the Idlewild airport on Long Island. Before getting underway, from the left seat in the cockpit, the captain briefed the first officer and flight engineer about what to expect. He would command the flight to Chicago.

TWA Flight 529 departed the Logan airport at 7:45 p.m. on Thursday night bound for its next stop. The busiest airport serving New York City, Idlewild had been built on a vast amount of acreage on Long Island, not far from the beach along Jamaica Bay. Although the field was known as Idlewild Airport during 1961, its official name would change to JFK International Airport in 1963 to honor deceased President John F. Kennedy. Throughout its many decades in operation, the airport had grown into one of the busiest passenger and cargo handling facilities in the world.

It was important for TWA to make sure that the airline's presence became known at such a large metropolitan airport. To accomplish that feat, the airline designed and erected a massive new passenger terminal. The intent was to communicate the public's confidence in modern air travel by flying aboard TWA planes. In addition, the airport's administration required the building of other nearby terminals that they owned and operated by individual airlines. TWA's terminal complex, by far the largest and most impressive of any of them, would be completed and opened to the public for the first time during the early months of 1962.

Shortly after Flight 529 was cleared to land at Idlewild, the passengers who boarded in Boston remained seated. It was almost 9:00 p.m. A few of the passengers who boarded in New York were also long-time residents of California. The allure of a laid-back California lifestyle had likely cultivated a desire to relocate to the Golden State. Some of them had already established professional careers or their own businesses there. Understandably, they were anxious to return home and assume

1. California Bound

those responsibilities once again. Some of the adults had brought along their children to visit family members living in the northeast.

An architect, along with his wife and four children, were among the passengers boarding Flight 529 in New York. Edward Chamberlain was anxious to return to his architectural design firm in California and to the family home in a quiet Palo Alto neighborhood. They had recently returned from a vacation trip to Europe. During World War II, he had joined the U.S. Air Force and been trained as both a pilot and a weather officer while serving his country.[14]

Another passenger boarding in New York happened to be a keypunch operator for a machine manufacturer in Manhattan. Single and never married, Monica Sun lived in a Salvation Army residential hall in the heart of New York City. She bought a ticket to enjoy the sights of San Francisco as a tourist, the first real vacation she had ever taken.[15]

Two of the passengers aboard Flight 529 planned to visit a close friend living in Los Angeles. The three men were former classmates who earlier attended the same college in New York.[16]

Following its brief stay at Idlewild, the plane departed on Thursday evening for Pittsburgh, the next stop for the Sky Club Coach flight. The plane landed in Pittsburgh within an hour. Unlike the busy airports in Boston and New York, Pittsburgh International Airport was far inland from the Atlantic Ocean. It was also 10 miles west of the busy Pittsburgh downtown area that defined much of the city. Opened in 1952, the airport soon became a busy hub for handling many of TWA's passenger and cargo flights.

Richard Maloney, an aerospace engineer, boarded Flight 529 in Pittsburgh. His childhood had been spent in Pennsylvania, but he was returning to his job in California's San Fernando Valley. He and his wife had visited family members living near Scranton. The couple brought along on this trip all five of their children, ranging in age from one to ten years old.[17]

Anton Skurcenski, a 40-year-old university professor and his wife also boarded Flight 529. As a student, he had graduated from the University of Pittsburgh where he and his wife first met. The couple got married in January 1943. After earning a doctorate in chemistry from the same university, he joined the faculty as a professor, teaching chemistry there for ten years. He also found time to begin another career as a ceramic chemist in California's aerospace industry. Late Thursday night, his brother drove the couple to the airport. Although they had flown to Pittsburgh aboard a jet, when it came time to return to California his wife wanted to fly in a slower plane.[18]

A 23-year-old soldier also boarded Flight 529 during its stop in Pittsburgh. Assigned as an ensign in the U.S. Navy, John Bartram was about to rejoin his fellow sailors following a 14-day personal leave. His ship in San Diego was moored in the harbor alongside similar vessels. He had graduated from the University of Rochester in 1961 after earning a bachelor of arts degree in physics. An accomplished student while in college, he joined the Naval Reserve Officers Training Corps on campus. The soldier's visit to the East Coast was especially important for him. After leaving home in Erie, Pennsylvania, he had driven to North Chili, a small Monroe County town in upstate New York. Upon arrival, he wasted no time in presenting an engagement ring to his 20-year-old girlfriend. She accepted the ring and would await his discharge from the Navy to begin their life together as husband and wife.[19]

Not everyone boarding Flight 529 in Pittsburgh was young, including Estella Woods, a 67-year-old woman who lived with a daughter in Southern California. She had visited her son's family, along with another two grown daughters, who resided in Binghamton in upstate New York. Following those visits, she changed her TWA flight to depart for California from the airport in Pittsburgh.[20]

Possibly the youngest person to board Flight 529 was only three months old when his mother checked both of them in at the Pittsburgh airport. Carol Walls had bought a ticket for return home to the Redondo Beach area of Los Angeles.[21] A former resident of Streator, Illinois, she had been visiting her hometown on vacation. However, another reason for the visit was to attend a funeral for her brother's young child who had died from a condition known as Sudden Infant Death Syndrome.

One more passenger also boarded Flight 529 in Pittsburgh before it took off at 12:05 a.m. Employed as an assistant district attorney for Allegheny County in Pennsylvania, Harry Savage planned to disembark upon the plane's arrival in Chicago. When the Constellation left the runway in Pittsburgh, he noticed something that didn't seem normal. During the takeoff, grinding noises could be heard in the cabin but the landing gear retracting didn't cause them. Approaching the airport in Chicago, a vibration started to shudder violently. The experience differed from the other times he flew on Constellations. Perhaps he should have notified the airline, but he didn't have enough time.[22]

1. California Bound

Adhering to a tight schedule, with the time now after midnight, Flight 529 departed the airport in Pittsburgh. Its next scheduled stop was Midway Airport in the Chicago area. No one knew it at the time, but Flight 529 would never reach Las Vegas, its next stop after Chicago.

2

The Crash

When it came to "red-eye" Sky Club Coach flights, it wasn't unusual for large families to take advantage of TWA's budget airfares. Many passengers who boarded Flight 529 were flying home from weeklong vacations or time spent visiting relatives and friends along the East Coast. TWA made it a practice to charge full fares to businessmen flying to last-minute meetings. But it also filled many of the seats with economy-minded family members. They were willing to fly from any one of a string of different airports during the nighttime hours. The Sky Club Coach flights were profitable for the airline and kept its planes in the air for decades.

Chicago's so-called "mile-square" Midway Airport supported both domestic and international air carriers for decades. Situated a dozen miles from the city's bustling downtown business district, Midway had always served as Chicago's primary airport and its experienced travelers had ranked it as the world's busiest. Although it handled millions of passengers during 1959, some of the airlines that had flown from there for years decided to move across town to newer O'Hare International Airport. As a result, the number of passengers traveling through Midway dropped more than 60 percent. O'Hare's modern terminal complex and longer runways could easily accommodate larger jets flown by the major airlines. Midway's shorter runways were impossible to expand as industrial and residential developments had restricted their length. Boxed in on all sides, it became clear that Midway would never be able to expand like other airports. Although some activities at the airport had slowed down, it was hardly deserted. TWA continued to be a major tenant, handling both passenger and cargo flights, as well as operating a large aircraft maintenance facility along one side of the airport.[1]

The number of flights arriving and departing past midnight at Midway wouldn't be a concern for Flight 529 coming in from Boston and

2. The Crash

the other cities. Only a handful of flights would be operating during the early morning hours.

Descending gradually from a darkened sky with landing lights lit, Flight 529 touched down on the runway at Midway at about 1:18 a.m. The plane was directed by ground control to a TWA gate along the terminal's concourse. During the touchdown, children strapped in seats near their parents were probably awakened by an ear-splitting jolt of landing gear tires hitting the ground. Along with their parents, they had boarded the plane several hours earlier at one of the East Coast airports where TWA offered its Sky Club Coach service.

Guided along a taxiway to its gate, dozens of sleepy and tired passengers would probably have liked nothing more than to stretch their legs, because the time in Chicago was now past 1:30 a.m. The plane's refrigeration system was able to produce only a limited amount of air to cool more than 70 people. The maintenance crews planned to repair the system sometime in the future, but not during the brief stop at Midway that night. The incoming captain, discussing this issue with his flight engineer, would have been likely to talk with captain Jim Sanders and flight engineer Jim Newlin in the flight operations office. They would take the plane to Las Vegas and Los Angeles. Regarding the refrigeration issue, they agreed that it didn't affect the plane's airworthiness.[2] Not considered a "safety of flight matter," its repair could wait.

After turning over responsibility for Flight 529's westward leg to Sanders, it's likely the incoming pilots and hostesses boarding in Boston would have hailed cab rides to home or checked in at a local hotel. They would get some rest in order to crew another flight during the long Labor Day weekend. Their flight from Pittsburgh to Midway had gone according to plan.

During the quiet early morning hours, the TWA employees on duty at Midway began handling both the fueling and loading chores. But for the passengers still sitting in the cabin, the rapid fueling and loading meant there wasn't enough time for them to disembark. Inside the terminal, the poorly lit concourse (its interior resembling a much older terminal) was furnished with rows of uncomfortable plastic seats with little or no cushioning. A retail shop stayed open throughout the night to pull in whatever business there was. Passengers could purchase newspapers, cigarettes, and candy. Further back, along a side of the concourse, was an item that most airports in North America were offering at the time: life insurance policies to anyone who was hesitant to fly on an airliner. It wasn't uncommon for travelers to operate its machines, selling insurance policies for $2.50 apiece. Passengers often paid for them with quarters before embarking on a flight.

Cigarette vending machines set up near the gates were easy to find. Although the area around the gate was largely abandoned at that hour, the odor of stale tobacco smoke would likely have become evident with passengers strolling around the concourse. Cigarette smoking was acceptable, although it was restricted to only the rear section of airliner passenger cabins. Throughout the 1960s, smoking was allowed aboard all commercial airliners in the United States. It wasn't until April 23, 1988, that it was banned by the FAA on all the nation's airliners.

Nine passengers, who had boarded the flight from other airports on the East Coast, began removing their belongings from the overhead bins and vacating seats soon after landing. Apparently, they had business or family matters to attend to during their time in Chicago. The only airline departure scheduled during the early morning hour happened to be Flight 529. Several ticketholders ready to board would be waiting inside the concourse. The hand on a nearby clock passed 1:40 a.m., as a TWA agent at the gate announced that Flight 529 was ready to board.

Five individuals who bought tickets would enter the cabin that night and slip into its empty seats. A majority of them were ticketed for California. Within a matter of minutes, every seat in the cabin would be filled. Some of the passengers lived in Illinois, while others had arrived earlier that day on other airlines from surrounding states.

One of the passengers, a 34-year-old businessman, planned to visit his parents in Los Angeles where he had grown up.[3] Another passenger lived near Muncie in Indiana. It was reported that he would be the last person boarding Flight 529 that morning, making use of a standby ticket.[4]

A 29-year-old woman from suburban Berwyn, in Cook County, Illinois, was a hospital nurse; she was on the way to San Francisco for a vacation.[5]

The final two passengers boarding in Chicago were active-duty members of the U.S. military. One of them, a 20-year-old coming from the village of Chicago Ridge in Illinois, was on his way to San Diego for submarine duty. He had enjoyed a two-week leave and visited his parents at their home.[6] Another 22-year-old passenger, having the rank of sergeant in the U.S. Army, had also boarded. He was traveling to California to join a unit of the 101st Airborne Division.[7]

2. The Crash

Of the group of children in the Constellation's cabin, 14 of them were 10 years old or younger. Most of them, along with their parents, were continuing on from Boston, New York, or Pittsburgh all the way to California.

All of the Constellation cabins had been outfitted with so-called "comfort" seats, although it's likely the passengers felt they were other than comfortable. After departure time was announced, the hostesses would prepare them for the next phase of the flight. A quick glance at a wall clock revealed it was nearing 2:45 a.m. Flight 529 would soon depart for Las Vegas and its other destinations in California.

Each of the crewmembers assigned to Flight 529 lived in coastal cities around the Los Angeles area. It explained why they decided to bid for this particular flight. TWA had domiciled them for flights scheduled to fly in and out of Los Angeles International Airport. Compared to more recent years, far less freeway traffic existed during the early 1960s. It proved convenient for airline crewmembers to commute to the Los Angeles airport from their homes in nearby beach cities.

For many years during the late 1940s, Jim Sanders had flown Constellations from the United States to Cairo, Madrid, Geneva, Paris and other locales overseas. After being upgraded to captain at TWA, he continued flying both its international and domestic routes. By the time he boarded Flight 529 at Midway, the 40-year-old aviator had flown more than 12,000 hours at the controls of this and other Constellations. Sharing his interest in aviation matters, his wife was also employed by TWA as a hostess. The couple lived in Manhattan Beach, a short drive from the Los Angeles airport.[8]

Dale Tarrant, the first officer who also joined the Flight 529 crew, had been hired by TWA in December 1955. Born during 1929 in Sturgis, South Dakota, 31-year-old Tarrant had attended Black Hills Teachers College before serving in the U.S. Air Force from 1952 to 1955. He lived in Redondo Beach with his wife, a former Western Air Lines stewardess. Tarrant's flying time totaled 5,344 hours, with 1,975 of them logged in Constellations.[9]

Thirty-eight-year-old Jim Newlin had joined TWA in 1951, beginning his career in the airline's maintenance base as an airframe and engine mechanic. He was promoted to flight engineer in 1954. A resident of Balboa Beach, Newlin was married; he and his wife were raising two children. He had logged 5,817 hours as a Constellation flight engineer.[10]

17 Days and 17 Miles Apart

Barbara Pearson, at the age of 25, had flown for TWA since August 1957. Living near the beach in the coastal community of Santa Monica, she expected to resign from TWA upon arrival in Los Angeles to devote her time to motherhood. Her baby was due in April 1962. She expected to meet her husband at Los Angeles International Airport upon arrival and tell him the exciting news.[11]

Nanette Fidger, age 20, had been employed by the airline since May 1961. She began flying for TWA on July 15 after completing the company's training program. Similar to Pearson, she intended to complete Flight 529 but then resign and get married.[12]

A product of the dusty Texas panhandle, young Jim Sanders was the kind of boy who drifted through his teenage years wondering where the rest of his life might take him. For a tall, lanky kid born in April 1941 and raised in the Texas flatlands, life seemed dull. Riding bicycles, playing cards with friends, and watching an occasional movie was all there was to occupy his time in the sleepy town of Abilene. Besides pulling weeds from the front lawn at 1310 Poplar Street, his parents' house, the only paying job that teenagers like him could find involved pumping gasoline into the automobiles of his neighbors at a nearby gas station.[13]

Entranced whenever he saw fast moving single-engine propeller-driven warplanes roar over his parents' house, Sanders set a personal goal to become a pilot, although this would have to wait a few years. He had heard about the military's urgent need for more fighter and bomber pilots. When he reached the age of 21, still intrigued with anything to do with airplanes, he volunteered to join the Army Air Corps.

Joining the military and completing training enabled him to pilot four-engine bombers. He and a crew left for Kansas under orders to pick up several newly manufactured Boeing B-17s at the factory there. His fellow pilots were preparing the planes to undertake bombing missions. They would soon fly deep over occupied Europe at high altitudes during daylight hours. The crews would be capable of destroying targets from five miles above the ground. In addition to Sanders as the pilot, nine other crewmembers would go with him on these missions.

Sanders and his flight crew would eventually fly 25 missions in a B-17 and never get shot down. Remarkably, only two of his crewmembers were injured by flak hitting the plane from enemy gunners. Discharged after brief hospitalizations, both men volunteered to return to their same duties in Sanders' B-17, a credit to the pilot's leadership.

2. The Crash

The roughest time Sanders experienced took place while flying a mission over the countryside in France. His plane had been badly shot up by flak. Part of its hydraulic system and the communication radios, oxygen system, and cables for moving its control surfaces were heavily damaged. One of the engines was hit and disabled, the result of a series of attacks from incoming fire. Sanders would later be awarded a distinguished flying cross, air medal, and three oak leaf clusters. But in his mind, the recognition should have been about surviving 25 missions without anyone being killed.

There was always the possibility that the B-17 crews could get shot down, captured, or in the worst case, killed. Recognizing those outcomes, the bomber crews flying over Europe were restricted to a maximum of 25 missions flying over dangerous enemy territory. Beating the odds, those crews would return to the United States for either reassignment or discharge from military service. Sanders decided to resign from the Army Air Corps and apply for a pilot job at the commercial airlines. He chose a major international airline called Trans World Airlines.[14]

Not long after joining the airline on August 30, 1945, Sanders went on to fly Lockheed Constellations. In February 1948, serving as a co-captain, he flew from Madrid in Spain to Idlewild in New York. A month later, he flew across the Atlantic from Paris to New York. The same month, he flew the same route to New York. The youthful pilot was logging more flight hours than the airline's senior pilots. At the age of 26, he loved taking those trips. There were many other transoceanic flights to Europe he flew and he accepted each of them without complaint. While flying over enemy territory a few years before joining TWA, he had dropped hundreds of bombs over the same countryside that he now flew over for his airline.

Based on his years of flying experience, TWA promoted Sanders to captain on June 18, 1954. By the time he commanded Flight 529 on September 1, 1961, his logbook revealed a remarkable 17,011 hours spent in the air, 12,633 of them logged in various model Constellations.

After more than six years as a seasoned TWA captain, Sanders prepared to command still another routine Sky Club Coach flight—Chicago to California, with a short stop in Las Vegas to refuel. The trip would involve flying through nighttime hours with a cabin filled with not only adult passengers but also 20 children. The crewmembers in the cockpit had children of their own and likely understood the difficulties that parents can often face while traveling with young

17 Days and 17 Miles Apart

children. Two military personnel also boarded the Constellation in Chicago, a common sight aboard many Sky Club Coach flights.

The weather forecast and planned route for the flight to Las Vegas and California were carefully examined by both pilots. It was fortunate the weather at Midway wasn't a problem: scattered clouds at 10,000 feet, a moonless night, three miles visibility with light haze and smoke, along with the wind blowing at eight knots.

Standing in TWA's flight operations room, Sanders would likely have welcomed first officer Tarrant to join in a conversation with Newlin. Hostesses Pearson and Fidger may have also joined in at some point. The projected flight time to McCarran Airport in Las Vegas was expected to be six hours and 23 minutes.

Outside the terminal, TWA's ground crew had kept busy throughout the plane's short stay at Midway. Enough fuel for its transcontinental journey was uploaded. Those 3,240 gallons of aviation grade gasoline were poured into four separate fuel tanks in the wings. The maximum allowable takeoff weight for a Model 049 Constellation was 94,794

TWA Constellation N86511 at McCarron International Airport in Las Vegas, Nevada, on June 24, 1961. Two months later on September 1, the same plane crashed near Clarendon Hills, Illinois, killing everyone aboard (courtesy American Aviation Historical Society [AAHS-38721]).

2. The Crash

pounds, well below a maximum allowable weight of 96,000 pounds. Both the passenger and cargo manifests were carefully checked to make sure the plane's center of gravity was within acceptable limits. It appeared that everything was in order.

The crewmembers seated in the narrow cockpit were now ready to begin the flight. After Jim Newlin completed a walk-around inspection of the plane's exterior, a TWA employee would likely roll back a loading ramp leading into the cabin. Returning to the cockpit, Newlin prepared to start the Constellation's four Curtiss-Wright R-3350 piston engines. Each engine was designed to deliver 2,200 horsepower on takeoff. Carefully moving toggle switches and levers along the side-facing engineer's station, Newlin's actions slowly brought each of the big engines to life.

Clouds of oily smoke pouring from the exhaust stacks of each engine quickly swept across the nearly deserted ramp, fading slowly into cool evening air. All four engines started successfully and, now idling, the crew was ready to taxi out to its assigned runway. With the parking brake released, a TWA employee standing on the ramp well ahead of the cockpit guided the airliner away from its gate. The Constellation would taxi to the threshold for Runway 22, having one of two parallel runways available for takeoffs and landings.

It is likely that first officer Dale Tarrant would have picked up a microphone to contact the FAA air traffic control (ATC) center. Under federal regulations, the crew was required to read back a clearance provided by a controller. Tarrant did so without error. Having completed that task, the plane could now be guided across the United States under so-called instrument flight rules, following a series of airway markers depicted on the plane's navigation instruments. The FAA defined those airways: "Rules and regulations established by the FAA to govern flight under conditions in which flight by outside visual reference is not safe."[15]

By this time the crew would be briefed by Sanders about the proper procedures to follow should an engine fail or fire break out during the takeoff. Even experienced crews live on the edge, anticipating system breakdowns. Never predictable, they cause each crewmember to take such briefings seriously. In an emergency, every second counts. If an agreed-on procedure isn't followed closely, it could result in passenger injuries or possibly death.

With the Constellation moving into position for takeoff, it would taxi onto a concrete run-up pad at the end of Runway 22 Left, arriving

17 Days and 17 Miles Apart

there in less than a minute. Sanders would then rotate a small wheel, known as a steering tiller. Positioned near his left leg, its rotation moved the nose around to align the plane with the active runway. Doing so also served to take advantage of a gentle breeze blowing in from Lake Michigan. The plane's parking brake was set, serving as a signal to run up the Constellation's engines, two of them at a time. Flight engineer Newlin would now check the RPM drops of each magneto, cycle the propellers to assure they feathered properly, and attend to dozens of routine tasks. The engines would be given a thorough workout, each emitting a healthy roar from their exhaust stacks. At the same time, the firing patterns of their 144 spark plugs would be closely watched on a built-in ignition analyzer on the flight engineer's panel.

Sanders and Tarrant would exercise the flight controls, moving their control wheels and rudder pedals to mechanical limits. Its purpose was to verify that the elevator, aileron, and rudder control surfaces had unobstructed travel. Passing this step satisfactorily, an additional test was performed. Should the elevator's hydraulic boost system fail (which rarely happened) pulling a handle up would disconnect its "power steering." This would enable the crew to manually move the elevator control surface. The de-boosting procedure had been covered, but apparently not stressed, as part of a pilot training program at TWA and other air carriers that operated Constellations.

The Constellation, equipped with tight cockpit seating for its flight crews, had a shift handle positioned alongside the right leg of the pilot, far from where a first officer or flight engineer could easily move it. They would not be able to quickly pull up the handle if the hydraulic boost failed. On the other hand, it would probably never need to be activated. When the handle was pulled up during a test that night, it likely moved smoothly without encountering any resistance and would have successfully shifted from hydraulic power to a manual mode.

All of the checklist items completed satisfactorily, Flight 529 would be ready to depart, pending a takeoff clearance from the control tower at Midway. In the passenger cabin, the hostesses would return to their seats near the cockpit door. With seat belt and no smoking signs still lit, the cabin lights would be switched off. The passengers could watch the lights of Chicago passing below when the plane began climbing away from the runway.

Cleared for takeoff at 2:00 a.m., each engine throttle lever would be moved forward. Doing so, it created an ear-splitting roar and vibration

2. The Crash

felt throughout the cabin. As the Constellation began to gain speed roaring along the runway, the pilots routinely focused their eyes on the tachometer and manifold pressure gauges. It is likely that the readings from those instruments were normal that night. The Curtiss-Wright reciprocating engines were producing 2,200 horsepower at 2,000 RPM during the takeoff. They powered 15-foot diameter, three-bladed Hamilton Standard full feathering, constant-speed propellers. The plane's takeoff could continue as planned.

With the runway's end fast approaching, Sanders would have moved his hand from the tiller to his control wheel. Tarrant would then announce they were reaching an important speed, known as the point of no return, to decide whether or not to continue the takeoff. This would be followed by another verbal notification, advising Sanders to "rotate." His control wheel would be gently eased back, with 48 tons of aluminum and steel being shifted from the landing gear assemblies into the plane's wings.

A control lever on the center pedestal would be pulled by Tarrant to retract the landing gear. Fully retracting the flaps came next. Everything must have appeared to be routine.

After thundering down the concrete ribbon for less than half a minute, the plane began climbing through a moonless sky to its assigned cruise altitude. It took to the sky in a graceful manner, gaining altitude slowly but surely. It then made a shallow right turn away from the runway. TWA Flight 529 was now heading due west at this point. The hand of a clock fitted to the cockpit instrument panel indicated it was 2:01 a.m.

With the throttles pulled back slightly from takeoff to a "maximum except takeoff" power setting, the level of noise in the cabin would have remained loud. For passengers who remembered other noisy takeoffs earlier that day, they probably assumed the noise would quiet down after reaching cruise altitude.

Soon after departing Midway, the pilots likely noticed something was amiss when they tried adjusting the elevator. Also, the response of their control wheels would have appeared to be less coordinated than usual. It may have felt like twisting the handle of a broken tool. Moving the round trim tab wheel on the side of the cockpit pedestal wouldn't have worked, nor would moving any other cockpit control. This was unlike the other Constellations the crew had flown. They needed to return to Midway airport without any

The cockpit of a Model 049 Constellation, similar to that of TWA Flight 529, had tight seating for a pilot, copilot, and flight engineer. During its flights to Europe, a navigator would be seated to the left of the flight engineer (courtesy American Aviation Historical Society [AAHS-38708]).

2. The Crash

delay. Over the years, Flight 529's crew had flown different Constellations and experienced almost everything—but never anything as strange as this.

Within another minute in the air, the pilots would lose all longitudinal control of the airliner. It was later determined there was no possibility the elevator shift handle could be pulled up when the control wheel was pushed forward at the same time. Everything was changing at lightning speed right before their eyes. The plane began making a series of unwanted excursions in the darkened sky, going up, then down, followed by more up and down movements again and again. It was much like a paper airplane being thrown from high up—first nose down, then nose up and repeating.

The erratic motion was known as a phugoid oscillation. It consists of a nearly constant angle of attack, but the airspeed and altitude changes, this taking several minutes to subside. While trying to bring the nose down, the plane would move in the opposite direction.[16] For Flight 529, the oscillations would have to stop in order to land the plane safely.

What had begun as a routine passenger flight from Boston was turning into a full-blown disaster. Even experienced pilots would have found it difficult to figure out what was happening. The crew believed they would have only one chance to reverse the instability. By this time, they likely concluded that the elevator control surface had jammed in a full-up position. This is why the Constellation was climbing erratically. Recalling their pilot training days at TWA, the pilots would know the elevator could be freed by pulling the shift handle up. This would enable them to manually move the elevator and hopefully regain control. But what was happening was very different.

A jammed flight control can be compared to an ignition key jamming in an automobile. The same outcome can occur with a frozen flight control system such as Flight 529 suffered. The crew would likely have applied as much pressure as possible to pull the shift handle up. For whatever reason, it still wouldn't budge. While one pilot may have continued to push the wheel forward, the other pilot would likely do the same with his left hand while pulling up the handle with his right hand. Designing a flight control system in such a way made no sense because pilots are trained to push their control wheels forward to exit stalling conditions. There is little doubt that the captain had verified the handle worked properly while Flight 529 waited for takeoff clearance at Midway. Less than 15 minutes earlier, everything worked fine. But now it didn't and made no sense. Flight 529 was losing altitude rapidly.

What took place in the passenger cabin is unknown. However, other inflight disruptions, such as violent clear air turbulence, have resulted in serious injuries and occasional deaths. There is little doubt that what occurred aboard Flight 529 was horrific. Both of the flight attendants would have sensed that something terrible had happened but couldn't do anything to stop it. Some of the ticketholders must have thought the same. They would have felt the rear of the plane dropping down violently from under them and then moving back up. Throughout the pitch-black cabin, a series of mysterious jolts would toss anything loose into the air. The passengers could have thought they hit a severe air pocket.

Firmly strapped in seats, the passengers may have become confused thinking about a roller-coaster ride that didn't stop. Desperate to learn what had happened so soon after takeoff, some of them would likely press their faces against the cabin windows. But they would see nothing but dark sky and dim city lights. Those lights were growing larger as the ground got closer. Especially for the first-time passengers aboard, nothing could be more frightening than what they were witnessing.

Failing to respond to any type of control movement, Flight 529 remained in a nose-high, stalled attitude while dropping lower out of the sky. Although the plane seemed to recover for a few seconds, another stall instantly took its place, continuing to throw the plane and its occupants around the sky.

Engine failures and fires had become commonplace for pilots operating Constellations. Their engines, originally developed to power Boeing B-29 bombers during the postwar years, were unreliable, faced with a half dozen major problems. Unfortunately, Model 049 Constellations used a very similar type of engine. None of the engines had caught fire, so it was unlikely that they caused this instability.

What was happening could only be described as unfathomable. The airliner was quickly falling out of the sky. Dropping as fast as a heavy rock, it was much like a roller coaster roaring down a narrow, unstable track and getting pushed off its side.

Drawing on thousands of hours of experience flying Constellations, the crew would likely not have given up. The pilots would have

2. The Crash

gripped the wheels in unison, using both hands. The nose needed to be forced down to stop the sickening series of stalls. Charged with adrenaline, they would have reacted instinctively, in a similar way to how they were trained. It would appear that nobody had taught the crew how to recover from this type of stall. Perhaps the information was buried in the rear of a pilot's flight manual. The technique was not likely to be disclosed during pilot training sessions at TWA.

The pilots may have thought about trying other options. But realistically, there weren't any. The elevator remained jammed at a dangerous angle even with both pilots pushing forward on their wheels. It would prove impossible for one of them to push a wheel and pull up the handle to switch the system to manual control. Neither pilot would have known it then, but pulling up the handle could disengage the hydraulic boost—but only if both pilots stopped pushing their wheels forward at the same time the handle was pulled up.

With far too little altitude left for a safe recovery, it would have taken a miracle to keep Flight 529 in the air. It meant that an earlier plan for returning to Midway was no longer an option. For now, an emergency landing in an unlit empty field was the only action possible. Totally occupied with the crisis inside the cockpit, the crewmembers didn't have enough time to contact the controllers at Midway or any maintenance experts at TWA. More than likely, they continued pushing the wheels forward, but finally realized that doing so was accomplishing nothing.

There was no more altitude remaining, as the plane flew low over the darkened countryside. Sanders would need to keep his eyes focused through narrow cockpit windows to identify city lights and streets in the residential neighborhoods below them. It was a long shot, but the crew would need to attempt an emergency landing. The Constellation cockpit was extremely tight for the crews, meaning its small windows at the front and sides didn't help with visibility. It would have taken two hands to even open a side window, even though doing so would to be futile.

With little forward airspeed and altitude remaining, the city lights would have grown brighter and bigger by the second. The plane continued its downward plunge, dropping like a rock falling into the shaft of an out-of-control elevator. With only seconds left in the air, Flight 529 hit the ground hard, exploded in flames, and in seconds, killed everyone aboard. In this rural farming area of southern Illinois, flames from the explosion lit the sky for miles around.

Within a few hours, radio and television stations, in addition to morning editions of the nation's newspapers, covered news of the disaster. It turned into a major story, especially because TWA had routes spread throughout the world. From Paris to New York to California, it was shocking news. The first television network to broadcast from the crash site was NBC.[17] Its reports during the morning hours terrified viewers—video of smoking, twisted wreckage and victims being placed under sheets before being carried away on stretchers. Shortly after dawn, other stations also began offering coverage.

The crash of TWA Flight 529 was reported on front pages of newspapers throughout the country (courtesy Mary Brown at Clarendon Hills Historical Society).

The crash site began to fill up with reporters and photographers. The crash continued as a page-one story with no indication it would be replaced with another. Wherever he was at the time, TWA owner Howard Hughes would likely not be happy.

Within the ranks of seasoned aerospace engineers, the boost system's design was considered too complicated to perform the simple function it was intended to accomplish. There was a belief that simplification or complete removal of the system could actually save lives. But

2. The Crash

airline owner Howard Hughes continued to believe the system worked the way it was intended. Much of the aviation industry caved in and didn't support any change to improve the safety of the Constellations then in service.

Unknown to the pilots attempting to control Flight 529 that night, there were other Constellations with a history of their hydraulic boost systems failing. During 1946, four of TWA's most experienced pilots were killed due to elevator control problems.[18] There were several other similar accidents, some documented, but many not. Now, 15 years after those events, a similar problem had reared its ugly head and caused the destruction of still another airliner. Flight 529's crew would not have been aware of those problems. Nor would people at the airlines who trained mechanics to maintain the systems, or even employees at the FAA for approving some of Lockheed's flawed mechanical systems.

Possibly only one pilot in the United States, who began flying various Model 049 Constellations during 1945, understood how the complicated hydraulic boost systems functioned. It was TWA's owner, Howard Hughes. Beginning at the time flight controls for his flying boat were developed during World War II, Hughes took extreme interest in boosted control systems using hydraulic power to move its heavy control surfaces.[19]

The hydraulic system was far more complex than other aircraft systems. The boost reduced the amount of force that pilots needed to exert the controls. The boost actuators for ailerons were located in the outer wing, while those for moving the rudder and elevator were tucked inside the plane's tail cone. Hydraulic pressure was supplied to actuator control valves in order for positioning actuators to control the surfaces. A so-called "feel system" provided the pilots with a force comparable to a conventional flight control system. Should a plane's entire hydraulic system fail, an electrical auxiliary boost pump would provide pressure to move the rudders and elevators. In the event of a total loss of electrical power, the controls could be operated manually. Because the elevators were the heaviest control surfaces in the plane, they were equipped with a shift mechanism to provide the pilots with greater mechanical advantage when being operated manually.

There was considerable doubt about incorporating a boosted control system in new airliners. Hall Hibbard, a vice president at the time Lockheed was formed, stated that a boosted system wasn't necessary because the competing Douglas DC-6 and Boeing 377 airliners didn't have such devices.[20] Due to its complexity, the system also added to the cost of Constellations. To prevent a major redesign of the plane, Hibbard decided to keep the systems. The decision would later haunt him when a number of Constellation and Electra crashes ended up killing hundreds of people. Louis Barr, a former Constellation flight engineer who had accumulated 7,800 hours operating every model of Constellation, offered his opinion about eliminating this type of control system: "In order to remove the system, extensive redesign would have been required."[21]

During 1949 the federal government issued an Airworthiness Directive (AD) requiring modification of the plane's elevator boost system. Airworthiness Directives (ADs) are legally enforceable regulations issued by the FAA (or another government agency) to correct an unsafe condition in an aircraft component, such as an engine, propeller or other airborne appliance. If the changes weren't made on a timely basis, the entire fleet of Model 049, 149, 649 and 749 Constellations would have to be grounded. The directive addressed a similar kind of malfunction that would later cause Flight 529 to crash—12 years after this warning was issued. In part, the directive stated: "Numerous instances of malfunctioning of the elevator booster system have been reported, causing longitudinal hunting of the airplane and, in one instance, injury to some passengers when operation of the elevator boost shifter mechanism was accomplished."[22]

On the day of the tragedy, an unknown number of people decided to not board Flight 529. Susan Stephens, a university student, was one of them. She almost boarded the ill-fated Constellation but changed her mind at the last minute. However, two other students she was traveling with, both attending another university, weren't as lucky and died in the crash.[23]

Another Constellation captain, Edward Betts, had been hired by TWA in 1945 following service in the Army. He had been at the controls of a B-17 during the war and retired from TWA in 1980 after a 35-year career. His last assignment was as a 747 captain on the airline's international routes. "Due to a change in pilot assignments for September 1, 1961, he barely missed commanding ill-fated Flight 529 during its final night in the air."[24]

September 1, 1961, will always be remembered for what happened in darkness, more than 60 years ago.

3

Nightmare

At 2:04 a.m. during an otherwise tranquil night, about nine miles west of the Midway airport, TWA Flight 529 cut a deep crater in a farmer's field, broke into pieces, and ejected its passengers onto acres of corn. Within seconds, an enormous fire engulfed what remained of its airframe, fueled by at least 3,000 gallons of volatile aviation gasoline. The Constellation had sliced through rows of corn stalks and soybeans, skidding across them for nearly half a mile. The intense impact and fire would take the lives of the five crewmembers and 73 passengers aboard.

Residents living in all directions from the crash site near Clarendon Hills could feel the ground shake. It caused them to suspect that the noise and vibration could be coming from Argonne National Laboratories, a sprawling Atomic Energy Commission research facility built to develop nuclear reactors. It was later determined that the facility was not at fault.

Portions of the plane's airframe ended up getting buried in a field near 61st Street. During its final moments in the air, the plane was seen flying low over the roofs of several houses. It struck the ground in an extreme nose-down angle, its landing gear and wing flaps retracted. The pilot was somehow able to guide the plane through the night's total darkness. There was no need to lower the landing gear, adjust the flaps, or even switch on the landing lights. After bouncing on the ground at least four times, its cockpit section dug into a moist agricultural field.

Dropping much like a lawn dart, what had once been a sharp-looking airliner vanished from view. A massive sheet of flames began consuming what was left of it.

A minute and 34 seconds after the pilots acknowledged its take-off clearance from a Midway controller, another controller in the tower began following Flight 529's progress. A few minutes after its departure,

17 Days and 17 Miles Apart

The Constellation impacted farmland just south of Clarendon Hills, at the top of this aerial photograph. The crash site stretched from 61st Street on the south, 59th Street on the north, and Bentley Avenue to the west, with Clarendon Hills Road on the east side (courtesy Mary Brown at Clarendon Hills Historical Society).

3. Nightmare

a flickering green image appeared on radar. It told him that the plane was now flying five miles west of the airport, proceeding on its assigned course. But after a few more seconds, the image disappeared from view.

Because its sudden disappearance could have been caused by a temporary glitch affecting the entire radar network, the controller ignored it, not realizing that something unthinkable had just happened. Grabbing a pair of binoculars to focus his eyes on the horizon, another controller saw a bright flash in the sky west of the airport. Curious, he radioed the captain of a Northwest Airlines plane, an air freighter preparing to depart Midway. After taking off, the controller asked him to report if he was seeing anything unusual. Circling over what looked like farmland several miles west of the airport, something caught his eye: hundred-foot-high flames thrown off from something burning on the ground. There was also plenty of black smoke rising from the same area.

There was little doubt that the flames and smoke resulting from the breakup of Flight 529. Its crash site was pinpointed as being nine miles west of the Midway airport, a short distance from Hinsdale, a village in DuPage County about 20 miles west of downtown Chicago.[1]

Humid weather during the last day of August in 1961 wasn't a surprise for the local residents there, especially people living on its farms. The area consisted of mostly farm houses surrounding large agricultural fields. An earlier thunderstorm that day was a frequent occurrence, the storm bringing rain showers, soaking soil in the area. During the early 1950s a handful of farmhouses were constructed near the fields, a common sight in the area. Seemingly endless rows of corn stalks and soybeans had been grown in those fields for decades.

One of the farmers living in the neighborhood also owned a house there. Jerry Broz maintained an agricultural field to grow its corn and soybeans. It was north of 61st Street, not far from where he and his wife had the house. As a fulltime farmer, Broz had spent many days, sometimes dawn to dusk, tending to the rows of crops that he was growing. Many residents of the area during the last century had earned a living by raising crops later put on sale to neighbors in nearby communities.

As midnight approached, Broz would have been too sleepy to turn on an evening newscast. Instead, he slipped into bed. Earlier that evening, once the thunderstorms passed through the area, he had opened a few windows around the house. It brought in a cool breeze. The hand on a clock near his bed indicated that it was the first day of September, a holiday for many workers. Over a long weekend, they would celebrate

17 Days and 17 Miles Apart

Labor Day. But for farmers like Broz, it amounted to nothing more than just another workday. Restful sleep was the only thing he wanted that evening. But that peace and quiet was about to end abruptly four minutes after 2:00 a.m.

Jettisoned from their bed, Broz and his wife awoke to an intense noise. Stucco adhering to their bedroom ceiling began cracking as the rest of the house shook. They assumed that the noise and vibration could have come from a low flying military aircraft. It was loud enough to scare the daylights out of them, as his wife recalled: "I heard the plane fly low over the house. My husband and I woke up and jumped out of bed."[2]

The plane turned away from their house slowly—but soon headed back. Watching the plane while still in the air, they decided to stand next to an open window along one side of the house. Groping through a foreboding, but cloudless sky, its shrill noise suddenly increased intensity. It was unlike anything they had heard before, sounding like a dozen freight trains roaring along their bedroom window. Like frightened children, the couple stood motionless, their eyes focused on the undisturbed acreage outside.

Flying in and out of darkness, the silhouette of a huge plane came into view, likely an airliner with flashing lights. Its engines sputtered at first but then sped up, producing an earth-shaking roar. Descending rapidly from as high as 1,800 feet above the ground, the plane appeared to stay motionless in the air with little or no forward movement. It was fast dropping out of the sky. Shedding pieces of its airframe, the plane flew over the roofs of several houses, turning north across 61st Street.

The plane's altitude now lower than ever, with nothing to arrest its vertical descent, its nose was pointing nearly straight down. No hope of recovery evident at this point, it looked as though the Constellation might smash into the rain-soaked field and dig into the soil. Sinking lower by the second, its vertical fin and rudder broke off from the fuselage. Not destroyed or even burnt, but resting on a patch of dirt near the street, sat the heavy tail assembly. It had ended up 33 feet from where the rest of the plane would soon hit. Lacking a major part of its tail, the rest of the Constellation pitched downward into the ground.

Major sections of the plane skidded along the rough surface of the agricultural field, pulverizing many hundreds of cornstalks planted there. The tail-less plane hit the ground with tremendous force, followed by

3. Nightmare

The horizontal stabilizer from the Constellation after it separated from the fuselage of Flight 529. Impacting the ground, the plane plowed across a field of corn stalks and soybeans (courtesy Mary Brown at Clarendon Hills Historical Society).

bouncing up and digging a path through the field. Its nose section, tilted down at a 20-degree angle, was pushed deeply into the earth. It would destroy the cockpit structure, and no doubt, killed its three crewmembers. What remained of the plane cut a swath through the soil, leaving behind a path of debris 200 feet wide by 1,100 feet in length.

The house belonging to Broz and his wife was only yards away from where most of the plane ended up. Although much of the wreckage didn't touch the ground where they were standing, his wife told a newspaper reporter: "We could see the wheels, the wings, everything falling apart."[3]

The Constellation's two-ton piston engines carved four deep craters into the soil. Hundreds of aluminum pieces forming structural parts of the airframe were scattered in every direction around the field. The first thought in Broz' mind was to rescue passengers trapped in the wreckage or thrown into the field.

Within seconds, aviation gasoline began pouring from shattered fuel tanks in the plane's damaged wings. A horrendous noise resulting from a massive explosion came next. Flames quickly consumed whatever had been left of the airframe. The flow of gasoline spread quickly, flames shooting high into the air, while fuel vapor began creeping into windows and yards of nearby homes. The smell of both burning gasoline and broken corn stalks was saturating the neighborhood. It was fortunate that Broz didn't walk around the unburned wreckage. He could have gotten burned because the fire was about to erupt.

The spewed fuel scorched the Broz house, melting some of its plastic window screens. The explosion fed an enormous ball of fire reaching an estimated two hundred feet in the air. The flames turned night into day for anyone living in neighborhoods surrounding the crash site. As for the Constellation, the fire melted and destroyed most of its airframe. The flames were so intense that some of the parts exploded into thousands of red-hot, odd-shaped pieces small enough to hold in a hand. The flames also consumed large amounts of clothing, likely belonging to its passengers. Throughout the field, the extreme heat was so intense that it withered hundreds of cornstalks after their tops were chopped off.

After a short time, the fuel that had earlier fed the explosion stopped flowing. The supply of fuel was now exhausted. A thundering noise that resulted from the initial impact had also faded away. All was quiet now, except for crackling noises coming from a dozen or so small fires burning around the cornfield. A large main landing gear assembly was thrown near a fence, broken off from one of the wings. Toward the rear of the Broz property, other sections of the plane had smashed into a corrugated steel storage shed only feet away from the house.

Bodies of its passengers were found strapped in their seats. Because most of the fuselage had disintegrated, some of them were ejected.

3. Nightmare

Because of severe bouncing on the ground after it first hit, the stress caused many items to break away from the fuselage.

Later that day, inside a shed not far from the Broz house, the first responders came across the bodies of three people. One of them was a young boy who had apparently been thrown onto the top of the shed's attic. Not far from the shed, other bodies were found scattered across the length of the field, sandwiched between the rows of corn stalks.[4]

By this time, Broz would have dialed the town's police and fire departments to tell them that an airliner had crashed on his property. Within minutes, the sound of fire engines, police cars, and ambulances could be heard roaring along a rocky, two-lane road leading to his property. The first order of business for firefighters would be to extinguish the flames popping up across the field. Ambulances weren't needed. The crews soon discovered that nobody was alive to rescue.

Broz, along with dozens of his neighbors living in the area, had never seen anything so shocking. In the minds of many residents, the disaster sounded like it was taking place in their own back yards. They would have memories of the awful crash for the rest of their lives. Charles George, a nearby resident, talked with a newspaper reporter: "I was asleep when I was awakened by a sound like a locomotive outside our window. I jumped up and saw a passing silhouette and then the plane crashed in our field. A tremendous wall of flames came rolling toward our house and stopped just short, singeing crops and trees."[5]

Some of the residents living near the crash site didn't waste time driving over to see it. They hurriedly got dressed. But the thick, black smoke and pungent smell of decaying flesh was far from what they expected. Arriving there within minutes, they saw an enormous scythe chopping a swath wider and longer than a football field. Shards of metal and fabric were scattered along with bodies of victims littering the field. The brief but intense fire had torched some of the bodies, rendering them unrecognizable.

The amount of carnage was gruesome, many bodies found dismembered and having burned limbs. Realizing there was nothing the neighbors could do to help, some of them ran home to strip blankets and sheets from their beds. Returning to the crash site, they used sheets to cover up whatever bodies they came across. There weren't enough sheets to cover all of the dead, so they unbundled stacks of newspapers to take the place of sheets.[6]

Scattered throughout the plowed field were possessions belonging to the people whose lives were snuffed out by the crash. An opened book, bathrobe, baby bonnet, shower clogs, and broken suitcases among them.[7]

Hearing sirens wailing in the distance, Broz and his neighbors saw the fire department get into action. It took only a few minutes. Several workers from a nearby carnival also showed up. They had been setting up lighting equipment for a Labor Day weekend event. But for now, they began moving portable arc-light equipment in place around the crash site. Its intense lights helped brighten the darkened cornfield during the pre-dawn hours.

It was likely that the explosion and fire had little to do with catapulting some passengers into the field. More logically, it was because of the horrendous impact resulting from its rapid vertical descent and sudden stop. The plane had instantly dug into unyielding earth, its wings breaking apart, the fuselage then snapping into large sections and countless smaller ones. The force was so great that bolts used to anchor the passenger seats to the fuselage had snapped, its seats thrown into the rows of cornstalks. For the most part, some passengers were still tightly strapped in those seats. What the first responders were witnessing resembled a battlefield scene of a movie littered with casualties.

The first detachment from the local fire department arrived on the scene soon after the crash. National guardsmen were later deployed to patrol the newly restricted area. Even though its troops kept their eyes on anyone trying to visit the site. Looters were already seen climbing over its barriers and walking throughout the field. Touching whatever bodies they found, they searched for money and wallets.

A group of unpaid volunteers from the Clarendon Heights Fire Department was there before anyone else. Most of its men had been asleep when the plane crashed several blocks from the town. Its earsplitting thud quickly got them out of bed. Crackling orange flames rousted most of the community, following the intense sound of its impact.[8]

Fire chief John Heidenreich would normally show up at his job in a few hours. He didn't that day. His firefighters had jumped out of their beds. The awful noise of the impact awakened them. They rushed to the crash site during that eerie dark night, the first firefighters to arrive there. Heidenreich told a newspaper reporter: "I grabbed my pants, a shirt, and my boots. My wife, Marilyn, began telephoning our men, and fire departments in nearby communities to give the alarm."[9]

3. Nightmare

Rescue crews from fire departments, government agencies, and Trans World Airlines kept busy at the crash site during the early morning hours of September 1, 1961. Note the white poles that represented the location of each victim (courtesy Mary Brown at Clarendon Hills Historical Society).

George Remkus, at the age of fourteen, along with his father, also headed over to the crash site. Both of the men lived a short distance from the fire department where they volunteered. Captain George Ernest, who helped lead the operation, was also there. While still in the air, small parts of the plane's airframe had fallen in the backyard of his house. Also at the site was Frank Trout, a 17-year-old teenager who lived adjacent to Clarendon Hills. Both he and his father had served as volunteer firefighters. The younger Trout told a newspaper reporter what he witnessed at the crash site: "I saw a lady, still strapped in her seat. She was holding a baby. But both were dead. There were small fires all over the field."[10]

As daylight crept over the horizon, the volunteers began gathering burned belongings carried by the men, women, and children who died there. They also placed wooden stakes throughout the field to mark where bodies of the victims were located. By the time sunlight brightened the day, nearly a hundred people, consisting of investigators, law enforcement personnel, or people tasked with removing the bodies, were onsite. They weren't alone. From the surrounding communities, hundreds of curiosity seekers began crowding the area. Cars were parked wherever their drivers could find a space. They wanted to view the destruction that had taken place in such a tranquil setting.

Representatives from the U.S. Post Office also arrived on the scene. Their task, undoubtedly an unpleasant one, involved retrieving whatever pieces of scorched mail were scattered throughout the field. Churches from local communities were called on to have their priests administer last rites to the dead. Several priests kept busy throughout the morning hours, moving from body to body.

Later that morning, black hearses began to line up along Clarendon Hills Road. The crash victims were wrapped in rubber sheets before moving them to the Cook County Office of the Coroner in Chicago for identification. The gruesome task consumed five days. DNA testing to identify accident victims would later come into existence to expedite the process, but not as early as 1961.

By mid-afternoon on Friday, Najeeb Halaby, a one-time Lockheed employee, record-setting test pilot, and second administrator of the fledging Federal Aviation Agency, arrived on the scene. Accompanying him were people to assist investigators working for the Civil Aeronautics Board. The public were already hungry to learn what had caused the crash. His intervention seemed strange, because at that time, the FAA had no authority to investigate airliner accidents. The CAB had sole responsibility for that task.[11]

A theory beginning to circulate suggested that a bombing could have occurred, although it hadn't been substantiated. An explosion was supposedly heard while the plane was in the air. However, seasoned accident investigators had learned long ago to dismiss such accounts. An initial evaluation by a medical team examining a few of the corpses had ruled out a bombing. The victims didn't show any burst organs, this being typical if they died from an explosion. The injuries appeared to be more like those occurring in fatal automobile accidents. If not a bomb, the question remained—what caused the crash?

TWA wasted no time gathering together a team of technicians and airport workers to assist other personnel collecting wreckage at the crash site. At TWA's corporate headquarters, phones in the public relations department began ringing off the hook during the morning hours on Friday. By then, the crash had become front-page news throughout the nation and much of the world.

3. Nightmare

The most important outgoing phone call was reserved for Howard Hughes, TWA's major stockholder and outspoken founder. There had been other crashes of Constellations over the years, many due to bad weather or pilot error, but Flight 529 was different. It was possible that a small part of the plane's control system had failed, causing the pilots to lose control and crash. But when it came to one of his plane's crashing due to suspected mechanical failure, Hughes closely followed every aspect of its investigation. However, at the time of the crash, he was also heavily involved with other business distractions. TWA wasn't making a profit, posting alarming losses on a daily basis. Even worse, almost a year earlier, he had been prevented from managing the airline, although he did remain its largest stockholder.

> On February 13, 1962, less than six months after Flight 529 crashed, lawyers for Hughes filed a countersuit against TWA in New York City. It stated that the airline's lending institutions had conspired to seize the airline out from under him. In the lawsuit, he asked the court to dissolve a voting trust that forced him out.[12] It also called for the court to restore his control of TWA and award him millions of dollars in damages. He challenged the authority of the voting trust—while owning most of the airline's stock. Not surprising, the court dismissed the lawsuit. True to form, Howard Hughes would never give up.

As daylight dawned in Chicago on the first day of September, the vice president of public affairs at TWA was charged with a task he preferred not undertaking. His job called for him to contact Hughes and tell him the horrible news: Flight 529 crashed and killed everyone aboard.

During the summer of 1956, when a United Air Lines Douglas DC-7 accidentally knocked a TWA Constellation out of the sky over the Grand Canyon,[13] Hughes' principal response at the time was to make sure that neither United or TWA got blamed for causing the accident. Instead, he agreed with the CAB that cited poor air traffic control as a cause.[14] What upset him most was the loss of a Lockheed 1049 Super Constellation, one of only ten of those type airliners in TWA's fleet.

Ironically, the Constellation's captain had asked air traffic control to cancel his instrument flight plan. He wanted to fly a thousand feet higher, his request quickly approved. With both the United and TWA planes now assigned to the same altitude, flying in and out of clouds, it put them on a deadly collision course. However, a CAB accident investigation report describing the crash focused on technical issues, rather than human factors. No reason was given why TWA management would permit its captains to deviate from a company approved flight plan. Aware of these facts, it was understandable that Hughes stopped offering opinions concerning the cause of this and other accidents.

The extent of it is unknown, but negative publicity concerning the Flight 529 accident could affect the price of the airline's stock and reduce his personal wealth. While Hughes' mind was sharp when it came to absorbing technical details, human beings ran a distant second with him. He was never able to share a joke or enjoy the friendship of children or adults. In essence, he didn't seem to need human companionship. Hughes displayed an amazing lack of concern for other people. He only liked those who could return a favor, especially if it was something that could provide him with whatever he wanted at the time.[15]

The only tribute to lives taken too soon, along with comforting its next of kin and offspring, would be a thorough investigation to determine exactly what had caused Flight 529 to crash. It would ensure that such an accident would never happen again.

The rescuers working near Clarendon Hills didn't realize that 17 days after this crash, a Lockheed Electra belonging to Northwest Airlines also crashed while departing O'Hare International Airport. It took the lives of another 37 people. The cause was suspected as being similar to what brought down Flight 529.

When it came to the TWA Constellation, also unknown at the time of its crash, lives were cut short because a careless mechanic had forgotten to install a steel bolt. He still worked in the airline's maintenance department. Surely, this and the crash itself, along with a tremendous loss of lives and an important airliner, might have gotten Howard Hughes' undivided attention.

4

Smoking Gun

During World War II, while functioning under strict government restrictions and rationing, TWA was able to still turn a profit. Only one class of passenger service existed at the airlines, with no discounts or promotional offers being offered. Its planes flew full loads of passengers for 12 hours a day, with their ground crews working up to 60 hours a week. Meanwhile, the pilots put in 100 hours a month in the cockpits.

Because TWA was responsible for much of the Constellation's early development, the airline was given priority when it came to delivering the airliners from the factory. It meant that the first 12 planes coming off the assembly line would go to TWA and no other airline. By the end of 1946, TWA had taken delivery of nine of the airliners for its fleet.

The excitement didn't last long at Lockheed, however. Due to an airline pilot's strike in 1947, TWA cancelled another order for eight more Constellations. Making matters worse for Lockheed the following year, the airline again cancelled orders for another 18 of the planes.

The Constellations that TWA passengers were boarding were nothing like the shiny new jetliners. Their noisy 18-cylinder piston engines turned four large size propellers. Inside the passenger cabins, there were no cocktails, free movies, or even comfortable seating. The cabins were packed as tightly as possible with passengers and carry-on belongings. This was the reason why TWA flights became known as the Sky Club Coach service. Even its pressurization system was manually controlled to assure that its passengers wouldn't feel any surges.

There was something else that passengers boarding the Constellation in Boston didn't know. This same plane had been involved in a major accident during its early years flying for TWA. Following that accident, it was repaired, rather than scrapped like other airlines might have done. The accident happened because two of its engines had failed in flight, forcing its pilot to make an unplanned emergency landing.

17 Days and 17 Miles Apart

Damage to the plane was substantial before getting rebuilt. It was the same Constellation that had crashed on September 1, 1961, in the field near Clarendon Hills.

There was another serious accident at another airline flying Constellations. It took place on June 18, 1946, with a Pan American Airways flight scheduled to fly from New York to London.[1] Shortly after becoming airborne, a fire warning light had lit for its number four engine. Two of that engine's fire extinguishers were activated, but the flames couldn't be controlled. During the plane's descent, its propeller continued to rotate slowly, even though it had been feathered. The flames continued to pour from the top of the engine nacelle. Minutes after the fire warning had first sounded, the entire engine swung downward and fell off from the wing. Oil and other fluids began pouring from several damaged hoses in the nacelle.

A successful belly landing was made on a grass field without any injuries. It was later discovered that a metal firewall surrounding the engine wasn't capable of preventing a fire from traveling into other areas of the wing. A fire in one nacelle could pass with little difficulty into two other nacelles. Due to a lack of fire extinguishing in the other nacelles, the leaking fuel and oil hoses could easily start a fire. The Constellation also lacked fire detectors in its nacelles. And a fire-extinguishing agent proved ineffective in controlling a large fire. If the engine nacelle had remained intact over time, the fire would have weakened the wing structure, causing it to fail, resulting in a crash.

The CAB investigators discovered that a driveshaft used to operate a supercharger had failed, the system designed to pressurize the passenger cabin. Driven by the engine, its shaft had snapped into several pieces. It also sliced apart the fluid-carrying hoses and tubing connected to fuel and hydraulic pumps. The immediate solution was to install a pipe-like housing around the drive shafts to prevent them from breaking. It became a serious problem that affected all Constellations then in airline service.

Another accident occurred three weeks later on July 11 when a TWA Constellation suffered an in-flight fire while flying over the coast of Pennsylvania.[2] The smell of burning insulation became noticeable to the crew in the cockpit. An external hatch was opened to air out the cockpit, but it only fed the fire. The Constellation crashed in a field. Only one of the six people onboard survived. The fire was later traced to a bolt that served as an electrical connection between the plane's

4. Smoking Gun

generators and its main electrical distribution system. The flames had entered the cabin from the forward baggage compartment, where the plane's hydraulic reservoirs were located. When hydraulic fluid leaked onto the insulation, a raging fire was the result.

These early events were frightening, but they occurred long before the crash of Flight 529. By the time of that fatal flight, it was assumed Lockheed had resolved several problems affecting the fleets of Constellations.

Trans World Airlines offered its customers a supposedly safe product: air transportation. But it failed to assume any responsibility for its lack of safety.

From California to New York, the crash of Flight 529 had shocked the nation. This was especially true among inexperienced air travelers. Finding its cause, and making sure that similar accidents wouldn't be repeated, was a responsibility of the Civil Aeronautics Board in Washington, D.C. Investigators at the CAB were determined to find a cause of the crash as soon as possible. They told the officials at TWA about the Constellation's missing bolt and cotter pin they discussed earlier. Whether the airline's executives and engineers believed it or not, that loss resulted in the elevator control surface jamming and its pilots losing all control. This simple understanding caused the investigators to dig into something even more complicated.

To more fully explore the loss of TWA Flight 529, the CAB convened a hearing at Midway Hotel in Chicago on September 27, 1962. Chaired by senior officials from the agency, with everyone under oath at the hearing, an aircraft mechanic employed by TWA expressed doubt that he worked on the ill-fated plane. Other than this mechanic as the sole suspect, the managers and executives at the airline had no idea who could have made a mistake. Out of the thousands of employees working at its maintenance facilities in the United States, one of them had forgotten to install a cotter pin to prevent a bolt from falling out. The supervisors routinely assigned work tasks to the mechanics but stayed away from mechanical work. At the end of the day, there was no evidence presented by TWA that showed an employee had started the deadly chain of events. In the minds of the CAB investigators, nothing they were hearing that day made sense.[3]

TWA quickly backed away from assuming any responsibility for the crash of Flight 529. Lockheed and the FAA did the same, the latter organization supposedly being responsible for aviation safety in the

17 Days and 17 Miles Apart

United States. Meanwhile, the investigators closely studied what they previously uncovered seeking any errors they may have made. They discovered something of interest. It was unknown what had taken place in the cockpit during the plane's final moments in the air. There were no radio calls to the control tower in Midway from either pilot, or flight data recordings for the investigators to examine.[4]

It was obvious to the investigators that TWA's persistent goal was to prevent multi-million-dollar litigation from the surviving family members. It was also clear that the pilot's total loss of control had occurred while the plane was still in the air. The airline sternly countered that opinion, continuing to state that the missing bolt and its cotter pin exited when the plane was on the ground. Based on everything the CAB had heard at the hearing, none of it made sense to the investigative team. However, TWA couldn't offer a logical reason why the plane's experienced crew could have lost control while flying in perfect weather conditions. They didn't even send a short message to the control tower or TWA's maintenance center.

On the surface, the airline's claim made sense with its executives and lawyers. By itself, the missing cotter pin didn't cause its airliner to crash. It was the loss of a bolt that brought the plane down, the pin only serving to restrain it. This controversy continued to fuel a chain of circumstance with outcomes that nobody could agree about.

The CAB investigators decided to query the administrator of the FAA. They had asked him to work with Lockheed to redesign an important part of the Constellation's elevator control system. Najeeb Halaby, the FAA's second administrator, refused to cooperate with the CAB request. He didn't believe that a dangerous problem existed. Hundreds of Constellations were flying daily, trouble-free passenger service and had done so for well over a decade.

President Dwight Eisenhower had signed legislation to establish the Federal Aviation Agency into law on August 18, 1958. It created an independent federal agency free from the existing Department of Commerce. The function and authority of the earlier Civil Aeronautics Administration was transferred to the administration's new FAA, it in full operation on January 1, 1959.

The FAA's first administrator was Elwood Quesada, a retired lieutenant general who had served in the U.S. Air Force. During World War II, his efforts contributed to using close air support tactics to achieve greater precision and speed. An impatient leader, Quesada was known

4. Smoking Gun

for a short temper, especially evident when other leaders wouldn't pay attention to his recommendations. Following retirement from the Air Force, he served as a vice president at Lockheed Aircraft Corporation from 1953 to 1958. This experience led to his appointment as the first administrator at the FAA.

One of Quesada's first actions was to bring 28,000 employees working at the CAA over to the FAA. All of that agency's staff, facilities, offices, equipment, and inventory were transferred, including its fleet of 90 aircraft. However, for the time being, the Civil Aeronautics Board retained authority over aircraft crash investigations. In 1961, the investigation of Flight 529 was one of them.

The CAB investigation at the crash site of TWA Flight 529 moved into high gear. Its investigators began sifting through the burnt cornfield for clues. In an attempt to uncover even the smallest pieces, the work consumed several weeks. It was hoped that the bits and pieces of debris, some of them scattered beneath dirt in the field, would assist learning what had contributed to the crash. Larger pieces of the plane ended up being tagged, segregated into piles, and trucked to a roped-off corner of TWA's maintenance hangar at Midway Airport. Anything even remotely connected to the crash was carefully collected and labeled. The CAB's work at the crash site was occasionally interrupted. Heartless scavengers began arriving not long after the first responders left. The investigators couldn't determine what pieces of wreckage had been carted off, or if any missing pieces might help with the investigative process.

Although they didn't provide much assistance, other aviation organizations offered to help with the investigation. They included employees from TWA, along with the Air Line Pilots Association, the Flight Engineers Association, Lockheed Aircraft Corporation, Curtiss-Wright Corporation and newly formed FAA.

Members of a CAB witness group began walking door-to-door throughout neighborhoods near the crash site. They talked with the residents, asking if they had heard or seen the limping Constellation during its final moments in the air. The witness group would eventually conduct and document about 150 interviews.

Concerned about the airline's image with the traveling public, TWA wasted no time to make a public statement. Charles Tillinghast, Jr., chief executive officer of TWA at the time, sought to calm his worried customers: "We are cooperating with federal and local authorities in an effort to determine the cause. This was the first fatal accident involving a TWA 049 type Constellation since 1947. During this period these airplanes have flown billions of passenger miles in complete safety."[5]

It didn't take long for the CAB investigators to come up with an educated guess about what could have brought the plane down. Although most of its airframe was pulverized into piles of metal strips, one of its largest airframe sections had escaped the inferno. It would become the most important clue the CAB would have—its tail section, commonly known as an empennage. It had broken off from the aft fuselage and slammed into the field about 33 feet from the rest of the wreckage. Its aluminum skin, structure, linkages, and control rods appeared to be undamaged. Even its paint wasn't scratched.

On a temporary basis, most of the plane's wreckage stayed in storage at a corner of the TWA hangar at the airport. However, the empennage received most of the CAB's attention, especially its rudder, elevator, and horizontal stabilizer. These were the only sizable pieces of wreckage that had survived the impact of the crash. The distance from the bulk of the wreckage to where the empennage ended up suggested that it had separated seconds before the rest of the plane dove into the field.

A part of the right-hand rudder control surface was found sheared off.[6] Extreme movement of the elevator could have easily hit the surface during upward travel. A deformed pattern, carved into the metal frame of the rudder, got the investigators' eyes. It became clear that the elevator, stuck in a full-up position, had rubbed against the rudder at some point.

Portions of the instruments and controls from the cockpit were recovered in the debris field. Although severely damaged, a shift handle used to disengage the hydraulic boost for moving the elevator was found in its "on" position. This meant that the hydraulic system was operational prior to the crash. At least, that's what the initial CAB examination revealed.

Prior to World War II, aircraft flight control systems consisted of simple devices. Ailerons, rudders, and elevators were coupled directly to control wheels or sticks in cockpits using cables, pulleys, and turnbuckles. During the war, the size and performance of newer planes, such as Constellations, had progressed to a point where the pilots needed more muscle power to move their cumbersome control

4. Smoking Gun

TWA Flight 529's severed stabilizer section is shown having an extreme upward angle of its elevator control surface, an important clue for investigators (courtesy Mary Brown at Clarendon Hills Historical Society).

surfaces. Lockheed developed the boosted flight control system to serve this purpose.

When it came time to expand the CAB's investigation, a number of hydraulic components, used to position the rudder and elevator control surfaces, were removed from the wreckage for testing in a laboratory. On a test bench, they functioned satisfactorily. However, the investigators noted something unusual. A small steel arm, normally connected to a steel link known as a parallelogram, wasn't found attached to anything. It may have become disconnected prior to the plane hitting the ground. A bolt, designed to attach the arm to the parallelogram, was also missing, as was its nut and cotter pin. A CAB investigation report provided the details: "Examination of the parallelogram linkage of the elevator boost located in the extreme aft section of the fuselage revealed a $5/16$ inch AN 175–21 nickel steel bolt was missing. This parallelogram linkage connects the pilot elevator input to the control valve of the elevator boost system."[7]

A crucial question needed answering: Did the force resulting from

17 Days and 17 Miles Apart

Due to the extreme impact of the crash, few instruments from the cockpit and cabin were recovered. One was an oil pressure gauge, used by a flight engineer to monitor engine temperatures. Together with switches and other cockpit instruments, it had been mounted on the Constellation's flight engineer's panel. The alarm clock had likely belonged to one of the passengers. It shows 2:04 a.m., the exact time that the plane impacted the field (courtesy Mark Reynolds).

the crash push out the bolt connecting the arm to the parallelogram? Or did the bolt fall out when the plane was still in the air? The horizontal stabilizer survived both impact and fire, but a critical part of its parallelogram didn't. If the empennage had been destroyed in the inferno, in common with other aircraft accidents, solving the mystery of why Flight 529 crashed would have consumed many additional weeks or months of research.

Appreciating the missing bolt's significance to the crash, the investigators scrambled to find it amid the crumpled pieces of metal, burnt fabric, and rusty control cables scattered throughout the floor in the TWA hangar. Every nut and bolt assigned to the parallelogram linkage had been accounted for—except the bolt they had been seeking. Speculating that it could be hidden from view under plowed-up dirt in the

4. Smoking Gun

cornfield, they revisited the site and sifted through shovelfuls of soil. A methodical ground search was conducted, hoping the bolt would be found. The team of searchers ended up going through several acres of charred dirt and debris where the Constellation shed its weakened tail and its engines dug deep craters in the earth. The painstaking work consumed much time, but no bolt was found. Once again, the CAB investigators left empty handed. It seemed likely that the bolt didn't have a nut or cotter pin securing it before the plane crashed. If the bolt had fallen out during its takeoff from Midway, the plane would not have been able to lift off from the runway.

Other parties to the investigation had a different opinion: the bolt exited when or after the plane hit the ground. This sharp difference of opinion began to build momentum.

The missing hex-headed bolt had been machined to a closer tolerance than a general-purpose fastener. It had an unusual feature—a small hole drilled through its shank to retain a cotter pin or thin piece of safety wire. Small slots drilled in its nut, known as castellations,

Fasteners identical to those installed in the elevator control linkage of TWA Flight 529. Parts shown include a AN-175-21 bolt along with its AN-320-5 nut and a AN-0380-2-2 cotter pin for securing the nut (author's collection).

17 Days and 17 Miles Apart

were used to secure the nut to a hole in the bolt. The cotter pin was extremely small—only a 16th of an inch in diameter by one-half-inch long.

An almost indistinguishable smudge of grease was found smeared across the small arm of the parallelogram. It became another potentially important clue. The CAB investigators, working with engineers brought in from Lockheed, conducted a close inspection, focusing on the arm that didn't have a bolt. Following the plane's earlier elevator maintenance in a TWA hangar, its nut could have unscrewed, allowing the bolt to drift out from its hole and splattering a thin layer of grease onto the arm. Although there were high hopes by finding this clue, the grease theory was later abandoned after realizing that it alone could not have resulted in the crash of Flight 529.

Sorting through all the collected evidence to date, a mechanic could have failed to install the bolt correctly during a maintenance visit in November 1960. Not everyone agreed. They responded that this wasn't logical due to the length of time between November and the month of the crash. Or a nut could have been over-tightened, stripping its threads. However, even a stripped nut, if a cotter pin had been installed, would be adequate to secure the bolt. The most logical reason for the bolt's absence was that a cotter pin had never been installed during one of those maintenance visits at TWA.

When the bolt fell out from the parallelogram, a valve controlling the hydraulic boost moved to its "open" position, causing fluid to flow to an "up-elevator" side of the system. The elevator control surface then moved to its maximum 40-degree angle, causing the plane to stall. The pilots had apparently used their hands to push the control wheels forward. Using his right hand, it's likely the captain tried pulling the shift handle up to switch from hydraulic to manual control. Unfortunately, the elevator remained stuck. It also seemed predictable that the pilots would continue to push against the wheels, preventing the boost system from switching to manual operation.

In the final accident investigation report for TWA Flight 529, the CAB made it clear what had caused the crash:

> If the pilot responds normally to a stall, several events will occur if the bolt worked its way out of the parallelogram. After the bolt comes out, the weight of the spool and the parallelogram lines caused full pressure to be applied to the up-elevator side of the actuator. The elevator travels up to its maximum hinge angle. The plane enters an accelerated stall.

4. Smoking Gun

When the stall decays toward a primary stall, elevator angle increases to 40 degrees. The crew would normally apply high forward pressure on the control wheels to get the nose down. While forward pressure is applied, they attempt to pull the shift handle. With the elevator at maximum deflection, held there by hydraulic pressure and forward force on the wheel, it becomes impossible to move the shift handle far enough to operate the shutoff valve. In essence, the increased forward force results in a higher force needed to pull the handle.[8]

Once the bolt fell out, the weight of the spool controlling its valve, combined with the additional weight of the parallelogram, would have kept the elevator in its stuck position. The plane would enter a dangerous stall condition. Nothing could save the Constellation at this point. The uncontrollable maneuvering of Flight 529 likely involved at least two kinds of stalls. A secondary stall can occur when the recovery attempt from a stall is too abrupt, but an accelerated stall can occur at any speed. Assuming that a plane's elevator is fully functional, it's a simple matter for a pilot to ease back on the control wheel and recover. In the case of Flight 529 this wasn't possible. Because the pilot lost all control of the elevator, there was nothing that the crew could do to pull the plane out of its deadly series of stalls.[9]

The pilots likely continued pushing against the wheels in an attempt to force the nose down. At the same time, they tried pulling the shift handle up, the elevator remaining stuck. The handle couldn't be moved, held in place tightly by hydraulic pressure and the force exerted by them pushing forward on the wheels. The combination made it impossible to move the handle far enough up to shift the boost to manual control.

Vibration resulting from the relentless stalls caused extreme damage to the empennage and stabilizer structure, causing the entire tail assembly to separate from the aft fuselage.

The CAB investigators assumed overall responsibility and developed their own theories about the crash. The FAA, that two-year-old organization headed by administrator Najeeb Halaby, kept its eyes on whatever information the CAB came across. Unknown to many observers at the time, Halaby was not only an experienced pilot, but was earlier assigned to Lockheed Aircraft Corporation in Burbank. A possible conflict of interest became apparent. During the time that Halaby worked at Lockheed, the company was manufacturing the Constellations now under scrutiny by CAB investigators.

17 Days and 17 Miles Apart

Halaby was only 16 years old when he made a solo flight in an open-cockpit biplane. During 1933 he went on to earn a pilot's license and later graduated from Yale University with a law degree. As an officer in the U.S. Navy during World War II, he served as a test pilot assigned to Lockheed. During the late 1950s Halaby joined a social circle in Washington, D.C. This move enabled him to interact with John and Jacqueline Kennedy. He ended up campaigning for Kennedy when the former senator ran for president. On March 3, 1961, after winning the presidential election, Kennedy appointed Halaby to head the administration's Federal Aviation Agency.[10]

Halaby's reputation as an independent thinker became apparent when he made decisions. When it involved issues involving Flight 529, fearing that other Constellations could also have missing or failing bolts, Halaby ordered his staff into action. The FAA issued an airworthiness directive (AD) mandating that all operators of Constellations inspect the elevator mechanisms for loose or missing bolts.

The text of the airworthiness directive penned by Halaby's staff was simple, specific, and demanded that the inspections be conducted immediately. The AD applied to model 049, 149, 649, 749, and 1049 series Constellations. It stated the following: "Effective September 20, 1961, for all persons except those to whom it was made effective immediately by telegram dated September 8, 1961."

The FAA's sense of urgency became obvious when it provided rationale for the request:

> As a result of findings during investigation of a recent Lockheed Model 049 aircraft fatal accident, it is necessary to require the following corrective action. Unless already accomplished within the last 50 hours' time in service, the following special inspection is required at the first layover or stop where qualified maintenance personnel and facilities are available and the inspection can be conducted without undue delay but not to exceed the next 25 hours' time in service after the effective date of this AD. Inspect to ensure that the 6 bolts, nuts, and cotter pins in the parallelogram linkage between the elevator boost valve and boost mechanism are properly secured and safetied.[11]

The message was blunt, to the point, and prepared unusually fast for a government bureaucracy. The executives at TWA grudgingly agreed with whatever the FAA announced. In the minds of the airline's executives avoiding negative publicity was the only goal at the airline. TWA and other Constellation operators had no choice but to comply with the

4. Smoking Gun

directive. The airline went on to announce its opinion concerning the matter in the airline's employee newsletter:

> TWA has completed the control system inspections on certain of its Constellations as ordered by the FAA following the tragic accident in Chicago. The inspection of TWA 049 aircraft was completed on September 1 and 2, some days prior to the official FAA request. The FAA had ordered TWA and the other seven airlines operating these types of Constellations to inspect the aircraft to insure that the five bolts, nuts and cotter pins in the parallelogram linkage between the elevator boost valve and boost mechanism are properly secured and safe tied.[12]

The TWA newsletter didn't mention if any missing bolts, nuts, or cotter pins were discovered by mechanics performing the inspections. Officials from the FAA had not monitored the inspection work in the airline's hangars.

By now, public outcry was demanding that Kennedy, Halaby and the agency take more action. At the time, it appeared like FAA had been siding with the victims who died in Flight 529, and not the airline or the plane's manufacturer. Under Halaby's leadership, this would later change.

Howard Hughes had more than a passing interest in the design of the Constellation. After all, he was Lockheed's first commercial customer for the planes. He had specified some of its smallest details, including a hydraulic boost system for moving its heavy rudders, ailerons, and elevators. Hughes had flown the Constellations that Lockheed had built for TWA over many years.

The Constellation was not designed to fly without a boost system, causing Lockheed to market it as a safety feature. Pumps driven by engines on the plane's left wing energized a hydraulic system that operated strictly its flight controls. A secondary system, powered by engines on the right wing, operated the landing gear, flaps, brakes, and retractable tailskid. Former TWA Constellation flight engineer Edward Betts had an opinion about this arrangement: "When everything functioned normally the system worked great. But it was also the source of a lot of logbook writeups for the tail kicking from side to side or up and down, which could be discomforting to passengers in the rear of the plane."[13]

It was well known that Lockheed Constellations were originally designed and built to move military troops and equipment during World War II. When the war ended, the airlines took an opportunity to convert the transports into airliners. While still in military colors, a comprehensive operator's manual was prepared to guide the actions of pilots flying the planes. It covered the hydraulic boost system in detail. There was also a warning about using the system, especially one for its elevator:

> Failure of the control surface boost system will be noticed by a stiffening of the controls. To shift the elevator control from the boost system to manual operation, pull the handle up. This operation shifts a linkage in the tail cone such that full movement of the control column moves the elevator only about a third of its normal travel. It also bypasses the elevator booster cylinder. The reduced elevator travel is sufficient for all normal maneuvers and for landing at a higher than minimum speed.[14]

The operator's manual went into even greater detail concerning the possible loss of all elevator control:

> A pull rod to the left of the pilot's control stand will disconnect the elevator booster and at the same time shift the elevator control linkage to provide a mechanical advantage for normal control of approximately 3 to 1 compared to the normal linkage. Because the pilot contributes but a small percentage of the total force required to operate the surface controls (the hydraulic system contributing the rest) it is obvious that if the booster system fails, full deflection of the surfaces can't be obtained even at very low airspeed.[15]

Whether or not the military information was included in civilian Constellation flight training manuals is not known. If not, it should have been.

At the time of the Flight 529 crash, many airlines were outsourcing so-called "heavy maintenance" to outside companies. Instead, TWA decided to invest in constructing and staffing its own in-house repair and overhaul facilities in key cities around the country. Inside the hangars, everything from minor inspections to major overhauls had been accomplished. To accommodate so much work, TWA employed thousands of technical personnel, many of them being members of a machinist union.

TWA's largest overhaul and maintenance base was located at Mid–Continent International Airport in Kansas City, Missouri. Flight 529 was flown there during May 1959 to undergo major maintenance. The work involved replacing several components of its hydraulic booster system, including those controlling the elevator. Upon completion, the work was inspected and documented as being airworthy. TWA placed the plane back in passenger service without delay. Further maintenance was accomplished during November 1960. It involved replacing

4. Smoking Gun

components that were dedicated to only the elevator control system. This included disassembling the troublesome parallelogram assembly. Five bolts that retained the assembly were replaced—including a bolt the CAB investigators were still seeking. Another inspection of the Constellation's flight controls took place during a routine check on August 7, 1961—three weeks before Flight 529 crashed. Nothing abnormal was noted during that inspection.[16]

Missing bolts weren't the only thing on the FAA's mind. During its investigation of the tail assembly, cracking of the horizontal stabilizer's rear spar was noted. Within two weeks after Flight 529 had crashed, the FAA issued another airworthiness directive requiring that all Constellation operators inspect the stabilizers for cracking. In a rush to get this accomplished, and fearing other Constellations could crash, the AD read:

> As a result of reports of numerous cases of cracking in the horizontal stabilizer rear spar-to-fuselage attachment, the following inspections must be accomplished within the next 400 hours' time in service after effective date of this AD, unless already accomplished within the last 4,300 hours' time in service and at intervals of 4,700 hours' time in service.[17]

The CAB investigators continued to be mystified. Not only were they concerned about what they knew—but also what they didn't know. They couldn't understand why thousands of mechanics and inspectors working for TWA didn't notice a missing cotter pin or loose bolt during any of the maintenance visits, particularly one conducted less than a month before the crash.

The Constellation series of airliners had an unusually checkered history, although the executives at Lockheed would never acknowledge it. Other than complying with airworthiness directives issued by the FAA, the manufacturer reported only easily solved problems affecting the hundreds of Constellations in airline and military service.

As far back as 1949, the government issued an airworthiness directive requiring the elevator booster systems be inspected and modified as soon as possible. Ironically, three years after the loss of Flight 529, the FAA issued another AD pertaining to a wide range of Constellations, including models 49, 149, 649, 649A, 749A, 1049–54, 1049C, 1049D and 1049E. In other words, the AD affected the entire fleet of Constellations. It called for inspecting the parallelograms to make sure their attaching bolts had been installed and tightened properly.

17 Days and 17 Miles Apart

Keep in mind that the earlier AD was issued during 1949—not immediately after Flight 529 crashed in 1961. Why nothing was done between those years isn't known.[18]

The military also suffered a fatal accident of a Constellation, in addition to another non-injury incident, while operating military versions of the plane.[19] It caused the CAB investigators to review their accident reports in detail. They uncovered a shocking similarity to what happened to Flight 529. Following the crash of a U.S. Air Force C-121, a transport version of the Constellation, the Air Force ordered that a research study be conducted to analyze failure modes of the plane's hydraulic boost system. Lockheed didn't pay for this study. The finding: when the booster shift system was tested and subjected to simulated air loads, pulling up the shift handle wasn't possible if more than a hundred pounds of force was pushed against the control wheels. Somehow circumventing this handicap while in flight, the pilots flying this C-121 didn't crash but landed safely after a harrowing ride down from a high altitude.

The crew of a U.S. Navy R7V, another militarized variant of the Constellation, weren't as fortunate.[20] It was flying from Ontario International Airport in Southern California to Moffett Field in Northern California during the evening of May 14, 1958. Its pilot attempted an emergency landing near the Taft Airport in the southwest San Joaquin Valley. The R7V had made several 360-degree turns with the plane's nose forced up at a high angle. Not regaining the altitude lost making those turns, it continued flying around in an orbit, losing more altitude, and coming dangerously close to the unpopulated farmland below it. Without warning, a severe pitch-up maneuver pushed the plane's nose even higher, causing a series of accelerated stalls. The R7V descended in a stalled condition, quickly dropping down from 12,300 feet while its pilots continued struggling in a futile attempt to pull it out of the stall. Flying far too low to recover, the Constellation slammed into the ground, killing everyone aboard.[21]

When the Navy investigators sifted through the R7V's wreckage, they discovered that its shift handle was placed in an "on" position. It had not been pulled up, likely because the pilots didn't have sufficient strength or didn't understand how the system worked. A result was the series of stalls. The investigation revealed that a clevis bolt, attaching its parallelogram to the spool of a valve controlling the boost cylinder, had come loose. It wasn't an identical bolt to the one missing from Flight

4. Smoking Gun

529, but the outcome was the same for its occupants. Uncontrolled movement of the spool had caused it to reposition the elevator, resulting in a nose that rose sharply.

The R7V had endured five successive accelerated stalls before it crashed. Its airframe had absorbed tremendous shaking brought on by extreme air loads. It eventually resulted in breakage of the plane's skin, stringers, and bulkheads throughout the aft fuselage. What happened to Flight 529 was similar. The R7V's horizontal stabilizer structure failed, causing the plane to turn into nothing more than a falling brick. The probable cause from its investigators stated that the accident was caused by failure of a linkage in the elevator boost system resulting in the elevator traveling to its full up position.

Expressing concern because the military was the top non-commercial customer for Lockheed, the company decided to perform a series of tests for the Navy. They were similar to what the Air Force had earlier conducted. The tests revealed that during extreme deflection of the elevator, moving the shift handle couldn't be accomplished if pressure was applied to either control wheel in the cockpit. A report authored by a Lockheed flight control engineer stated in part:

> A study of the curves reveals the marked effect of [control] column forces on shift force, but also that there is a reasonable amount of column force allowable. The conditions permitting a shift to manual have considerable latitude, depending upon surface moment, restraining column force, and surface angle. Within these limits many opportunities would be present permitting a shift to manual position.[22]

Combining this finding with what the CAB investigators learned about Flight 529's final moments, the engineer's report described a hit-and-miss approach to design an emergency control system for a modern airliner. For the CAB investigators, it was shocking. Assuming that an elevator's pitch control had jammed, as it did with Flight 529, the CAB disputed the Lockheed test report by responding: "Particularly in an unmanageable regime, and if a corrective mechanism is available, a pilot should be offered a positive correction, not opportunities-within-limits."[23] Lockheed should have stated that the design of its boost control system was not failsafe, and modify the system to avoid suffering frightening stalls and fatal accidents.

Recovering from a steep nose-up attitude should be a simple matter, a straightforward procedure for most pilots. But the investigators discovered another dangerous design peculiarity in Lockheed flight control systems. By shifting from boost to manual operation, the control's mechanical advantage also changed the relationship between the control wheels and the mechanism positioning the elevator. As a result, the control wheels in the cockpit would be pushed aft, in unison with movement of the elevator. When the system's hydraulic valves were operating normally, the elevator remained free to move either up or down, assisted by air pressure pushing against it. Of course, forward pressure was not being applied to the control wheels so the shift to manual operation could be completed successfully.

In order to test both the hydraulic and boost control systems, Lockheed engineers built a full-scale mock-up of those systems. To simulate engine operation, four hydraulic pumps were driven by 90-horsepower V-8 piston engines. To represent high-altitude flight conditions, frozen boxes were placed around the engines, exposing the systems to subzero temperatures that Constellations often encountered. Two hundred hours undergoing cycling, amounting to at least 1,000 cycles for each hour operated, were undertaken. This gave the boost system a thorough test. For part of the test, a control wheel from a cockpit was repeatedly turned around an arc, followed by pushing it fore and aft.

Following all of the experimental research, the engineers and executives at Lockheed decided that the system's design was adequate, as did the FAA. As for what the U.S. Air Force and Navy thought about this, it remained a confidential matter. It was assumed that the pilots of Flight 529 had applied plenty of forward pressure to the control wheels in their attempt to exit the series of deadly stalls. The captain likely tried to pull up the boost shift handle several times. Because the elevator was stuck at a dangerous angle, it was too late for the crew to recover.

No other pilot, regardless of flying experience, could have gotten Flight 529 under control and landed safely. Seventy-eight people boarded a plane that would soon be missing an important bolt. If a nut or its cotter pin had been installed, it's likely that everyone would arrive at the destinations safely. Instead, they died during a dark night in a muddy cornfield. It had nothing to do with pilot error, bad weather, engine failure, or sabotage. It was pure negligence on the part of TWA—and a design flaw that continued to exist in the flight control systems of every Constellation that Lockheed built.

5

Who Did It?

As a passenger, would you risk your life boarding an airliner that had been involved in a number of serious accidents and then rebuilt? What if it had flown hundreds of trips across the Atlantic Ocean to countries in Europe? Do you think that an airliner's electrical, hydraulic, and flight control systems could fail while you are in the air? If any of these issues bother you, be careful what airline you choose for an upcoming trip. Flight 529 had experienced all of these issues during its long life at TWA.

It took more than a year for investigators from the Civil Aeronautics Board to pull together the facts needed to hold a public hearing and determine a cause for the Flight 529 crash. At times, some of the testimony could have turned into a showstopper. Some of the players may have made it look like an unstructured criminal trial. If it was really a true trial, the defendants would likely be TWA and Lockheed with plaintiffs played by the CAB investigators, and in a strange sense, people left behind from those who died in the crash. As with real courtroom proceedings, and at least in this situation, lawyers for the airline set the stage, TWA well known as one of America's premier international air carriers.

A mechanic testifying at the CAB hearing, backed by TWA vice presidents and senior managers had little to say when asked about their employee's connection to the crash. When questioned under oath, the mechanic didn't remember installing a cotter pin or a missing bolt. The lawyers from TWA instantly switched the focus, stating that the bolt had fallen out after the plane crashed, rather than when it was still in the air. This was the only "new" piece of information that TWA would offer. Lawyers for Lockheed Aircraft Corporation backed up the airline's claims, stating the Constellation was a proven airliner and considered safe in all respects. In essence, it amounted to nothing more than corporate doubletalk.

17 Days and 17 Miles Apart

The TWA mechanic, not identified by name in a CAB accident investigation report, testified that he installed the plane's parallelogram linkage in November 1960. The CAB team wondered if he screwed in the missing bolt and cotter pin. "I am sure all bolts were installed, properly torqued, and safetied," he responded when asked whether the bolt was installed by him or someone else.

Possibly seeing Ray Dunn in the audience (who would attend all trials and hearings involving TWA safety or liability), and going back to what he said earlier, the mechanic quickly corrected himself: "I do not remember specifically working on plane 555...." TWA had numbered the crashed plane as ship number 555. He had either developed a weak memory or made the comment to avoid condemnation from his employer, several TWA executives being in the room. Either way, the statement contradicted his testimony a few minutes earlier.[1] It was clear that he was no longer a credible witness.

The CAB recommended that the mechanism for shifting the Constellation's elevator hydraulic boost to manual operation should be modified by Lockheed. The CAB pointed out that the instinctive action of pilots was known to be sequential in nature, rather than simultaneous. The recommendation called for redesigning part of the mechanism to relieve hydraulic pressure before a need to pull up the handle and gain manual control. It differed from the amount of force applied to its control wheels in the cockpit. It seemed like a simple request, but TWA executives, the FAA, and lawyers at Lockheed didn't see it that way.[2]

Mountains of evidence were presented to support the CAB's findings. Of primary importance, the agency continued to ask that Lockheed modify the hydraulic boost system in all Constellations. However, the FAA and officials at Lockheed continued to reject that request. After months of meetings, interviews, and research, Lockheed remained steadfast in its decision: the elevator control system in Constellations would not be changed. The decision wasn't much of a surprise even though the existing design could prove dangerous and result in fatal accidents.

Actually, a missing cotter pin was not what caused Flight 529 to crash. It was the loss of control resulting from a missing bolt. The pin had only "contributed" to a loss of the bolt. After stating this opinion, the TWA lawyers would play down the mechanic's role in the disaster. The mechanic could have forgotten to install a pin, but by itself, it would

70

5. Who Did It?

not have resulted in a crash. The airline continued to stress that the bolt had been ejected only after the plane hit the ground.

Flight 529 had flown many thousands of hours without an accident, at least according to what TWA offered. The intent of its reasoning, of course, was to shield the airline from assuming any liability for the crash. Its lawyers and executives were skilled in twisting well-honed statements coming from the CAB investigators, particularly its words about to be released in a final accident investigation report prepared by the agency.

A year of onsite and laboratory analysis conducted by CAB employees was now history. Its investigators had examined anything even remotely connected to the loss of Flight 529. Assessing each possibility, only three of them stood out as suspects—a bolt, nut, and cotter pin. After announcing a cause of the crash, the investigators discovered that much of the aviation industry didn't agree with its conclusions. Of course, some of them had reputations to worry about or money that could be lost. They included Trans World Airlines, other airlines, aircraft and equipment manufacturers, Lockheed Aircraft Corporation, and even an administrator at the Federal Aviation Agency. TWA's competitors had watched the investigation unfold. They secretly hoped that their airline passengers wouldn't pay attention to so much publicity.

In the minds of CAB investigators, it felt as though they were communicating with a wall at times. They began to wonder if a lack of concern for a cause might be a cover-up for wrongdoing. Or more likely, was TWA trying to avoid a string of expensive lawsuits? After all was said and done, plenty of well-documented evidence ended up damming the reputations of both TWA and Lockheed. Throughout the lengthy investigation, both of those companies expressed little interest in spending time and money to improve the safety of Constellations. Their ignorance of the official findings made no sense with the team of experienced CAB investigators.

The difference of opinion involved nothing more than a simple disagreement—did a bolt fall out while the plane was in the air? Or was it already on the ground? Of course, if it had fallen out immediately after takeoff, the pilots would have lost control and crashed while departing from the airport. Ruling out this possibility, what type of mechanical failure could bring down such a large plane? During the investigation, there were no comments from TWA and Lockheed to answer this and other questions.

17 Days and 17 Miles Apart

There was no doubt the bolt fell out several minutes after the take-off from Midway, but certainly not over or near the airport. The plane had likely been in the air, but what caused one of the airline's most experienced captains to lose control and crash? Representatives from TWA and Lockheed did not offer an explanation.

During the 1960s, most accident investigations centered more on the actual failure of mechanical parts than what led to their failure—the so-called human factor. The mechanics and inspectors who had worked on Flight 529's elevator mechanism said the work was accomplished correctly, even though they couldn't back up that claim with any evidence.

Supporting his mechanics, Dunn, the executive managing all maintenance operations at TWA, didn't concur with the CAB's findings. The amount of formal education the executives and mechanics had at TWA wasn't unusual. The only requirement was an employee had to show intense devotion to a job, loyalty, and a willingness to work whatever hours were needed to get the work done.

At the time of the Flight 529 crash, Dunn was in charge of all maintenance and engineering activity at the airline. A quiet, humble, and dedicated employee, he had joined TWA in 1935. Largely self-taught, he remained with the airline, ascending through its ranks while the company grew larger over its decades in business.[3]

TWA's expansive Mid–Continent (MCI) overhaul base in Kansas City, Missouri, involving a worldwide work force totaling 6,500 employees, about 3,500 of them based at MCI. Nearing the early1960s, the facility had been charged with the care of 200 piston and turbojet powered airliners. On file at the base could be found IBM computer cards having complete records for every functioning component in TWA airliners, including the Constellation that crashed. By running the cards through a computer system, the mechanics could determine exactly when vital parts from each plane had to be inspected or replaced during its visit to the facility. When the CAB investigators examined the files for Flight 529, they discovered the IBM system had not been at fault. Instead, it was nothing more than carelessness caused by one of the 6,500 employees.[4]

During his final years at TWA, Dunn was thought to be a logical successor for the president's position at the airline. Not only was he popular with Hughes, but also with TWA president Charles Tillinghast. Considered to be the president's right-hand man, Dunn was eventually

5. Who Did It?

promoted to a senior vice president and system general manager position. However, his loyalty always remained with Howard Hughes.[5]

The employees at TWA, wherever in the world they were based, were directed to never discuss the crash of Flight 529 with anyone outside of the airline. It was many years later, long after Hughes' death in 1976, that some of them offered opinions concerning what had caused the crash.

The author corresponded with David Kent, who as a child lived in an area where Flight 529 had crashed. "The airline would not admit culpability where there wasn't a 100 percent certainty," he said. "Every TWA mechanic and, likely the pilots for the airline, would tell you that the airline was at fault." Bill Aitken served as the head mechanic at TWA in the Midway hangar at the time of the crash. Kent talked with him. "I could not get Bill Aitken to tell me that much, but I suspect it had something to do with his position as main liaison between the feds and TWA."

Kent also offered comments from another TWA employee. "Jack Dusak would've told you that it's prima facie evidence that they left the cotter pin out of the boost mechanism linkage. That very assembly begs the installation of a cotter pin. Leaving that little piece of hardware out is the only factor that could have led to this crash."[6]

Unfortunately, none of the former TWA employees are still alive. Assuming that the cause had nothing to do with a missing bolt or pin, the airline never offered an explanation why the Constellation became uncontrollable in the air and crashed. If a missing pin or bolt wasn't the cause, it had to be something else. The question remained unanswered: What caused the plane to become uncontrollable while in the air? Nobody at TWA would answer that question, or maybe didn't feel comfortable doing so. It might have been because there wasn't an answer making sense with the CAB investigators.

The evidence continued pointing to negligence on the part of a mechanic or possibly an inspector handling a chosen work task, likely both of those people. But everyone continued to deny any culpability. If the bolt had been found at the crash site, a metallurgical analysis in a laboratory could have revealed the length of time it was lodged in a bushing and roughly when it fell out. It would be like finding a spent bullet during the course of a crime scene investigation—without a suspect for what happened being firmly in mind.

Because an inspection of the elevator control linkages in TWA's

17 Days and 17 Miles Apart

other Constellations revealed they were installed properly, it became obvious that the action of only one individual, rather than several, resulted in the crash. It was not a systemic failure of TWA's maintenance procedures. A mechanic could have become distracted for any one of several reasons. This meant it had not been intentional. The parallelogram linkage was difficult to inspect in a cave-like recess of the plane's tail cone. A flashlight would be needed to illuminate its interior. It would require a mechanic to squeeze his fingers around a tiny cotter pin to insert it into the small hole of a bolt and secure it in place.

It was unusual that the CAB's strong conclusion in its accident investigation report made no reference to a maintenance error: "...the probable cause of this accident was the loss of an AN-175–21 nickel steel bolt from the parallelogram linkage of the elevator boost system, resulting in loss of control of the aircraft."[7]

The key word here is "probable." This word is found describing accidents cited in reports from the CAB and later the NTSB. Without an admission of guilt from any of the parties, and lacking a missing bolt or pin to enter into evidence, the investigative findings seemed to be more conjecture than fact in the minds of some observers.

Months after the hearing concluded, TWA executives and their lawyers remained resolute in their positions regarding the bolt issue. In the October 16, 1961, edition of *Skyliner*, the airline's employee newspaper, TWA reported in blunt terms that the CAB investigators had everything wrong. It stated: "CAB investigators were of the conclusion the bolt may have come off in flight. TWA officials contended the bolt came off on impact."[8]

None of the airlines watching the investigation unfold were eager to share information with either the CAB or FAA. Backing the leadership of its pilot and mechanic unions, TWA resisted making such information exchanges. This remained adversarial throughout the investigation of Flight 529. The relationship became so trying that the Civil Aeronautics Board, pilot and mechanic unions, and the airline itself, set up field offices as far away from each other as possible.[9]

Following the hearing and after publishing its accident investigation report, the CAB wound up its investigation of Flight 529, satisfied with its work. Its teams of investigators, engineers, and pilots had gathered evidence, unearthed clues, and offered the traveling public and aviation industry what it believed to be a sole cause of the crash.

Exactly when and where the bolt fell out continued to be an

5. Who Did It?

unknown, resulting in no shortage of opinions. In an attempt to save face, the representatives from TWA changed its story somewhat by stating the bolt had been sheared into pieces from extreme impact of the crash. The airline offered no further comment, especially from Charles Tillinghast, TWA's latest president who had been hired months earlier. He had little or no aviation background. Within the bureaucracy at TWA, the corporate communications staff remained mum as well. Howard Hughes however, received regular updates during the CAB's investigation.

In an email, the author asked retired TWA executive Jerry Cosley about this matter. Although interested in discussing other issues affecting the airline, when it came to Flight 529, he replied "no comment."[10]

A little over six months after the crash of Flight 529, the FAA responded to a CAB recommendation asking Lockheed to redesign the hydraulic boost control. After all, Halaby's career revolved around aviation interests beginning early in childhood. Here was his response:

> On March 8, 1962, the administrator advised the board that his agency was having the Constellation flight manual amended to include "procedures for turning off the elevator boost with an uncontrollable elevator." The Administrator further advised "in view of the excellent service history achieved by this aircraft since 1946, he believes there is insufficient justification to require design changes to accomplish your total objective."[11]

Disagreeing with that response, here's how the CAB responded:

> Although turning off the elevator boost provides a possible means of regaining control, it appears helpful to assure that a pilot will recall and execute successfully the flight manual instructions when confronted unexpectedly with a violent structure-damaging maneuver instantaneously resisted by pushing on the control wheels. The Board, therefore recommends on August 24, 1962, that further consideration be given to modification of the shifting system.[12]

By January 1, 1959, the FAA had absorbed many of the functions with thousands of employees coming from the older Civil Aeronautics Administration. It had been operating as an independent agency responsible for determining the cause of airline accidents.

Throughout his brief time at the FAA, Halaby was called on to decide a number of major issues. One of them had to do with Lockheed, designer and manufacturer of not only Constellations, but turboprop L-188 Electra airliners. The Electra had been designed and built

17 Days and 17 Miles Apart

with serious design flaws that resulted in several fatal crashes. One of them involved an Electra that departed O'Hare International Airport, not far from where Flight 529 had crashed. Because the faulty design of every Electra was clearly the responsibility of Lockheed, the company continued to struggle in the aviation marketplace to try and remain in business.[13]

Early in his career, Halaby worked at Lockheed Aircraft Corporation, as did former FAA administrator Elwood Quesada. Both of the men knew people who were still employed at the company. As such, Halaby felt obligated to help Lockheed overcome its current financial woes in any way he could. One way was to take any pressure off its engineering staff and not task it with redesigning the Constellation's boost control system. The same group of engineers had been assigned to remedy the Electra's many other faults.

Halaby's letter to the CAB noted that a pilot's flight manual for the Constellation was being revised by Lockheed to include "procedures for turning off the elevator boost with an uncontrollable elevator."[14] He had taken into account the safety record of all airline Constellations beginning when the first one entered commercial service, a "probable" but not conclusive cause of Flight 529 crashing, and the likely cost to the airlines if Lockheed were to modify the shift mechanisms. These reasons were why he vetoed the CAB recommendation.

In his role as FAA administrator, Halaby appeared to ignore the frantic environment that likely existed in the cockpit of Flight 529 during its final moments in the air—and why this type of crash could happen again. The human element had not been factored in—only added costs to Lockheed and its airlines, and the remote possibility that this particular system could fail again. In essence, the agency was more attuned to studying parts failing than people and processes causing them to fail. It would take years for the FAA to appreciate how a simple error made by a mechanic could bring down an airliner. However, it became obvious that the FAA had taken into account the boost system problems affecting military C-121 and R7V Constellations. Halaby may have considered them to be little more than "unusual" events.

The few words in Halaby's letter were not what the hard-working investigators wanted to hear—or family members and friends of passengers who perished aboard Flight 529.

A position paper prepared by Georg Kohne, a retired senior captain at Lufthansa German Airlines, and experienced Constellation pilot,

5. Who Did It?

offered clarification about the plane's safety issues. Kohne, along with several other pilots and flight engineers, had been involved in a project to restore and fly a Constellation in scheduled service. He wrote:

> The Lockheed Constellation series may well be the most attractive and interesting design of all airliners. However, its safety record does not at all qualify for any positive ranking. Many, way too many Constellations were lost in operation ... frequently caused by poor ergonomic design or a demanding, complicated or misleading system layout being at least a contribution, if not the root causes.[15]

The Civil Aeronautics Board's mandate from Congress was clear when it came to aviation accident investigations. It read: "Investigation and determination of probable cause of civil aircraft accidents; and suggesting corrective action to improve safety in air commerce."[16] The CAB was satisfied doing its job and didn't appreciate outside intervention. The most important word in this statement was "suggesting." The agency didn't have authority to require an airline or government agency to make changes for improving safety.

A lack of sufficient manpower at the CAB became even more serious during 1961. It was able to assign only a limited number of experienced investigators to determine why Flight 529 and many other planes were crashing. The agency was operating on an extremely small budget, failing to gain additional taxpayer support from members of Congress. Lacking that support in order to survive, its leaders fought for every taxpayer dollar that the agency could get.

In a 1960 annual report to members of Congress, here's what the CAB's leadership revealed: "The workload entailed in the investigative work of fiscal 1960 represented a 74-percent increase over fiscal 1959 and was met only by a large amount of uncompensated overtime devoted by a dedicated corps of investigators."[17]

Weak oversight at the CAB found its way into a methodology today employed by the FAA to oversee aircraft certification practices. Two fatal accidents involving Boeing *737* MAX jetliners during 2018 and 2019 brought the agency's process into sharp focus. Manufacturers such as Boeing were handling much of the certification work—without direct supervision from engineers working directly for the FAA.[18]

In common with most of the citizens in America filing income tax returns, aircraft certification was, and still is, a largely honor-based system. It continues to depend on the knowledge of employees working for the manufacturers it monitors. It does not rely on engineers working at the FAA to review and approve the systems of newly designed airliners.

The system didn't work well a half-century ago when 856 Constellations were built and doesn't work well today. It's been called many things over the years. Today it's known far and wide as Organization Designation Authorization—ODA for short. In a strange way, Flight 529 became a victim of that antiquated system.

6

Howard Hughes

Throughout his entire lifetime Howard Hughes had an overpowering desire to become a legend in the world of aviation. Going back as far as 1935 with the H-1 racing plane that he designed and flew, Hughes set a world speed record of 352 miles per hour. Two years later he flew coast-to-coast in the record time of 7 hours and 28 minutes. The following year he became famous by setting another record flying around the world in 91 hours, 14 minutes, and 21 seconds.[1] These events were publicized in newspapers and on television throughout the world.

In addition to owning TWA during World War II, Hughes planned to mass-produce military planes to support America's war effort, but the war ended before the project got underway. He also expected to build three huge flying boats, but ended up making only one of them, it not capable of sustained flight. Whether known as an accomplished aviator or brilliant engineer, Hughes had the perfect background to own and manage a major airline. For him, Trans World Airlines represented more than owning real estate, airliners, or setting records. He created and expanded the airline into a worldwide empire. Based on having this success, he felt that the rest of commercial aviation would soon follow in his footsteps.

Gaining control of TWA during the airline's infancy and tightly managing its operations for decades to come provided great satisfaction for Hughes. Rather than assuming an executive position at his airline, he always managed its operations from behind the scenes. He never thought about becoming its president or even serving as a member of its board of directors. Remotely, he ruled the airline with an iron hand. Over the years he hired two presidents for TWA, but later fired them before they had even met. Lastly, he never attended a single TWA corporate board meeting, but did produce written agendas for others to follow at those meetings.[2]

17 Days and 17 Miles Apart

In addition to aviation, at an early age Hughes became fascinated with moviemaking, especially if a film involved something about aviation. In his mind, he possessed talent as a producer, director, writer, and even a film editor.[3] After buying RKO studios in Hollywood, the executives there disagreed with his management style. They resented his telling them what to do and when to do it. Far worse, the company was losing market share because movie production was continuing on a sharp dive. After dozens of the executives resigned, Hughes decided to shut down the entire studio and dissolve its operations. He also sold RKO's national theater chain to General Tire and Rubber Company in July 1955.[4]

Of all the businesses Howard Hughes owned or controlled during various times of his life, TWA was where he made the greatest contributions to advance commercial aviation. He expected that TWA's international traffic would grow significantly during future years, and would require bigger and faster airliners. During 1939 he prepared several sketches depicting a new type of plane to carry a larger number of passengers than the existing airliners.

Hughes presented the concept to Bob Gross, chairman of Lockheed Aircraft Corporation. Gross was pleased with what he saw, and eager to land more business from airlines such as TWA. He directed vice president Hall Hibbard and chief engineer Kelly Johnson to design and build a prototype of the proposed plane.[5] What emerged was the nation's first high-speed, piston-powered passenger airliner. The new plane was named Constellation, and soon hailed as the most advanced airliner of its time. The plane would enter scheduled airline service during 1945.

Hughes guided TWA's course by making a sizable investment in the airline. Transcontinental and Western Air, as it was known at the time, had been formed during the early 1930s from the merger of four smaller air carriers. Young Hughes had an excellent background to gradually take over control of the airline. By 1944, he acquired more than 45 percent of all TWA stock, giving him controlling interest. Not satisfied with even this level of ownership, he continued buying more shares until they totaled 78 percent.[6]

In addition to Hughes ownership, the airline had thousands of minority stockholders, many owning only a few shares. Hughes ignored all of them. Chief executive officers at other major airlines owned only a fraction of their company's stock. It caused them to rely on shareholders for guidance concerning their airline's operations. Hughes used a

6. Howard Hughes

different approach by doing whatever he wanted and not paying attention to other stockholders.[7] He looked forward to supervising the creation of its advertising campaigns, developing powerful messages and deciding where to place the advertisements. He even planned the advertising budget for TWA's marketing department.

Hughes was TWA's sole owner at the time Flight 529 had crashed. He continued as its major stockholder for several more years, long after the CAB accident investigation was concluded. Although his control of the airline's operations abruptly shifted from him to a group of financial backers, thousands of longtime TWA employees remained loyal to the industrialist. One of them was then in charge of maintenance and engineering in Kansas City, Missouri. Managing the airline's gigantic repair facility there, its leader handled whatever requests Hughes wanted. The billionaire industrialist continued to believe that he was in control behind the scenes.

Throughout his many years in the aviation business, Hughes made it a point to brief anyone interested in learning how complex mechanical devices worked, and under what conditions they could fail. The hydraulic boost systems in his fleet of Constellations were among them. Most important to Hughes was his airline's reputation for "safety." If its safety record was ever questioned, his enormous investment in TWA stock could drop like a rock. The airline could disappear; so he didn't want to take such a risk.

During the middle of the last century, Howard Hughes was one of a small number of billionaires who owned a number of major corporations in America. Surprisingly, much of his fortune didn't come from owning TWA or any other enterprise. It came from a profitable manufacturing plant in Houston, Texas, called the Hughes Tool Company. Being the sole owner of both TWA and the tool company, on a regular basis Hughes received millions in profits from the Texas-based company. Recognizing a potential tax problem, he was forced to make a decision and avoid federal income taxes: invest in a newly formed corporation, put the money in an existing corporation, or pay federal taxes on the profits. Rather than paying taxes to the government, he chose TWA as an entity to park the money. In order to benefit TWA, the profits would be used to purchase new airliners required to expand its operations to more cities throughout the world.

The tool company's moneymaking secret was based on the leasing of a single patented product line. That is, a drill bit that has three revolving and interlocking cutting surfaces. The unique tool was widely used for drilling through thick rock or gushers from newly discovered oil deposits. Invented by Hughes' father at the turn of the last century, the bit obsoleted all previous types of tools.[8] They could be found in countless oil fields throughout the world. Howard Robard Hughes, Sr., had moved to Texas in 1901, expecting to strike it rich from an oil boom already underway there. Using his ability as a miner working in Missouri, he walked from one oil patch to another. During this time, he also accumulated a substantial financial nest egg. In 1908, he patented the revolutionary drill bit, built a sizable manufacturing plant in Houston, and produced the expensive bits.[9] The future empire and son Howard's accumulation of wealth were now assured after the device was patented.

Although TWA wasn't allowed by the tool company to register title to each plane that it flew, the airline was obligated to pay it a hefty "fee" for operating those planes. The tool company could write off the cost of buying the planes, along with depreciation for them, on its corporate tax return. Other than the income coming from the drill bit leases, the only other major source of income for the tool company came from the fees coming in from the airline.

When it came time for Hughes to buy the latest jets for TWA, he continued using money from the tool company, leasing them to the airline on a long-term basis. This arrangement enabled the tool company to treat the investments as capital gains—to avoid an excess profits tax with the IRS. At the airline, the lease payments were charged off as normal business expenses.

Aside from controlling TWA, beginning during the early 1940s, Hughes purchased 1,300 acres of vacant land in Culver City, not far inland from the coast around Los Angeles. It would function as the headquarters for his growing Hughes Aircraft Company.[10] Hughes also had a 9,000-foot-long runway plowed out from acres of its nearby agricultural fields. It would be used to conduct tests of new or modified airplanes. Hughes later constructed several large buildings for housing his aircraft design and production facilities. Throughout years to come, the Culver City plant had also become home to all of his company's aeronautical operations. In the 1950s that same company would grow into one of the nation's major defense contractors. It designed and produced many different sophisticated electronic systems to aim and fire guns in fighter and interceptor aircraft.

6. Howard Hughes

During the first six months in 1942, German submarines had sunk a total of 681 ships attempting to cross the Atlantic Ocean on their way to Europe. The ships had been used for transporting supplies and fuel to support America's war effort overseas. Upset with such a loss, billionaire industrialist Henry J. Kaiser decided to approach Howard Hughes with an idea to build giant airplanes to replace ocean shipments.[11] The planes could fly over the ocean rather than sail across it. Hughes liked what he heard. It didn't take long for the men to form something called the Hughes Kaiser Corporation. As a result, the Hughes Aircraft Company was awarded a government contract to build three of the planes, soon called flying boats.

At the start of the project, the aircraft division of Hughes Tool Company in Culver City consisted of nothing more than a small group of engineers and mechanics. That group had designed and built the H-1 racer in the 1930s but were now involved with developing a new military plane called the D-2.[12] It was designed to be a fast, high-altitude bomber built from only wood. However, the work was plagued with problems from the start. Finding the right kind of glue to assemble the plane proved almost impossible. Even worse, the specific type of engine required for it wasn't available during the war years. Facing so many problems, Hughes was forced to change its design from a bomber configuration to a twin-engine fighter.[13] However, before construction of the prototype was completed, the military brass told Hughes that the plane didn't meet their requirements. Annoyed with the government's decision, Hughes and his team continued to work on the D-2 during spare time. Not happy with other mandated changes, Hughes fell out of favor with the government.[14]

Pushing the unsuccessful D-2 program aside, Hughes substituted the flying boat project in its place and pushed it along toward completion. He and a team of engineers at the sprawling Culver City plant designed a plane capable of transporting 750 troops. The wings were fitted with eight 3,000 horsepower Pratt & Whitney piston engines, its wings 20 feet longer than a football field. The plane was designated the HK-1.[15]

On November 2, 1947, with Hughes as its only pilot, the flying boat glided slowly along a three-mile-long stretch of water in the Long Beach Harbor, just outside of Los Angeles. Hughes surprised everyone in attendance by lowering the wing flaps, causing the plane to rise slowly into the air, reaching several feet over the ocean for about a mile. The event was widely publicized as the first flight of America's one and only flying boat.

Shortly after the war ended, a Congressional hearing was conducted in Washington to review how much taxpayer money had been spent on various wartime projects. The flying boat was a project under scrutiny. During one of only a few appearances before a government body, Hughes dominated the hearing and deflected allegations that could upset a less confident witness. The industrialist wasted no time to defend his actions and those of his employees, especially the people working on the flying boat project:

> I can tell you that I designed every nut and bolt that went into this airplane. I carried out the design to a greater degree than any other man that I know in the business. In fact, I am frequently accused of going too far and not delegating enough of the work to other people. I worked anywhere from eighteen to twenty hours a day on this project for between six months and one year, and this, coupled with the F-11, the feed chute, and the other work I did during the war, resulted in me being so completely broken down physically that I was sent away for a total of seven months for a rest after the war.[16]

There was one thing guaranteed to get Howard Hughes' undivided attention. During the 1940s he had made sure that a hydraulic boost system was installed in the flying boat to move its heavy control surfaces. During that same time, he required that the Lockheed Constellations he had ordered for TWA have a similar type of system. Not known at the time, the later investigation of the Flight 529 crash revealed that its elevator boost system had failed. Not far from the O'Hare airport, Northwest Flight 706 also crashed due to the failure of a similar type boost system that controlled the plane's ailerons.[17]

On September 1, 1943, the Army Air Force requested that a long-range, high speed, high altitude, land-based photographic reconnaissance plane be developed for the Army. A contract was issued to the Hughes Tool Company to develop and fly such a plane.[18] Upon being awarded the contract, Hughes made sure that work on this plane became a priority, his employees preparing the unique plane for its first flight in 1946. Designed from scratch as a reconnaissance aircraft for taking photos over enemy territory, its project was designated as the XF-11. Two 8-blade contra-rotating propellers driven by two Pratt & Whitney piston engines powered it. Together they produced a total of 6,000 horsepower.[19]

When parked near the runway in Culver City, the twin-tailed plane

6. Howard Hughes

conveyed a sleek appearance sitting on its tricycle landing gear. The first XF-11 was expected to make its first flight during late spring. Hughes expected to make this and subsequent test flights alone. When the day for its first flight arrived on April 15, he made sure that the plane was ready to fly. The engines were started while Hughes released its brakes, eased up on the throttles, and the big plane moved toward the runway from its parking spot. Arriving at the end of the runway, he turned it around to face a breeze blowing in from the Pacific Ocean. Setting the brakes, he ran through the plane's checklist, lining up on the unpaved grass runway and advancing the throttles to takeoff power. Releasing the brakes, the XF-11 rolled down the runway, gaining speed rapidly. Soon airborne over Culver City, the plane continued to climb, making a wide left circle around his airfield. For a new plane, it handled well, the instrument readings all appearing normal.

Over the next 40 minutes he continued to circle the airfield from about 5,000 feet. Without any warning, the plane suddenly yawed and dropped down to 2,500 feet, falling extremely fast. None of this was expected and Hughes considered bailing out. But the plane was soon too low, well under 1,000 feet. Instead, he flew north where it roared over the rooftops and swimming pools of a ritzy collection of mansions in Beverly Hills. He was also flying over a fairway of the Los Angeles Country Club where he had earlier played golf many times.[20]

Little altitude remaining, Hughes knew he was about to crash. To brace himself, he planted both of his feet high against the top of the instrument panel. He decided to flare the plane onto the roof of a large home directly ahead of him. Instead, the plane hit another home at an angle, the plane's tail and wing separating. After striking a power pole only seconds remained for him to continue in the air. The XF-11 struck the roof of the home, bounced and skidded sideways for several feet. The flames immediately turned into an explosion, fueled by a large quantity of gasoline flowing from its tanks.

Although soon rescued from the cockpit, Hughes nearly died in that crash. It happened at 6:42 p.m. on Sunday, July 7, 1946. After getting pulled from the cockpit, he would spend 35 days as a patient at Good Samaritan Hospital in Los Angeles. A team of doctors providing his care documented the extent of his injuries:

> His chest was crushed. He suffered fractures of seven ribs on the left side, two on the right, a fracture of the left clavicle, a possible fracture of the

nose, a large laceration of the scalp, extensive second- and third-degree burns on the left hand, a second-degree burn on the lower part of the left chest, a second-degree burn on the left buttock, cuts, bruises, and abrasions on his arms and legs, and many small cuts on his face. His left lung had collapsed and his right was also injured. His heart had been pushed to one side of his chest cavity. He was in severe shock.[21]

Nobody in the hospital thought that he would survive the night. Fighting those odds, he was lucky. Stuck in a hospital bed for so many weeks, he had several things on his mind. First, he wanted to publicize his longstanding reputation as a skilled aviator. As the owner of a major airline, he owed an explanation to his customers and loyal airline employees about his recovery. He also wanted to explain why the XF-11 had crashed.

During his convalescence, Hughes was given morphine to lessen the pain. His personal doctor was willing to supply whatever kind or quantity of narcotics he wanted. As the weeks went by, Hughes switched from morphine to codeine.[22]

Hughes began developing eccentric behaviors and an increasingly reclusive lifestyle not long after the XF-11 crash. These character changes could have resulted from treating the chronic pain, increased deafness, or an obsessive-compulsive disorder. According to the Mayo Clinic, OCD "features a pattern of unwanted thoughts and fears (obsessions) that lead you to do repetitive behaviors (compulsions). These obsessions and compulsions interfere with daily activities and cause significant distress."[23]

During times of crisis, Hughes was known to withdraw from anything that didn't interest him, losing touch with reality, and displaying a bizarre behavior. Making matters worse, he continued to use some of the drugs on a regular basis. Hughes' hearing was severely damaged after surviving at least three major airplane crashes.[24] He also suffered from extreme weakness, likely caused by those injuries. The use of modern hearing aids brought on continuous headaches, but provided him no improvement in hearing. The headaches, and the fear of catching a disease, contributed to slowly turning him into a reclusive way of living.[25]

The XF-11 accident investigation report concluded that a pitch-change mechanism for the rear propeller on the plane's right side had failed due to a loss of its lubricating fluid. The propellers were designed to use separate hydraulic systems at the front and rear, operating independently of the plane's engines. The loss of more than 40

6. Howard Hughes

ounces of fluid from either of the systems would cause the propeller blades to change into reverse pitch. This resulted in Hughes losing control of the plane. The final report from the military accident investigation board assigned primary blame on the propeller malfunction, but it also faulted Hughes for the way he conducted the test flight.[26]

Remarkably, once again taking charge in Culver City after more than a month in bed, Hughes pushed the flying boat project toward completion and readied the second XF-11 for testing. The contra-rotating dual propellers that were fitted to the original plane had been replaced with individual 16-foot-diameter, four-bladed propellers. On April 5, 1947, Hughes made a successful test flight of the second XF-11.[27] By now, the government had cancelled a production order for the planes.

Board members at the nation's airlines were forced to make difficult financial decisions during the late 1950s. There was a pressing need to replace their piston-powered transports with new jets. They didn't have much choice because longtime business travelers were demanding a major upgrade in service. They wanted to arrive at their destinations in half the time that older airliners required, and not bounce around the sky while flying in bad weather.

As the longtime sole owner of TWA, Hughes had weathered a number of difficult issues that affected his company. Adding to its list of problems, he was facing a cash shortage during the first quarter of 1958. When he was at the helm of the airline, he tightly controlled every aspect of its operations. But now, in common with other airline presidents, he had to place orders for new jets built by Boeing and General Dynamics. There was only one problem: he wasn't sure how to pay for them.

The nation's major aircraft manufacturers were keeping busy assembling the jets and marketing them to airlines in other countries. Almost all of the airliners destined for those airlines had been designed and built in America. It was a different era in commercial aviation. Even today, only one company, Boeing Commercial Airplanes, continues to manufacture passenger jets for sale in the United States and other countries.

Hughes continued to procrastinate when it was time to buy the fleet of jets.[28] He was distrustful of other people asking him to make crucial decisions such as this one. Although United Air Lines, American Airlines, and several other competitive airlines were already flying jets, Hughes had not taken delivery of even a single plane and didn't even place any orders for them. The manufacturers were offering TWA's competitive airlines coveted early delivery positions for the jets they had bought. Continuing to procrastinate placing the orders, and lacking enough money to pay for the jets, he grudgingly provided some of the needed financing.[29] For the time being, the money would be used to make at least some down payments. But the amount of money needed didn't meet his expectations because a recession was impacting the entire nation. During the mid–1950s, his tool company had earned profits of $25 million to $30 million. By spring 1957, a world oil glut resulted in a sharp decline of drilling, resulting in less of a demand for drill bits. Its earnings dropped to $20 million for 1957 and less than $15 million during 1958.[30] His tool company's cash balance, only two years earlier, had now been exhausted.

At this point, TWA found itself in a difficult situation. While other airlines were adding new jets to their fleets every month, TWA wasn't getting any of them. It was so bad that the airline's creditors could have forced it into bankruptcy. Securing loans to assure timely delivery of the planes became an unwanted headache. TWA required hundreds of millions of dollars to pay for the planes it needed to order. If the airline didn't pay for them on time, the manufacturers would not schedule any deliveries of the jets to TWA.

Unfortunately for Hughes, even more money was needed to make even partial payments for the jets. He again planned to use some of his own money to get the planes into passenger service.[31] Otherwise, he would be forced to seek outside financial help. Lacking enough money, he was forced to seek assistance from the nation's financial establishment in New York City. The Equitable Life Assurance Society was willing to help him.[32] However, it insisted that TWA, and not the tool company, own title to the jets. For a long time, Hughes had used profits from the tool company to buy planes for the airline. The fees paid by the airline to the tool company would no longer be acceptable at Equitable. Hughes likely felt he was being manipulated by the financial industry and didn't like it one bit. He was caught in a squeeze.

Equitable Life always had maintained an arms-length relationship with Hughes over the years. In 1946 it provided a $40 million loan to the airline to help buy a fleet of 40 new Constellations from Lockheed. Hughes had come to regret that loan, mostly because Equitable periodically offered him unwanted advice about how to run the airline.[33] He ignored the advice, but continued to be upset because the outsider tried

6. Howard Hughes

to call the shots for him. This time, however, the terms of a proposed loan to buy the jets was very different.

Here's a simple explanation offered by Jack Real, the author's one-time boss in the Hughes empire, and one of the industrialist's loyal acquaintances. In his own book he stated:

> The lenders inserted into the loan documents an undisguised threat to Hughes' rule. As the price for their $105-million loan, they warned Hughes that if he defaulted or forced changes in TWA's management, he would be required to place his airline stock in a ten-year voting trust that gave the lenders the right to select a majority of the trustees. Those trustees then would assume responsibility for management of the airline.[34]

For the first time since the advent of civil aviation, a recession during 1958 and 1959 sent many of the nation's airlines into a tailspin. Airlines like TWA also needed more credit to buy the needed jets. Making matters worse in 1958, an earlier skirmish between Hughes and his financers took place. It had to do with a $12 million loan made to the airline from Equitable Life Assurance and a group of bankers headed by the Irving Trust Company.[35] The airline needed the money to meet its payroll. When the loan was due, Hughes tried to negotiate an extension. Equitable agreed with one condition. A voting trust would need to be set up.[36]

Hughes disagreed with the condition and paid off the loan himself. He wouldn't allow Equitable, or any other lender for that matter, to tell him how to run his business. A company using a trust could result in a traumatic experience for everyone involved. Some loans made to other airlines via a voting trust prevented them from building new passenger terminals, borrowing more money, buying more planes, or even relocating its ticket offices, until at least some of the debt had been paid back. There was often a clause noting that the lenders had a right to appoint a new management team if the existing one failed to satisfy its demands.[37]

Many of TWA's old-timers had intense loyalty to Hughes and would be offended by any newcomers such as New York financial experts hiring into the airline. They had kept in mind that Howard Hughes still owned more than 78 percent of the airline's stock.

When it came to TWA, the lenders would be allowed to take over control of the airline if any changes in its management were not corrected within 90 days. Hughes, of course, remained upset. He tried to find more reasonable lenders. Because his reputation was extremely poor on Wall Street, most of them stayed away from him.[38] Running out of options, he eventually caved in, signing up with Equitable and its host of associated lenders.

On December 15, 1960, a representative acting on behalf of Howard Hughes, signed the Equitable voting trust agreement.[39] After many years serving as the airline's leader, Hughes lost control of the corporation that day. The lenders were never happy with his actions. If he tried to switch the top executives at the airline, Equitable could use the power of its voting trust to stop him. The trust would also prevent him from buying or selling any TWA shares for at least ten years.

The airline was not in the best shape. When 1961 ended, TWA was headed for the largest one-year operating loss in its history. Voting trust or not, the future didn't look good.

Hughes disliked anything that restricted his actions or disagreed with his opinions concerning airline operations. The CAB's investigation of Flight 529 stayed on his mind. He was not accepting the theory that one of his mechanics made a fatal mistake. After all, the Constellation was an older plane that he probably flew many times. Much like what can happen to an aging automobile, older planes were known to also have mechanical problems. It was bound to happen because the plane was manufactured many years earlier. He distanced himself and the staff from anything to do with the CAB or FAA. Although he was no longer directly managing the airline, he still owned the entire operation and continued to enjoy the respect of every employee he hired.

Losing control of TWA turned into an unending nightmare for the industrialist. It would affect his thinking and actions over time. After so many years at the helm of a major airline, he was forced to relinquish control of everything he had built up over those years.

A new president, unknown to Hughes, would take over control of his empire. It was Ernest Breech, a former chairman at Ford Motor Company. When Breech announced that TWA's board of directors would meet, Hughes made sure that his handpicked board members would not be there. It meant a quorum couldn't be formed. Learning about his move, Breech canceled the meeting. Embarrassed by Hughes' behavior, he decided to hold a special stockholder's meeting instead. He removed the directors appointed by Hughes and replaced them with people free from his tight control.[40] Hearing about this move, Hughes would become infuriated.

When TWA announced that it would sell $100 million shares of

6. Howard Hughes

debentures, Hughes openly questioned the move, even filing a complaint with the Securities and Exchange Commission. It was a bold attempt to block the sale.[41] In March 1961, when TWA acquired $187 million worth of jets from Boeing, Hughes believed that the current management team had no authority to buy them.[42] Not wanting to lose a big sale, the aircraft manufacturer agreed with TWA's position and delivered the jets that the airline had ordered. At this point, Howard Hughes was no longer a Boeing customer.

Although Hughes still owned, and indirectly controlled TWA, it became known that his management powers had been clipped by the voting trust. But not everything changed at the airline. Unknown to the lawyers who were retained by Equitable to watch for unpredictable moves, his longstanding relationships with thousands of key employees meant that the airline's operations stayed the same as they were in the past. It was as though Hughes was still in charge, even though most of the employees never even met the man. In his mind, he was still their boss, at least the people he had hired decades earlier.

For well over a year Hughes fought every action from the airline's latest management team. He likely remained upset over how the CAB handled the investigation of Flight 529, its actions making the airline look like a low-class criminal.

Keeping all of this in mind, regardless of whether Hughes was in charge or not, why didn't the airline accept full responsibility for the Flight 529 crash and move on with other matters? It's a mystery carried on from decade to decade. Of course, taking responsibility could open up a Pandora's box full of lawsuits. As it stood, the airline's publicized lack of guilt meant that few independent law firms would have an interest in initiating lawsuits against TWA. Of course, it was well known that the aging industrialist would never enter a courtroom for a trial. The airline had successfully skirted any responsibility for what happened during the early night of the crash. However, in doing so, it also caused the next of kin and offspring to become furious. Without proper compensation to cover burial expenses or other costs related to the deceased, it continued to be annoying. It's still unknown whether Hughes had made this and other decisions to ignore the actions of CAB investigators.

Howard Hughes was someone who ran RKO into the ground, nearly plunged TWA into bankruptcy, lost control of his airline, never successfully got an airplane in production, and his hotels and casinos in

17 Days and 17 Miles Apart

Nevada lost money. He wanted to stamp his imprint on everything associated with his life. However, the history is clear that his enterprises seldom made money or even brought him happiness.[43]

    None of these events would be of interest to the paying passengers boarding hundreds of TWA flights every day. For most of them, Howard Hughes was a famous aviator and rich filmmaker in Hollywood, but not much else. Few of them knew that he owned the airline and plane they were about to board. For them, an airline was an airline, whether United, American, Continental—or even Trans World Airlines.

7

Scary Flights

Registered with the Federal Aviation Agency as N86511, the plane assigned to Flight 529 was among the oldest Constellations owned and operated by TWA. The airline had taken delivery of it on December 19, 1945. Six weeks later its passengers could be seen enjoying flights from New York to France, the plane being nicknamed the Star of Paris. A tradition at TWA and other airlines of that era involved painting the names of cities that its planes served on the sides of their fuselages. The flights to Europe during February 1946 represented a major milestone for the airline. They were the first scheduled transatlantic passenger flights departing from LaGuardia Field in New York and landing at Orly Field in Paris.

During later years, as more advanced Super Constellations and a first generation of jetliners joined TWA's fleet, N86511 was reconfigured to carry a maximum of 81 passengers. The company's Sky Club Coach service kept busy, attracting a budget-minded segment of air travelers. There were few creature comforts aboard the planes, but they got the job done, day after day.

Although continuing to log thousands of hours in the air, the plane assigned to Flight 529 served as a reliable workhorse for more than 15 years. Over that period of time, it transported hundreds of thousands of paying passengers. But it also recovered from several serious crashes.

When passengers boarded Lockheed Constellations in the 1950s, they may have assumed that the planes were designed to carry people just like them. It was an incorrect assumption. If it weren't for World War II, none of the airlines would be flying them during the postwar years. They had been designed and built to move soldiers and equipment during the war and nothing else.

On January 9, 1943, the first Constellation rolled out from a final assembly building at the Burbank airport in California for a test flight.

Its manufacturer, Lockheed Aircraft Corporation, had planned to deliver the plane to the U.S. Army for further testing and government acceptance. The military designated the plane as a C-69.

The Constellation was the first four-engine transport that Lockheed designed and built. Other than its beautiful, contoured shape of the fuselage, the C-69 also became known for its dozens of faults. The Army was demanding that Lockheed modify the few planes it had already taken delivery of. The military considered them unsafe. As a result, they were no longer used to transport military personnel to bases outside of the United States.

Before the first C-69 was delivered, Lockheed was facing serious problems with its Curtiss-Wright R-3350 engines. On February 20, 1943, less than two weeks after the first C-69 had been delivered, all of them were grounded because of engine problems. So many issues were identified that the engineers at Lockheed were upset with the Wright Engine Division of Curtiss-Wright. Many of those problems involved engine ignition systems. Lockheed accused the engine maker of not properly testing the system in a laboratory or during actual test flights. Another serious problem involved the unscrewing of cylinder heads from its mounting base while flying. There was loud backfiring and even some in-flight fires.

Faced with a growing list of customer complaints, a team of engineers at Lockheed got busy. More than 500 problems had required their attention. Working around the clock for weeks, each C-69 on the company's assembly line, or having been grounded by the Army, was modified. Having no choice in the matter, Lockheed was forced to pay for the changes and modifications. Satisfied for now, the Army gave the plane a green light so it could once again transport personnel to other countries.

One of the passenger-carrying flights taking its personnel across the Atlantic Ocean took place on August 4, 1945. The plane flew from New York City to Paris. Unfortunately, its notable speed record didn't last long. Six weeks later on September 18, the same plane became a victim of an accident. A flight crew, under contract to operate C-69s for the Army, was at the controls. As the plane flew eastbound high over the flatlands of Kansas, one of its engines caught fire. Unable to extinguish the blaze, an emergency belly landing was made on a cornfield outside of Topeka. Fortunately, there were no injuries. However, the plane exploded in flames and was declared a total loss. It was unwanted

7. Scary Flights

publicity for both the Army and Lockheed. Because of this accident, the Army again grounded every C-69 in its inventory. In an attempt to work with the Army officials, Lockheed offered a series of changes, some of them mandatory, before the C-69s could once again go back on flight status.

At the time the C-69 offered little comfort and safety. Its interior and cockpit lacked basic amenities. Back in the cabin, uncomfortable metal seats could barely support the posteriors of the wartime soldiers. Cockpit seating wasn't much better. The plane had minimal toilet facilities. There was no refrigerated air conditioning, resulting in either steaming or freezing temperatures throughout the cabin. Finally, the scant use of fiberglass insulation failed to reduce the intense noise and vibration produced by its troublesome piston engines.

On one hand, the engineering team at Lockheed continued to attempt pleasing its important military customer. At the same time, the company was expecting to modify the C-69s for sale to the nation's airlines. There was a rush to comply with the existing government standards and adapt the plane for air carrier service.

In order to certify C-69s for its airline customers, Lockheed decided to modify one of the existing military planes. To quickly move the conversion program along, a meeting was arranged between Lockheed and the unhappy Army officials. Both of the parties agreed that Lockheed would be allowed to convert existing C-69s into civilian airliners—and also not build more of the planes for the Army. Lockheed ended up buying a number of unfinished C-69s from the government, some of them sitting on the idle assembly lines in Burbank or parked outside in hot weather gathering dust. Lockheed also acquired all of the government-owned tooling that was used to assemble the planes. The tooling hadn't been used for several months, being stored alongside a production line in the factory.

After making all required modifications, the upgraded planes destined for the airlines were turned over to engineers at the Civil Aeronautics Administration. The agency would conduct its required certification testing. Without earning a type certificate from the CAA, the airlines would not be allowed to operate the airliners. To earn that coveted certification, the CAA told Lockheed to make several other modifications of the existing planes to increase the safety level for its passengers.

The engineers and managers at Lockheed already knew about

most of the plane's discrepancies. They had attempted to correct them prior to handing the plane over to the CAA. But they couldn't do much about the engines; they were trouble prone, with many planes catching fire while still in the air. New fire detection and extinguishing systems would be required by the CAA to prevent those fires. An early version of the Curtiss-Wright R-3350 engine also powered the wartime Boeing B-29 bombers. Known for frequently catching fire, many of those bombers ended up crashing. In an attempt to distance Lockheed from Curtiss-Wright, it told people that Lockheed only manufactured airplanes and not engines. Solving the fire-prone engine issue was the sole responsibility of the engine manufacturer. The officials at Lockheed knew that the commercial airlines would not accept recurring problems with the engines, nor would the evaluators who worked for the CAA.

Lockheed discovered that there were still more improvements requested by potential airline customers. They included improved cabin heating and cooling systems, along with upgraded insulation in cabin walls to lower its noise level. Replacing the C-69's tiny portholes with larger windows had to be changed, it needed to increase passenger comfort and improve visibility. Finally, the entire cabin interior needed to be redesigned using material having bright colors. The bare-metal military appearance was considered passé. The Army had no interest in making any of these improvements, let alone paying for them. Its only goal during the war was to move its troops and equipment around the world, whether its personnel were comfortable or not.

A transport category type certificate covering civilian Constellations, it Approved Type Certificate A-763, was awarded to Lockheed Aircraft Corporation on October 14, 1945. The airlines could now operate the first of the planes in scheduled passenger service. What were now Model 049 Constellations had been modified on the same production line where the C-69s earlier rolled out for the Army. Certifying the plane as an airliner kept the production line active well through May 1947, turning the former military transports into passenger-carrying Constellations. TWA remained at the top of Lockheed's list of customers, being the first airline to take delivery of a Constellation coming off that assembly line.

During the later years of Constellation production, other versions of the plane were approved under its original type certificate. However, newer Constellations, those equipped with stretched fuselages and

7. Scary Flights

longer wings, needed government approval under a completely different type certificate.

If anything, a large size elevator control surface was a necessity for the Constellation to help its pilots land heavily loaded planes in airports with short runways. During the war, government officials had initiated the requirement before they bought any C-69s from Lockheed. It would help maintain tight control of the plane during its final approach. The need to carefully coordinate the elevator, rudder, and aileron control surfaces kept pilots busy during the few seconds that the planes were directly over the runway and about to land. There was also another big issue. Because Curtiss-Wright R-3350 engines were powering all the Constellations, if any one of its engines were shut down and its propeller feathered, a dramatic improvement in rudder and aileron control was another requirement. The needed pressure was far more than had been required in planes built by other manufacturers. The distance existing between the fuselage and engine locations along the wings were requiring an increase in control. This had also been influenced by a larger diameter of the propellers. Taking all of these factors into account, a larger elevator control surface was considered essential.

In order to move the ailerons and elevators, along with its three rudder surfaces in the tail to guide the plane through the sky, a hydraulic boost system became an integral part of the Constellation's flight control systems. A manual override could be activated if the system ever failed. Long cables for moving the surfaces were connected to control wheels in the cockpit. Each cable was attached to a separate hydraulic actuator near its control surface. When it was necessary to activate the manual override, switching off the hydraulic pressure allowed its control surface to be moved manually. A force-return feature provided artificial feel to help the pilots sense their maneuvering.

There are several reasons why the Constellation was equipped with a tail having three separate rudder control surfaces. If the plane had been designed with a single vertical tail, it would be difficult to make it taller. The purpose was to control any yawing of the plane should one of the engines fail. Another reason for not having a single vertical fin had to do with ground handling. Being towed in and out of hangars at some airports could pose a problem. During the 1940s many of their hangar doors were too low to accommodate larger planes like Constellations. It called for dividing the load between three vertical tail surfaces, each smaller and lighter than a single tail surface. From a maintenance standpoint, rudder surfaces on either side of the elevator were also interchangeable. However, the tail fin at its center was not.

The Constellation's brakes were hydraulically operated, as was the landing gear's retraction system. The landing gear struts retracted forward into the engine nacelles. In the plane's nose, a strut restricted rearward travel until reaching the bottom of the forward fuselage. When fully retracted, all of the wheels and the wheel wells were fully enclosed, covered by doors sealing them.

Another life-saving feature called reverse pitch was added to the propellers of Constellations a few years after World War II. Because many post-war airliners were larger and heavier than earlier planes, wheel braking was a serious need. Improving existing wheel braking wasn't a solution. A complete redesign of the system was needed soon after reverse thrust braking became commonplace. Immediately after landing, the pilot would move the propeller control lever past a feathering setting into reverse pitch to trigger its powerful braking force. Compared to using only wheel braking, the landing distance of a Constellation was shortened by as much as 40 percent using both wheel braking and the reverse thrust.

Accidents involving Constellations such as Flight 529 weren't the only problems affecting the planes. Their heavy weight and immense size depended on hydraulic boost to move the control surfaces. To reduce the pilot workload, Lockheed had installed the systems in all of its airliners. Unfortunately, they didn't always work the way its manufacturer wanted.

Constellations were considered to be the most complex piston-powered airliners of their day. It meant there was greater potential for mechanical failures compared to simpler systems existing in competitive airliners. When it came to Flight 529, the elevator boost system is what had failed. It was something that simple. During an early test flight of another TWA Constellation, half of its hydraulic system failed. Five minutes later, the other half did the same. A highly experienced captain at the airline was in the cockpit and was able to move its controls without the help of hydraulic boost. However, it took the combined strength of both pilots pushing on their control wheels to save the day.

TWA faced an unpleasant history when it came to the number of crashes it was required to report. It also suffered from an abnormal number of serious maintenance oversights from the late 1940s through the 1960s. A number of accidents occurring during these years involved

7. Scary Flights

maintenance failures that ended up killing both flight crews and passengers. All of the accidents involved Lockheed Constellations.

Serious problems with the Constellation flight controls surfaced shortly after the planes first entered commercial service. In addition to routine control system problems, the fatal crash of a TWA Constellation raised public concerns on May 11, 1947. Because its wreckage proved difficult to retrieve from the bottom of the ocean, the Civil Aeronautics Board was unable to determine exactly what had caused it to crash.

During the early morning hours, the out-of-control plane slammed into Delaware Bay. Perched along the northeast seaboard of the United States, its waterway drained into the Atlantic Ocean. The purpose of the flight was to teach a new group of TWA pilots how to fly its Constellations. Four men were aboard, all of them killed after the plane hit the water and exploded.[1]

The Constellation had been flying approximately 2,500 feet over the surface of the ocean on a straight and level course. Without any warning, it began turning to the left. Continuing in that turn, the angle of the plane's left wing was soon pointing almost straight down. Its nose also dropped with a sharp dive resulting. At the same time, the instructor pilot tried recovering from the dive, its engines emitting a loud roar. Flying too low over the surface of the ocean, the Constellation smashed into it within seconds. Its nose was pointed down at a 45-degree angle on impact. Two or three muffled explosions followed an intense fire that poured thick black smoke into the air.

The plane had been flying normally until it entered the uncontrolled left turn. The bank angle increased sharply and the nose dropped as the plane entered an unforgiving dive. Training flights for TWA crewmembers had been conducted with and without the plane's hydraulic boost system engaged. The reason for demonstrating the system to newer pilots was to familiarize them with how the system worked. The specific intent of the instruction was to show them how to move the flight control surfaces manually.

Every effort was made by the CAB investigators to recover the plane's wreckage. It was important to determine whether a structural failure or equipment malfunction had caused or contributed to the accident. Only small parts of the plane were eventually salvaged from the ocean. Whether its loss of control had resulted from a failure of its flight controls, or because the crew used an incorrect technique, continued to be a mystery.

A CAB accident investigation report, dated February 5, 1948, provided a probable cause statement: "The Board finds that the probable cause of this accident was loss of control of the aircraft for reasons undetermined."[2] The brief CAB statement was inconclusive, especially the use of words such as "reasons undetermined." It became obvious the investigators found nothing that could have caused the crash.

A frightening experience took place during an instruction flight in another TWA Constellation. The plane had been flying at 7,000 feet when its elevator boost system was switched from hydraulic to manual control, this intended to provide practice for the trainee pilots aboard. Unfortunately, the plane immediately snapped into a 30-degree left bank. A gradual loss of altitude followed, the plane descending to 5,000 feet. The instructor pilot had a choice: feather the throttled engines or increase their power. He chose to increase the engine power.

The instructor made an attempt to roll out of the steep bank. But the plane wouldn't respond to his control inputs. The rudder trim tab was adjusted but didn't help. As the bank steepened, the nose dropped sharply. The instructor tried assisting his trainee pilot to recover, but nothing they tried lessened the bank angle. Throttling back two of the engines worsened the situation. Both pilots pushing forward on the control wheels achieved nothing.

When the wing's bank reached a dangerous 80-degree angle, the instructor tried moving the boost system's shift handle. Successful in doing this, he was fortunate that the plane was now flying at a normal attitude angle. The Constellation had lost at least 2,000 feet during its uncontrollable descent. If any more altitude had been lost, it's likely the plane would have crashed.

The CAB investigators were well aware that Constellations relied on boost systems to move their unusually large control surfaces. Although it was possible to fly the plane manually without the boost engaged, it wasn't a recommended procedure. The mechanical advantage provided by the system was needed to lighten the control forces. It became a common practice for the pilots at TWA to activate it. In this case, the startled crew was lucky that the Constellation didn't crash. No one was hurt. However, the incident brought to light a serious design flaw of Lockheed's complicated flight control system.

While investigating the May 11 crash into Delaware Bay, the CAB investigators came across another dangerous incident.[3] It had to do with the failure of the elevator hydraulic boost system of another TWA Constellation, cruising at 19,000 feet when the incident occurred.

7. Scary Flights

Unexpectedly, the plane jumped into a steep climb the pilots couldn't overcome by pushing their control wheels forward. During an attempt to stop the climb, the pilot even pressed his shoes against the control wheel to increase the force that was being applied. Not effective, he then tried pulling up the shift handle for the boost system, but it appeared to be jammed. He then throttled back two of the plane's engines, but it didn't make any difference. At the same time, for unknown reasons, a trainee flight engineer decided to switch off all four of the plane's hydraulic system shutoff valves. The pressure developed by the system is what powered the Constellation's flight controls.

The plane now entered a steep dive, even with the engines throttled back. The pilot again tried pulling up the shift handle. This time he was lucky because it moved. Once again controllable, the Constellation slowly resumed level flight. But for its crew in the cockpit, they were subjected to a hair-raising experience for those few terrifying minutes.

A teardown inspection of the valve controlling the plane's boost system revealed it was defective, restricting movement of the elevator control surface. It resulted in the loss of control. Specifically, a small shaft fitted to the valve mechanism had unscrewed and restricted any movement. The elevator could travel in one direction, but couldn't reverse when forward pressure was applied to the control wheels.

The crew was lucky to have had sufficient altitude for a safe recovery. An incorrect procedure used by an inexperienced flight engineer caused him to close the shutoff valves, freezing the flight controls. If the pilot had not been successful pulling the shift handle up, a crash would have likely resulted. The CAB investigators took this situation seriously, as they did all loss of control incidents. Shortly thereafter, an airworthiness directive (AD) was released to warn the operators of all Constellations about a possibility of the valve mechanism freezing. The AD was issued toward the end of 1949:

> Numerous incidents of malfunctioning of the elevator booster system have been reported, causing longitudinal hunting of the airplane and, in one instance, injury to some passengers when operation of the elevator boost shifter mechanism was accomplished. Also, in other instances, it has sometimes been impossible to actuate the shifter mechanism, probably as a result of frozen moisture accumulating on the mechanism.[4]

The directive applied to Lockheed Model 49, 149, 649, and 749 aircraft, requiring an inspection of the elevator boost system shift mechanisms. Frozen moisture inside the device could make it impossible to position the shift lever. The steps required by the directive were unique, but also time consuming to implement. They involved lubricating the system's control valve, checking the elevator shift handle function, and updating pilot instruction manuals for all Constellations.

Problems with boost systems were well known among the engineers at Lockheed. During the postwar years, Lockheed had passed up several opportunities to permanently correct the system's shortcomings. The mechanics at TWA were not happy because the system had become a high maintenance item. The airline was occasionally forced to cancel passenger flights due to problems with those systems.

Another TWA Constellation crashed on December 28, 1946, during a landing approach to Shannon Airport in Ireland. Out of the 14 passengers aboard, nine were killed, along with four of its nine crewmembers. The plane exploded after smashing into a grass-covered island about two miles from the end of the runway.[5]

The Constellation was flown on a regular schedule between Paris and New York City via Ireland and Newfoundland. It departed Paris an hour before midnight on December 27, its flight plan calling for an arrival at Shannon or an alternate airport in Prestwick, Scotland. The alternate field information was provided in the event that Shannon had been closed due to bad weather.

Approaching Shannon in the questionable weather, the Constellation flew about 600 feet over the airport's northern border. Continuing on this heading, not far from the airport's boundary, it descended to 500 feet. The plane then made a turn to the left, lining up with the centerline for Runway 14. Close to the ground now, it passed over a dirt hill that was blocking most of the airport's runway lights. During this turn, the plane lost another 150 feet of altitude.

The ground's unyielding surface couldn't be seen from the Constellation's cockpit. The outside vision was almost completely obscured. Without warning, the tip of its left wing dug into the ground, followed by the rest of the plane. A fuel tank in its wing then exploded, spreading flames throughout the interior. The severity of the crash landing was unexpected as was a fire spreading so quickly. The plane had skidded across rough terrain, followed by a fire consuming the entire airframe. The flames killed many of the passengers and half of its crewmembers.

Because the visibility was nearly zero, its captain relied on an altimeter reading to determine the plane's height above the ground. Neither

7. Scary Flights

pilot knew it at the time, but the readings from both altimeters in the cockpit were incorrect.

Learning about the altimeter discrepancy, the CAB investigators examined the altimeters that had been fitted to the Constellation's pilot and co-pilot instrument panels. For an unknown reason, the hose connections to both of the instruments were found reversed. It meant that the instruments were receiving pressurized air from the wrong source. It should have come from a source approved by the instrument manufacturer.

> Maintenance records for the plane revealed that its instrument panel assembly was disassembled at a TWA maintenance facility on December 10, 1946. During the reinstallation, its hoses were switched inadvertently. A safety test of the system, required by FAA regulations, would have revealed if air leakage existed. A document, initialed by a mechanic handling the safety test, indicated the test had been performed. However, it became clear that it was never accomplished. It was an unforgivable error because innocent people died in the crash. The CAB accident investigation report of April 21, 1947, provided details: "It can be concluded that the mechanics involved failed to make the tests as required and nevertheless initialed the maintenance forms to indicate compliance with that requirement."[6]

The CAB also presented a probable cause for the accident in the same report:

> The board determines that the probable cause of this accident was an error in altimeter indication, the primary reason for which was the reversal of the primary and alternate static source lines what left the pilot to conduct his approach to the airport at a dangerously low altitude. A contributing factor was the negligence of maintenance personnel in certifying to the satisfactory functioning of the static system although the tests required to determine such a condition were not accomplished. A further contributing factor was the restriction of vision from the cockpit resulting from fogging of the unheated windshield panels.[7]

There were more unexpected concerns about this accident. During November of 1950, the widow of 44-year-old Alexander Pekelis filed a lawsuit based on the death of her wealthy husband. He had died in the crash.[8] The lawsuit was an unusual one for the airline. TWA sought to use a "Warsaw Convention" ruling to minimize its financial exposure. The ruling stated that an airline would not be liable for maintenance or pilot errors if it had taken "all necessary measures to avoid the damage." It also limited the liability of an airline to $8,300 per passenger.[9]

17 Days and 17 Miles Apart

The lawsuit contended that his death had resulted from the plane's faulty altimeters and a mechanic who neglected to perform an FAA-required safety test. The TWA representatives in the courtroom, including maintenance executive Ray Dunn, stated that the circumstances under which the mechanic had acted did not amount to "willful misconduct."

Much of the discussion during the trial questioned why both of the altimeters were hooked up incorrectly. When the pilots lowered the plane's landing gear to land, the altitude displayed on the altimeters registered a much higher reading than the plane's actual height. A hose that supplied air pressure to the instruments should have been connected to carry air pressure from outside of the plane's nose. Instead, it transferred pressure from an enclosed space housing the nose landing gear. Because the hoses had been switched, with both altimeters using air pressure coming from the wheel well rather than outside, the readings were at least 400 feet too high.

The hose connections to both altimeters had been reversed sometime between December 16 and 18 by the same mechanic who had earlier reinstalled the instrument panel. However, the error wasn't discovered until a week later. A crew working on the plane on December 25 found it strange that no one had noticed the fatal error. Something else was even more peculiar. The TWA mechanic had signed a document stating that the system's safety test was performed. Of course, it never happened and the statement was a lie. Not only were the hoses for the altimeters reversed, but also the failure of a mechanic to carry out the mandatory safety test was unexpected. Thirteen people lost their lives due to his negligence.

As noontime approached on July 11, 1946, still another TWA Constellation on a crew training flight also ended up crashing. The accident took place about a mile northeast of the Reading Airport in Pennsylvania.[10] Inside the plane's forward baggage compartment, a fire had spread quickly, causing its pilots to lose control of the plane. Heavy smoke began engulfing the entire interior. The pilots unable to control the spread of its flames, a crash landing became the only option available. Five of the crewmembers aboard were killed in the crash, with the instructor pilot ending up injured. The tremendous impact and flames demolished all of what was left.

Sixteen minutes after departing the airport in Reading, the instructor pilot smelled an odor that resembled burning insulation. A

7. Scary Flights

trainee flight engineer decided to open a door leading into the passenger cabin. Upon opening it, he found the cabin to be filled with thick black smoke. An attempt to extinguish the fire proved ineffective because it had grown large in size. The engineer, also learning about a potentially dangerous condition in a fuel induction system of an engine, made another mistake. He erroneously associated that condition with smoke filling up the cabin. On his own, he decided to feather an engine that he thought had been contributing to the smoke. However, the instructor pilot didn't agree with this action. The pilot immediately descended and flew toward the Reading airport with all engine throttles pulled back to idle power settings.

During the plane's descent, another trainee flight engineer opened up a crew hatch to vent smoke building up in the cockpit. But rather than venting it to the exterior, the opened hatch resulted in bringing more deadly smoke into the cabin. At this point, with so much smoke inside, it proved impossible for either pilot to read the flight instruments or even see through the clouded windshield.

Flying blind and low over the ground, the instructor pilot opened a window on the right side of the cockpit. Slipping into the copilot seat, he tried controlling the Constellation's flight path with his head moving partially outside the window. Not able to be sure of the plane's direction and using movements of the control wheel, the instructor was able to crash land the plane in an abandoned field. It came to a slow stop. The crash landing was soon followed by a horrific explosion. Within seconds, the Constellation and its occupants were consumed in flames. The instructor pilot was lucky to have escaped, but the other crewmembers died in the crash.

Investigators from the CAA soon arrived at the scene. Over the days to come they found nothing suspicious, until discovering an overlooked part of the plane's electrical system. Specially designed electrical components had been installed in sections of the airframe. The engineers at Lockheed referred to them as through-studs. They were intended to provide an airtight connection for the electrical cables transferring power throughout the Constellation's metal structure. The cables had been stretched through sections of the wings, routed to electric generators driven by the engines. Three of the studs were installed along sides of the forward baggage compartment.

Six through-studs recovered from the wreckage had suffered severe arcing. Two of them were completely burned. The investigators suspected that the flammable insulation found adjacent to cables routed in the baggage compartment could easily catch fire. The temperatures of dissimilar metals used to manufacture the studs were too hot to touch if electricity had been traveling through the cables. It would result in continuous arcing. If the studs had come into contact with any flammable material, it would result in a fire.[11]

None of the through-studs had been manufactured in accordance with required specifications. Lockheed's quality control personnel did not inspect the devices before its workers on an assembly line installed them in new Constellations. Both steel and aluminum types of washers were used to assemble the defective parts. Lugs used for connecting to electric cables were made of either copper or aluminum, while the nuts were made of brass and steel to hold everything together.

For the electrical engineers at Lockheed, it was turning into a nightmare. The CAA's investigation report provided details: "The almost indiscriminate use of materials of different compositions aggravated the high contact resistances of the studs and, therefore, increased the likelihood of pitting."[12]

The sloppy installation of the defective through-studs and its cabling is what ignited the flammable material. The arcing became so intense that it caused some of the studs to break into pieces. Retrieved from the wreckage, four of them showed "intense local heating attributable to electrical arcing." A heavy-duty direct current generator, driven by an engine on the left wing, had failed to function properly during one of the Constellation's previous flights. An inspection conducted a day before the accident flight revealed that a cable leading to the generator had broken off from its mounting hardware.

A final report from the CAA concerning the accident provided details:

> It is apparent that electrical arcing had been caused by a defective through-stud installation and that such arcing was of sufficient duration and intensity to ignite the forward baggage compartment lining while in flight. In view of the condition of the baggage compartment lining in other Constellations, it is likely that leakage of hydraulic fluid has also taken place in the forward baggage compartment and that the fuselage lining was saturated with fluid.[13]

An inspection of Constellations in TWA's fleet revealed that hydraulic fluid was found leaking into other baggage compartments and saturating its insulation. The fluid apparently fed the fire. Exactly how it was ignited remained a mystery, although all of the evidence pointed to through-stud arcing. The replacement of electrical connectors became a top priority at Lockheed. The fix also called for making sure there was no arcing of its cables or any rubbing against the fuselage skin. Upgrading the forward baggage compartment soundproofing came next.

Another change was intended to prevent any leakage of hydraulic fluid from saturating the compartment's plastic liner. Otherwise, it would accumulate in a puddle. Finally, different types of fittings and plastic liners were investigated and installed throughout different areas of every plane. Fire extinguishing systems were not installed as standard equipment in the baggage compartments of existing Constellations. Making matters worse, an air circulating system in the passenger cabin was found to be directing its airflow into the baggage compartment. It was a deadly design because it could sustain a raging fire rather than extinguish it. Lockheed was required to redesign the system. The CAA went on to mandate that smoke detector systems be installed in each engine nacelle and baggage compartments of all Constellations.

The CAA investigators were upset with the quality of work they saw during a tour of the Lockheed plant in California. They kept in mind that poor quality control and inadequate inspection is what had cost people their lives:

> For the third time within the past year, a major accident has occurred in an air carrier aircraft which could readily have been avoided, had an adequate fire-detection system been installed. In each instance, the fire originated in inaccessible or remote areas of the aircraft and was able to develop to sufficiently severe proportions before detection to render a safe emergency landing impossible. A smoke-detection system would, without a doubt, have made it possible for the flight crew to take corrective action soon enough to permit a safe return to the airport.[14]

Unusual to mention in a CAA accident investigation report, the investigators devoted much of its content to what they witnessed at Lockheed:

> It is difficult to understand that such a situation could have been permitted to persist over an appreciable period of time without corrective action having been taken. The Lockheed Model 049 provides ample accessibility for ground inspection of the forward baggage compartment and failure to observe such a condition as must have existed prior to its last flight indicates the inadequacy of inspection policies then in effect. That the above situation was not an isolated incident became readily apparent after this

accident when similar conditions in forward baggage compartments were observed in several such aircraft. It was observed that insufficient coordination existed between the Civil Aeronautics Administration, the aircraft manufacturer and the air carrier operators, and that in several instances field inspectors were insufficiently informed as to malfunctioning observed within newer aircraft. The existence of inspectional deficiencies assumes particular significance in the light of the fact that the Constellation was provided a "service test" while in military employment during the war, and that such service test will not be available to the same extent for types of aircraft presently in the pre-production stages.[15]

The report ended with a probable cause for the accident:

The Board determines that the probable cause of this accident was failure of at least one of the generator lead through-stud installations in the fuselage skin of the forward baggage compartment which resulted in intense local heating due to the electrical arcing, ignition of the fuselage insulation, and creation of smoke of such density that sustained control of the aircraft became impossible. A contributing factor was the deficiency in the inspection systems which permitted defects in the aircraft to persist over a long period of time and to reach such proportions as to create a hazardous condition.[16]

At both Lockheed and its airline customers, worse news was about to arrive. The CAA decided to ground every Constellation then in service: "Under the emergency authority vested in the Administrator of Civil Aeronautics and in view of the deficiencies disclosed as a result of this accident, the CAA, immediately following the accident, suspended the airworthiness certificates of the Lockheed Model 049 for a period of 30 days."[17]

If not accomplished earlier, the electrical systems and associated components of all Constellations were redesigned and modified at the plant, the work paid for by Lockheed and its suppliers. The insulation was upgraded to prevent damage from wire chafing and protect it from contacting metal surfaces. An inventory of defective through-studs was discarded and replaced with properly manufactured and tested devices. In addition, weak aluminum conductors carrying electric power from the engine-driven generators were replaced with thicker copper cables. Finally, all fuses and switches throughout the plane were replaced to prevent the possibility of an electrical short circuit occurring in the future. Until the system updates were completed, the planes had not been allowed by the CAA to fly passengers or cargo. It was an expensive lesson for Lockheed and its suppliers. The changes amounted to a major

7. Scary Flights

redesign of the Constellation's electrical power control and distribution systems.

When passengers became aware of the Constellation's shortcomings, air travel at TWA and some other airlines took a dip. It proved difficult for the airline business to recover until all of the problems were resolved.

On August 30, 1950, another TWA Constellation experienced a worse problem near Cairo in Egypt. The flight had originated in Bombay, India. Its final destination was New York City, but it needed to make several stops for refueling.[18] After departing the Bombay airport, the plane arrived in Cairo during late evening hours to refuel before departing.

Shortly after departure, a fire from an engine failure on the right wing caused the captain to turn around and attempt a landing in Cairo. The Constellation had been on a pre-planned course for over 10 miles. Because the fire had spread rapidly, its flaming engine suddenly burned off from the mounts and fell away from the wing. It caused the captain to reduce the plane's speed while losing more altitude. Portions of the airframe continued to burn during its descent. The wing now almost fully covered in flames, the captain decided to make a left turn to line up with the runway in Cairo. By this time, the entire right wing was in flames. Recognizing the seriousness of what had happened and it being an extremely dark night, the captain decided to attempt an emergency landing on the desert floor, about 52 miles northeast of the Cairo airport.

Crashing during the moonless night, it struck the ground extremely hard at a relatively flat angle. The Constellation's fuselage shattered into pieces from the impact. Whatever was left of its airframe continued to burn. Its nearly full fuel tanks in the wings had burst open on impact, causing thousands of gallons of fuel to splash out, thoroughly saturating the sandy soil.

The crash and fire ended up causing the deaths of all 48 passengers and seven crewmembers aboard. The bodies and debris were scattered over a wide area stretching more than 700 feet.

During the CAA investigation, an inspection of TWA's maintenance records uncovered a significant oversight. The defective Curtiss-Wright R-3350 engine on the right wing had been running unusually hot during earlier flights, according to what the TWA mechanics recalled. Following the engine's complete disassembly, a probable cause

17 Days and 17 Miles Apart

for the accident was determined: total failure of the engine's master rod bearing. It had resulted in the uncontrollable fire and the deaths of all its occupants. TWA's maintenance department apparently dropped the ball. The R-3350 engines had been known to be trouble prone and the airline's maintenance team knew all about it. Because 18-cylinder reciprocating engines had a long history of running too hot, with it well documented, the defective engine should have been replaced prior to the plane undertaking long international flights like one from India to New York City.

On July 26, 1947, a Constellation that would later also crash as Flight 529 was damaged at the Shannon airport in Ireland after sliding off the surface of a wet runway. Upon landing, its wheel brakes were unable to reduce the speed of the heavy plane. Halfway down the runway it was still decelerating. The speed required it to turn off from the runway to slow down if the plane had a steerable nose wheel. Unfortunately, it didn't have that feature. Nor did it have reversible propellers.

The brakes on the right-hand landing gear assembly had failed, causing the plane to slide off the runway into a deep pile of mud. Without delay, the engineers got busy correcting a major shortcoming, affecting this and other Constellation landing gear assemblies. A strut damper was installed to absorb fore and aft shock loads when a plane landed. In addition, all Constellations were later modified with steerable nose wheel steering and reversible propellers, including the one later flown as Flight 529.

On November 18, 1950, the same airliner later crashing as Flight 529 was involved in still another accident. TWA Flight 94 departed Los Angeles International Airport (LAX) with a load of first-class passengers. They included actress Elizabeth Taylor and her bridegroom, Conrad "Nicky" Hilton. Other notable people seated in the passenger cabin were movie director John Ford, actress Nancy Olson, actor Ward Bond, and Nate Blumberg, head of Universal Studios.[19]

Raining steadily throughout the night, the weather was barely legal for the Constellation's takeoff from Los Angeles. The visibility amounted to only one-half of a mile. Soon after departing Runway 25 the weather became even worse. They were climbing to cruise altitude when the cylinders of its inboard engine on the left wing began overheating. Making matters worse, a cylinder head temperature gauge monitoring the inboard engine on the right wing also moved into a red zone. Both of their propellers were feathered and the engines shut down.

7. Scary Flights

The TWA captain needed to land the plane as soon as possible. But his communication radio could only transmit and receive messages on an airport's tower frequency. Facing fog, drizzle, and an overcast sky, returning to Los Angeles wasn't an option. The only airport with a runway suitable for landing Constellations was Long Beach Municipal Airport. But light rain was falling at that airport, too.

Flying on only two engines rather than four, while transporting a load of important passengers, baggage, and full tanks of fuel, required plenty of concentration on the part of its flight crew. The plane had a system installed for dumping fuel over the ocean should an emergency occur. However, the captain didn't want to open its nozzles. The malfunctioning radio could create a spark and ignite fuel vapors exiting the nozzles. It wasn't a risk worth taking, especially with so many Hollywood personalities in the cabin.

An instrument approach into Long Beach kept the captain in the fog until the plane broke out midway along the runway. It had passed through half of the runway's length before slowing down. Landing during bad weather, with two of its four engines shut down, continued to present a challenge. The runway's moist surface worsened the landing because of a stiff tailwind and its heavy landing weight. Lacking reversible propellers to stop, the pilots pressed on their brake pedals, skidding along the runway's surface before careening 300 yards across its end. The plane then struck a railroad track and abutment, knocking off its right-hand main landing gear assembly. Poor braking on the slippery surface had pushed the plane's nose around 180 degrees. The Constellation now facing the same direction from where it came, this was followed by an abrupt stop in a muddy ditch. The passengers were likely a bit rattled but certainly happy to have escaped injury.

In addition to the right landing gear getting sheared off, there was considerable damage to the underside of the wing and lower fuselage structure. A later inspection revealed that the master rod bearings of both Wright R-3350 engines had failed. Their propellers were found frozen solid and couldn't be rotated by the investigators.

It was amazing that during 1947, the same plane had crashed at the airport in Shannon, Ireland. It landed on a slick runway that broke off its right-hand landing gear assembly. A problem with engine overheating had resulted in the crash. The engineers at TWA concluded that the engine failures had occurred due to using diluted engine oil. This condition blocked the flow of lubricating oil to vital engine components, this causing the engine to seize.[20] This type of lubrication, widely called oil dilution, is used to temporarily decrease the viscosity of engine lubricating oil. Reciprocating piston engines could be started when the outside air temperature was extremely cold.

Much like the crash in Long Beach, the mechanics at TWA repaired the damage and released the plane for passenger flights in March 1951— carrying a new name called the Star of Dublin. For 10 years, the plane provided transportation for untold thousands of passengers, finally being assigned to fly passengers as Flight 529.

On June 3, 1954, this same Constellation experienced still another in-flight emergency. It suffered from a cracked cylinder head of an engine on the left wing. The captain landed the airliner as soon as possible to avoid igniting a fire while in the air. He was well aware of the TWA crash in Egypt years earlier that killed everyone aboard. His plane was flying from Chicago to San Francisco but needed to make an emergency landing at a small airport in Sioux City, Iowa. Although damage to its airframe was substantial, no one aboard was injured. Once again, the plane was repaired and placed back in passenger service. This was the third incident that passengers were forced to endure.

Most TWA employees were pleased with these outcomes. After all, there were no injuries, deaths, or expensive lawsuits. On September 1, 1961, the fatal crash of Flight 529 would change everything.

The government investigators, Lockheed, and even the morgue in Chicago, were about to get more business, although they surely didn't wish for it. On September 17 a near-new Lockheed Electra turboprop crashed after departing O'Hare International Airport. It was only an hour commute from where Flight 529 crashed. Everyone aboard the Electra was killed. Much like what had happened near Clarendon Hills, a reason for the crash would point to another case of sloppy maintenance.

8

Difficult Day

It had been many years from when the first Constellations were delivered to the world's airlines. Embracing modern technological advances and the advent of powerful turboprop jet engines, Lockheed Aircraft Corporation designed and built another all-new airliner. The result was its L-188 Electra. A group of engineers at Lockheed, who had earlier designed venerable C-130 transport planes for the U.S. Air Force, undertook design work for the commercial Electra. The overall size was similar to that of the Constellation, but its powerful engines were expected to provide far faster cruising speeds. It was hoped that the Electra would become the fastest airliner in commercial airline history. Cruising at speeds over 400 miles per hour to get to their destinations faster, its passengers enjoyed roomy seats, comfortable air conditioning, and a low cabin noise level. Compared to the Constellation, the Electra had everything its passengers could ever want.

The Electra had a conventional all-metal airframe structure, but larger in size than most other airliners. It could transport a maximum of 86 passengers seated in a coach-class arrangement. To assure a high cruising speed, the four turboprop engines each developed 3,750-shaft-horsepower. It was a requirement demanded by the nation's airlines. The engines produced almost twice the horsepower of Pratt & Whitney R-2800 piston engines found on other airliners of that era.

American Airlines became Lockheed's first customer for the Electra, placing the plane in passenger service on January 23, 1959. During evening hours on December 3 of that year, the plane departed Chicago for LaGuardia airport in New York. Approaching the airport during overcast weather, its pilot was cleared to make a visual approach over the East River on its way to the airport. Moments later, the plane struck the surface of the river just short of the runway.[1] Out of the 73 people on board, 45 died in the crash. Since the plane was almost new, it had

17 Days and 17 Miles Apart

logged only 302 hours in the air. Considered to be an "all-new" airliner within the aviation industry, the crash was felt to be nothing more than an isolated incident. However, two other crashes that were yet to happen would change that earlier opinion.

Northwest Airlines took delivery of its first Electra on July 19, 1959, followed by an inaugural passenger flight on September 18. The airline had ordered 18 L-188C Electras, each of the planes configured by Lockheed to carry 72 passengers and five crewmembers.

A seven-month-old Northwest Electra became the victim of another fatal accident on March 17, 1960. Heading from Chicago to Miami, it crashed not far from the town of Cannelton, Indiana, disintegrating while in the air high over an empty countrywide. The plane broke into large sections, the entire right wing one of them. The rest of the plane plunged straight down into the ground. All 63 people aboard were killed.[2] The crash was the third disaster involving an Electra in little more than a year. Its loss was a terrible blow for the time-honored domestic airline whose planes could be seen flying throughout the United States and the rest of the world.

At this point, the FAA got involved. There was no explanation as to why so many Electras were crashing. Behind the scenes, pressure was building among frequent air travelers to ground all of them. Following its inspection of 52 Electras, the FAA decided to limit their cruising speeds but nothing else.

The Electra's wings and engine mounts appeared to be sturdy—but were later found to have serious structural faults. That discovery caused Lockheed to undertake a major modification program. Satisfied that the manufacturer had solved all of its apparent problems, on December 31, 1960, the FAA removed the speed restriction it earlier imposed. The planes returned to passenger service on February 24, 1961, being renamed Electra IIs.[3] Assuring that the Electras were safe following major modifications at Lockheed meant that the plane's airworthiness was approved by the FAA.

In addition to earlier Electra crashes, another Electra was about to join them. Two weeks after TWA Flight 529 crashed in a rural area of southern Illinois, another disaster occurred outside of Chicago, not far from the major city. It was Flight 706 operated by Northwest Airlines.

For local residents, who spent most of their winter months staying in Illinois, the weather there was far from pleasant. Piles of melting snow and freezing temperatures were expected. The only relief from the

8. Difficult Day

extreme weather was to drive to a balmy southern state or board a plane for Florida. Northwest Airlines took advantage of that air travel market by offering a number of flights to cities in Florida. Flight 706 happened to be one of them.

There was no doubt that 1961 was a terrible year for both Trans World Airlines and Northwest Airlines. Worldwide, there had been a number of deadly crashes involving airliners, but September was an especially bad month for them. In addition to the loss of TWA 529 and Northwest 706, on September 10 a total of 83 people died in the crash of a chartered airliner near Shannon airport in Ireland. Two days later, on September 12, another 77 people lost their lives when their airliner crashed near Rabat in Morocco.

Sunday morning, September 17, 1961, roughly an hour's drive from

A recent aerial photograph of the TWA crash site reveals how much of the nearby land has been developed. The vacant grassy area in the middle of the photograph is where Flight 529 crashed in 1961 (courtesy Mary Brown at Clarendon Hills Historical Society).

where TWA Flight 529 crashed 17 days earlier, the loss of Flight 706 shook up travelers around the world. Owing to widespread news coverage of the TWA crash, another airliner crash happening in the same month was too much for many people to comprehend.[4]

Five crewmembers, scheduled to take Flight 706 to Florida from Chicago, left Minneapolis on Saturday afternoon. Being nonrevenue passengers, they boarded an Electra for a short flight to Chicago. They would stay overnight in a hotel there, scheduled to fly to Florida on Sunday morning. After completing their flight to Florida, and spending Sunday night there, they planned to fly back to Minnesota on Monday and prepare for another flight.

The sky remained clear during the early morning hours on Sunday. At 7:47 a.m., another crew left Wold Chamberlain Field in Minnesota with a handful of passengers. At 8:07 a.m. the Electra touched down at O'Hare International Airport. The incoming crew turned the plane over to another crew, planning to take it to Florida.

Fourteen passengers, arriving at O'Hare from suburbs around the Chicago area, were eager to board. When its departure time was announced in the terminal, they wasted no time filing into the plane and electing seats. Counting the number of passengers continuing on from Minneapolis, the cabin would soon become half full. Preparing for departure, both of its stewardesses went through the airline's routine safety instructions, followed by greeting each boarding passenger. Although the plane was designed to carry a maximum of 72 passengers, only 32 of its seats were filled. Everyone aboard now seated, it was time to depart Chicago for Florida.

Inside the Electra's cockpit prior to departure, its three-person crew kept busy studying checklists and adjusting controls. Ralph Hagstrom, the captain of Flight 706, lived in the Twin Cities area of Minnesota's Mendota Heights. He had been a pilot at Northwest Airlines for 19 years, beginning his career there on April 11, 1942. Married with five children, he previously resided in Superior, Wisconsin. The captain's flying time totaled 15,898 hours, 314 of them being logged at the controls of an Electra.[5]

At the age of 33, Richard Anderson, Flight 706's first officer, lived in Minnetonka Beach, Minnesota. Married, he and his wife were raising two young girls. He joined the airline as a pilot during 1954. Altogether, he had logged 6,643 hours, 90 of them in the cockpit of an Electra.[6]

8. Difficult Day

Wayne Fuller, the flight engineer, lived in South Saint Paul, Minnesota. He began his career as a mechanic at the airline during 1948 and promoted to flight engineer in 1955. Married, he and his wife were also raising five children. His flight time totaled 3,368 hours with 556 of them being logged as an Electra flight engineer.[7]

Stewardess Rosemary Bilski lived in Mendota Heights with her parents and a younger brother. She joined Northwest Airlines on June 29, 1957. Originally, she wasn't scheduled to fly aboard Flight 706. The Saturday before this flight, she decided to trade her shift with another stewardess and fly to Florida on Sunday. Her goal was to build up flight hours so she could attend a University of Minnesota football game. During her four years as a stewardess at Northwest, she also worked as a fashion model on a part-time basis.[8]

Jeanette McKenzie, the other stewardess that morning, also lived with her family in Minneapolis. Hired by Northwest on April 8, 1960, she had quit an office job for the opportunity to work as a stewardess.[9]

Assigned to fly Northwest Flight 706, the Electra was almost new, being registered with the FAA as N137US following its manufacture on June 14, 1960. Although the plane had gone through the Lockheed Electra Action Program (LEAP) on January 31, 1961, it wasn't delivered to the airline until June 22 of that year. It had logged only 614 hours in the air. The flight crew at O'Hare appreciated that it went through the LEAP program at Lockheed.[10] It meant that the wings and engine mounts were strengthened to prevent the kind of earlier accidents the Electra became known for. Eight months earlier, an Electra flown by another Northwest crew crashed in a deserted agricultural field. The crash was caused by structural failure of its right wing, the airliner disintegrating while in the air. This and other safety issues apparently resolved now, the flight crew at O'Hare was confident that it was safe enough to fly aboard.

A number of passengers were planning to visit friends or family members while visiting Florida. Although Flight 706 was scheduled to land at only three cities in that state, not all of the passengers lived in those areas. Instead, some of them expected to visit Largo, St. Petersburg, West Palm Beach, Fort Myers or Boca Raton. Many of them were older, a number retired, while others just relished an opportunity to visit family members there or enjoy Florida's warm weather.

Some of the passengers brought along family members. The

17 Days and 17 Miles Apart

president of a manufacturing company boarded in Milwaukee. He accompanied a teenage son, the young man expecting to enroll as a freshman at Florida Southern University.

Joyce Coutu, at the age of 28, kept her eyes on four young children while they boarded. Along with her husband, she lived in Waukegan, Illinois. Their children ranged in age from four months to five years, none of them having flown before. Both she and her children looked forward to visiting her parents in Tampa. After watching them board the Electra, her husband decided to stay at the airport until they departed. He walked over to the airport observation deck to wait.[11]

Another husband and wife looked forward to vacationing in Florida. The man had retired as a truck driver for a major oil company. His wife won the trip to Florida by entering a contest at a local grocery store. Their son had dropped them off at the front of the terminal. To watch them take off, he planned to wait on the observation deck.[12]

Nancy Foss, who traveled to Chicago from Arcadia in Southern California, brought her two-month-old daughter. She looked forward to enjoying her visit to Florida.[13] Marion Eckstein was on her way to West Palm Beach after attending a high school class reunion.[14] Twenty-two-year-old Janice Duffy, a resident of Lake Forest, Illinois, had worked as a teacher.[15] She was the daughter of an executive at a stock brokerage firm, but he didn't accompany her on this flight. Others boarded the plane that morning, all of them looking forward to spending time in Florida.

Developed on more than 7,600 acres of vacant land a few miles from a bustling business district in downtown Chicago, O'Hare International Airport was first known for a large aircraft factory there. During World War II, thousands of workers at the airport had built hundreds of four-engine Douglas C-54 transport planes for the military. They would be used to fly troops and supplies to support the overseas war effort. The airport's name was permanently changed to O'Hare in 1949. Although Midway Airport served Chicago travelers as their airport of choice for decades, its runways weren't long enough to safely accommodate the latest jets. Due to this restriction, O'Hare gained a majority of airline passengers during the late 1960s. From 1963 to 1998, O'Hare turned into the world's busiest airport, a logical successor to Midway.

The Electra was reported to be in excellent mechanical condition that morning, as expected for such a new airliner. Its earlier crew had no

8. Difficult Day

concerns with it after the flight from Milwaukee. Set to depart Chicago for Florida, the plane's final destination was Miami, after making intermediate stops at Tampa and Fort Lauderdale.

In its cockpit, the flight engineer brought the Electra's four Allison turboprop engines to life. The process took only a few minutes. Meanwhile, the captain looked over his flight plan, while the first officer contacted the O'Hare control tower to request a taxi clearance. The request was soon approved, and they taxied away from the terminal and maneuvered the Electra onto a taxiway leading to runway 14 Right for takeoff. It was now 8:55 a.m.

Upon reaching the far end of the runway, with all of its systems operating properly, the tower cleared Flight 706. Its weight was lighter than usual because fewer passengers had been boarded. Rapidly gaining speed along the 11,600-foot-long runway, and passing an 8,000-foot marker, the Electra gradually lifted off.

Almost immediately after leaving the ground, the right wing began tilting down. It surprised the flight crew. The angle of the bank had changed so quickly that whatever small amount of altitude the plane gained after taking off was lost. It was unlikely that the passengers in the cabin understood what was happening. The plane was stuck in this unusually steep bank. Getting steeper by the second, the wing was now pointing almost straight ground. The wing was about to smash into the ground.

Unlike other fatal accidents, its captain was able to provide an important clue for CAB investigators—a tape recording of his message with the control tower, even though it was less than eight seconds long. While stuck in the steep bank, its captain was able to transmit a short, garbled message. His final words, signaling impending disaster, came across loud and clear in the control tower. He said: "We're in trouble [break] uh and all units holding this is Northwest alert. I still don't have release right turn in no control."[16]

It became apparent the captain was attempting to solve a control problem at the same time.

Northwest Airlines Flight 706 continued flying in this manner for several more seconds. Veering across the ground in a northwesterly direction, its right wing sliced through several 38,000-volt power lines. They had been built along a railroad embankment that bordered the southeast boundary of O'Hare airport. The wing then struck a concrete wall; much of its airframe started to break apart. Shedding metal

17 Days and 17 Miles Apart

and pieces of plastic, Flight 706 roared across the soggy earth at nearly 100 miles an hour, bouncing up and down several times. The Electra's momentum caused it to slide across an empty meadow, plowing through the unpopulated area where small trees and bushes were growing. Coming to a sudden stop, its nose dug deeply into the marsh. The fuel tanks in the plane's wings ruptured instantly, spreading waves of liquid kerosene across the soil and splashing against what remained of its fuselage. Bluish flames were visible for miles around. Although seemingly distant from civilization, the crash site was only a short distance from the busy airport.

Only a few clues were left behind for the investigators. Part of the plane's tail became imbedded in the marsh. It looked much like a sign, the only recognizable part of the plane that had survived. Its separated tail stood tall near the end of the trail, with the earth surrounding it littered with small pieces of wreckage. Human bodies and baggage were scattered throughout the field. Either the impact or resulting fire killed everyone aboard.

The Electra's final resting place was far removed from where it had first hit the railroad tracks and skidded across the dirt. Explosions snapped the fuselage into pieces. There was little left of the plane when it stopped moving.

It became clear that the Electra had taken off from O'Hare, climbed into the air quickly, its right wing tilting downward, and a crash had followed within seconds. Its takeoff was considered normal but the uncontrollable right turn began shortly after departure. Instead of finding a way out of that unwanted turn, the Electra was faced with its tightening. The wing hit the ground and the plane exploded. It was never higher than a few hundred feet.

Everyone aboard died on impact. The site of the crash was less than an hour's drive on a freeway leading to Clarendon Hills. The Electra smashed into a largely deserted, grassy meadow just outside of O'Hare airport boundaries. However, unlike the crash of Flight 529 a dozen miles from Midway where it departed, Flight 706 smashed into the ground immediately after taking off. Its 37 passengers and crewmembers were killed, compared to 78 people who had lost their lives 17 days earlier. This latest crash upset many of the first responders and volunteers because it was so close to their own homes.

When Flight 529 crashed near Clarendon Hills, the small town relied on its own fire department and nearby residents. The crash scene

8. Difficult Day

at O'Hare was different. The airport, not far from a major city, had its own fire department, police department, and other emergency services available to help. It took only minutes for their personnel to arrive at the scene.

Officials from the federal government, led by CAB chairman Alan Boyd, along with FAA administrator Najeeb Halaby, arrived in Chicago from Washington on Sunday afternoon. They walked through the damp marshland, where pieces of charred metal and scraps of paper had been ejected, much of it mixed up with pumpkins, tomatoes, and squash growing in the area.

"There is no reason to believe there was an explosion due to a bomb or some type of sabotage," Boyd told the media. "There were no strong wind gusts at the time of takeoff. We had no reason to question the structural integrity of the Electra." Boyd was well aware that his agency was charged with investigating the loss of Flight 706.[17]

Flames and smoke coming from burning kerosene continued to rise into the sky. A fire department vehicle from the airport began pumping thousands of gallons of water from its tanker truck, most of it directed on the blazing wreckage. The intensely hot flames could be seen hundreds of feet above the trail. It was too hot to begin any rescue work. Later that morning, among the other people arriving at the site, were several priests moving among bodies in the field to administer last rites. The first responders also noticed that half of the bodies were still strapped into their seats, some of them thrown clear of the wreckage.

The CAB investigators speculated that both the Constellation and Electra may have crashed because their flight controls somehow jammed, referring to the elevator and aileron control surfaces. It would take nothing more than a missing cotter pin in the Constellation or a piece of thin wire in the Electra to bring the planes down. Of course, the Constellation was an older plane, but the Electra was almost new.

During the CAB investigation that followed, problems with the Electra's automatic pilot were dismissed as being unlikely. The autopilot was placarded as being inoperative on the cockpit instrument panel. The system had been disconnected while going through the extensive LEAP program while the plane was at Lockheed in Burbank. Regarding the chance of an asymmetrical flap failure, the system had a switch in the cockpit to automatically align the angle between the left and right flaps, even if they differed by as little as two degrees. This wasn't a concern because even if the switch failed to work, a pilot could easily override the system. The search for a cause of the crash continued.

When it came to the plane's ailerons, the investigators spotted something unusual. A series of fracture marks on the surface of the hydraulic boost unit for the right aileron was clear. It meant that the aileron could have jammed prior to the plane hitting the ground. It was found locked in a six-degree position instead of the one normally used.

The CAB investigators determined that a cable designed to physically connect the control wheel from the first officer to the aileron boost unit had been disconnected. It would have prevented the pilots from correcting the Electra's steep bank. The investigators found out that the cable was disconnected two months before the accident during routine maintenance at a Northwest Airline's maintenance facility. Safety wire was not used to retain the cable's connector. It was not replaced. Without any safety wire in place to retain the connector, it slowly unscrewed, falling out seconds after takeoff. Its purpose was to ensure that the control cable operating the aileron had the correct amount of tension.

Six weeks before the O'Hare accident, a scheduled maintenance task at Northwest Airlines called for replacing a so-called hydraulic boost package that controlled an aileron on the Electra's right wing. It became necessary to remove the short length of safety wire.

Several mechanics assigned to three different shifts had worked on changing the boost package. The CAB investigators were lucky to have located a mechanic who had disconnected and removed the piece of safety wire. But they never found someone else who had failed to reinstall it. Because the safety wire was not reinstalled, the boost system control cable eventually worked loose, resulting in the aileron jamming, while the Electra continued in a fatal turn.[18]

It was hoped by the CAB investigators that Lockheed would modify the flight control systems of all Constellations in worldwide service. Instead, they were never modified and those planes went back into carrying paying passengers. Expected to serve as an aviation industry watchdog, the FAA (today the Federal Aviation Administration) declared that any problem associated with Constellations was considered "cured."[19] No further action was taken.

8. Difficult Day

Shortly after Flight 706 crashed, the past history of the entire Electra fleet was questioned in detail. Something also didn't add up with the O'Hare and even the Clarendon Hills crashes. An unanswered question had to do with whether a human being triggered them? Because both of the crashes took place only weeks apart, could they have been coincidental? Or perhaps, did both airliners crash due to sabotage? As time went by, no one in the aviation industry or government agency wished to talk about these issues, especially one having to do with sabotage.

The crash of Flight 706 occurring so close to the loss of Flight 529, the CAB investigators wondered if a broken part could have caused both of them to crash. Or had they resulted from pilots losing control? Were they caused by a negligent mechanic forgetting to install part of their flight control systems? Or had someone in their cockpits pushed a wrong button?

While the investigators continued to comb through the cornfield outside Clarendon Hills, the negligence of an airline mechanic looked like the answer. Unfortunately, the investigation of Flight 706 would not prove to be that simple.

The detective work associated with both of the crashes ended up consuming more than a year. From early on in the investigation, the CAB determined that a TWA mechanic had forgotten to attach a cotter pin to a bolt in a link controlling the elevator control surface. Incredibly, an unrelated mechanic, working for Northwest Airlines, neglected to attach safety wire to a cable controlling an aileron. In the investigator minds, both these crashes, similar to each other, seemed too coincidental. If they hadn't been the result of negligence, did they represent an attempt to destroy the nation's air transportation system? Only time would provide an answer.

The CAB, short of leadership and not having enough seasoned accident investigators, meant it needed more time at the crash sites than had been expected. Errors caused by airline pilots were relatively simple to identify. But determining the role of little-understood mechanical issues required far more time. Engineers John Leak and Wesley Cowen headed the CAB investigative team. They began to examine details behind the crash of Flight 529 before doing the same at the site of Flight 706 near O'Hare. Leak had been managing the Technical Services Section of the Engineering Division at the CAB's Bureau of Safety. Cowen had joined the agency as an investigator over a year earlier. Both of them were about to face a tiresome work schedule.

17 Days and 17 Miles Apart

There had been some similarities common to both of the crashes. They were suspected of experiencing flight control problems at a low altitude soon after their takeoffs. In a cornfield, the CAB investigators were fortunate to have recovered the Constellation's tail section, it containing a mechanism to operate the rudders and elevator control surfaces. It helped determine a cause of the crash. Would the investigators be this lucky at the crash site of Northwest Airlines Flight 706?

A small group of people waiting on the airport's observation deck would become witnesses. Watching his mother and father board the Electra and taking off from the runway, one man prepared to leave for home. The Coutu woman's husband was there, too. In the distance, seeing flames and smoke climbing high into the sky, both of them worried about their family members. Joyce Coutu and the couple's four children did not survive the crash. Shocked with what he witnessed only a mile away, her husband tried running across the airfield to reach it burning in the distance, but the airport police restrained him.[20] Other people standing around the deck had also witnessed the crash but didn't exhibit that same intense emotion.

There were other witnesses to the crash of Flight 706 who lived or worked in the immediate area, some providing statements for CAB investigators. They described its flight as appearing to be normal with nothing out of the ordinary. That is, until the plane struck a row of power lines. A witness lived in nearby Bensenville. His home was located directly south of where the Electra first bounced against the ground. He saw the plane coming from the east with its right wing on fire. His daughter watched the crash. Nolan Miller, a construction worker at the airport, also witnessed the crash: "I saw the right wing hit a high tension line just outside the airport boundary and the whole body of it lit up in a huge blue arc. Then it went down ... enveloped in flames."[21]

The Cook County morgue was kept busy after Flight 529 crashed, charged with obtaining identifications and processing the bodies of its 78 victims. Now, after only two weeks, its team handled the bodies of another 37 victims coming from Flight 706.

In the morgue, Joyce Coutu's husband waited to identify the bodies of his wife and their four children. She had been dressed in a pink sweater, blue dress, and white boots, he recalled. Using this and other information, the coroner and his colleagues could identify all of the bodies.

8. Difficult Day

Wiping tears from his eyes, the man from Waukegan picked up a pen and signed each of five death certificates while there. His mother, along with three relatives, helped him enter a waiting car to go home.[22]

When it came to TWA Flight 529, an improperly assembled linkage caused the elevator to fail. It was surprising that the Electra was equipped with a similar type of hydraulic boost system. Did the flight controls in the Electra fail the same way they did in the Constellation? The CAB considered this possibility while continuing their investigations at both of the crash sites. The investigators wondered if there might be a link between Sunday's crash and that of the loss of an Eastern Air Lines Electra a year earlier at the airport in Boston. Fifty people died in that crash. The plane failed to gain altitude soon after taking off. It hit a flock of birds that caused all its engines to flame out at the same time.[23]

At the time, determining exactly when and why aviation accidents happened could seem like throwing darts. The causes could be almost anything. But Flight 706 was different from other accidents in an important way. Lockheed had strengthened the accident's plane's airframe with major structural upgrades only months before the crash. If its LEAP upgrade program failed to correct every known structural defect, it could destroy Lockheed's reputation for safety and permanently ground the entire Electra fleet.

The officials at Lockheed had reason to be worried. The CAB officials were faced with finding a cause of the Electra crash as quickly as possible. Could it be that those structural modifications didn't correct all the problems? Or had the crash been caused by nothing more than the missing piece of safety wire? The senior executives at Lockheed hoped that bad news was now behind them. Unfortunately, they found out that it wasn't.

9

Coincidence?

In addition to designing and building 856 commercial and military piston-powered Constellations, Lockheed Aircraft Corporation also developed a turboprop-powered L-188 Electra airliner during the 1950s. It was expected to replace older Constellations then in service at the airlines, many of them being flown by TWA pilots. Because the planes were nearing retirement, Lockheed was successful in turning this opportunity into a sizable profit, selling Electra's to replace older Constellations.

Major technical issues began affecting the entire Electra fleet soon after its passenger service began at airlines around the world. Some were victims of unexplained fatal accidents. Both Lockheed's board of directors and its many shareholders began to fear that the planes could end up being grounded by the government. They worried that the Electra could be the last propeller-driven airliner the company would manufacture. Needless to say, the engineers in Burbank began working overtime, searching for the reason why such a popular airliner continued to crash. Lockheed's future success as a corporation, along with its many thousands of engineers and other employees, depended on finding a cause. In Washington, D.C., government regulators were held under a gun by citizens and elected representatives alike to find the cause and develop a fix. Frequent air travelers demanded that Lockheed either fix the planes or let the government ground all of them. Similar to the electrical demons and grounding haunting early model Constellations, Lockheed found itself on a hot seat once again, while trying to understand and solve the Electra's perplexing problems.

Not long after the first Constellations were delivered to the airlines, technical problems began to cloud the plane's otherwise remarkable performance. Its unreliable and often unproven piston engines, combined with unpredictable electrical problems, added to its unsavory reputation. Because a number of Constellations had crashed, one might

9. Coincidence?

wonder how many were the result of failing hydraulic boost systems. The number could be surprising. Unknown to the public, the systems were maintenance nightmares. Airline mechanics hated their complexity and poor reliability.

In common with power steering systems in modern automobiles, aircraft boost systems operate in a similar manner. Power steering relies on hydraulic pressure to change the direction of a car's front wheels, and in the case of an airplane, its flight control surfaces. Eliminating these systems would result in an airliner carrying less of a payload. Aboard military versions of the Constellation, the boost systems proved useful to substantially lower a pilot's workload. Understanding these benefits and listening to its airline customers, Lockheed decided to continue installing the systems in all of its aircraft.

During World War II, while the engineers at Lockheed kept busy solving problems with the Constellation, the immense size of the plane's control surfaces proved difficult to position. Many airliners built by Lockheed's competing manufacturers used steel cables to link the surfaces to control wheels in their cockpits. Because the planes were smaller and lighter than Constellations, boosted controls weren't a necessity. However, there was another concern during the system's early development. The engineers weren't sure how much force was needed to move the heavy control surfaces. Adequate data weren't readily available to figure out how much force was required. The test engineers at Lockheed spent considerable time exploring different ideas. After all, the Constellation's horizontal stabilizer was nearly half the width of a wing for a twin-engine DC-3 airliner built by Douglas Aircraft Company. To move the Constellation's elevator, 50 to 80 pounds of pressure would likely be needed. Although a force as low as 25 pounds had been tested, it proved inadequate for use in a large airliner. An 80-pound force was eventually selected.[1]

The Constellation was originally designed to fly in and out of airports having short runways. To ensure safe operation, the use of boosted controls seemed like a logical solution to handle this requirement. But the complexity resulting from combining the existing flight control systems and hydraulic boost systems proved troublesome for engineers at Lockheed and mechanics at the airlines.

In Washington, D.C., another issue had prevented the widespread use of boosted controls at other aircraft manufacturers. Discontent with the systems had been brewing for some time among engineers at the Civil Aeronautics Board, that agency founded in 1940. Aside from other issues facing Lockheed, the boost system required approval from this agency before its planes could be placed in service at the airlines. The CAB engineers worried about approving such a complicated system. Beginning during the early years of powered flight, control systems using only cables proved trouble-free in other commercial aircraft. They wondered if they should take a chance and approve this new concept.[2]

To settle the difference of opinion and enable Lockheed to market its Constellations to the airlines, the manufacturer developed a way to disengage the boost system from hydraulic power should it fail. A handle in the plane's cockpit could be pulled to provide manual control of the elevator should an emergency occur. Every Constellation built by Lockheed would be equipped with it.

To minimize the possibility of another Constellation crashing, the CAB investigators suggested that some changes be incorporated in the boost system. This required the government to issue an airworthiness directive. The AD called for reworking the boost system components prior to a plane's next scheduled engine overhaul.[3] It involved lubricating valves controlling the control surfaces. Drilling holes in actuating rods and packing other assemblies with grease were further steps. The airworthiness directive was issued in 1949—long before TWA Flight 529 crashed in 1961.

Based on earlier concern about using boosted controls, the CAB was also fearful of using a shift lever in the cockpit to disengage the system. The airworthiness directive requested, prior to a next scheduled inspection, that each of the levers be checked for proper functioning. The FAA was aware that a manufacturing defect could render such systems inoperable. Finally, the same airworthiness directive required pilot flight manuals for all Constellations be updated with the following words: "Outline the shifting techniques to be followed when shifting is desired."[4]

The Constellation assigned to Flight 529 had been certificated by the CAB before carrying paying passengers. However, the money-starved agency didn't have sufficient manpower to approve the design of every new aircraft submitted for certification. A shortage of skilled inspectors, investigators, and engineers at the agency was nothing new during its years in Washington, D.C. In Burbank, the executives at Lockheed kept an eye on its decisions and prepared to take advantage of anything resulting from its changes.

9. Coincidence?

Every administrator at the Civil Aeronautics Board during postwar years assumed that data submitted by engineers at the manufacturers had been approved by managers and considered free to distribute. This was not always true. Doing this at Lockheed would entail a time-consuming process, but one easy to circumvent.

Over several decades, the agency used a so-called "designee" system to assure its regulations were followed closely. Within Lockheed's factory environment, a group of employees were designated to approve the company's test procedures and examine engineering data intended for a select number of eyes at the CAB. Although the agency was entrusted to approve all new aircraft designs, many of those tasks were delegated to engineers working at Lockheed or even its suppliers. Staffers at the agency reviewed the submitted data and issued type certificates supposedly valid for the entire life of a plane. The original Constellation was a good example of this happening.

The designee system created problems long before the Constellation and Electra programs came into being. The existing regulations prohibited a CAB administrator from certifying airliners if an unsafe problem was uncovered. In addition to the Constellation and Electra, piston-powered Douglas DC-6 and Martin 202 airliners were awarded type certificates even though they had design deficiencies.

TWA owner Howard Hughes offered his own opinion about hydraulically boosted controls during a Congressional hearing on August 7, 1947. He had been invited to appear before a Senate subcommittee in Washington, D.C., to defend his company's development of the flying boat. Taxpayers in the United States had paid for this project. Here's what he told the politicians during the hearing:

> Now this airplane has crossed a barrier in size. That barrier I consider to be one where the control system can no longer be operated by a man, even an emergency. Now, up to this time, we have had airplanes, which involved a booster system, like the boost on your brake on an automobile, just to make the controls easier to operate. But if that system ever failed, the pilot was still able to operate the controls manually, in an emergency.[5]

During 13 months of passenger service at the airlines, three Electras had crashed, killing the 163 people aboard them. Learning about this frightening trend, it didn't take long for public confidence to vanish. Some members of Congress, refusing to travel aboard an Electra, demanded that the planes be grounded until a cause of the crashes was determined.

17 Days and 17 Miles Apart

Although previously popular with both passengers and airlines, the mid-air disintegration of an Electra flown by Braniff Airways startled just about everybody. The crash occurred while the plane flew at a normal cruising speed at high altitude over the Texas countryside on September 29, 1959.[6] Its cause remained a mystery for months. Making matters worse, on March 17, 1960, a Northwest Airlines Electra crashed into a field in Indiana, its cause also a mystery.[7]

After examining potential causes of all these crashes, Lockheed decided to analyze the entire Electra concept and its design approach. This task, actually requested by the government, discovered the existence of two previously unknown problems. When air pressure had been applied to ribs in the wings between the fuselage and outboard engine nacelles, its skin became heavily distorted. None of this was noted in its original type certification documents. Secondly, resistance of the engine nacelles to atmospheric turbulence differed from what the earlier certification document noted. Bending of the Electra wing due to turbulence could increase dramatically, possibly leading to failure of its wing structure.

Overall responsibility for the Electra's safety rested on the leader of the Federal Aviation Agency. Elwood Quesada retired from the U.S. Air Force, later accepting the administrator role at the agency. During his time on the job in Washington, 113 Electras were flying for seven airlines in the United States, transporting 25,000 passengers every day. An additional twenty planes were operated by airlines in other countries. If Quesada were to ground all of them, older piston-powered airliners such as Constellations would be needed to replace them on a temporary basis.

Prior to his appointment at the FAA, Quesada served as a vice president at Lockheed Aircraft Corporation during the 1950s. However, he had no love for either the company or its executives due to an undisclosed disagreement. It could be said, unlike the actions of FAA successor Najeeb Halaby, he would not go out of his way to help the company. "As for my former connection with Lockheed, I left them with ill will," he told a writer.[8] On the other hand, Quesada was well aware of the economic impact that Lockheed would suffer if the Electra was grounded. He decided to keep them in the air—with one restriction. Its cruising speed was reduced to 275 knots. Quesada believed that a slower speed would lessen stress on its airframe.

Actually, the Lockheed engineers had imposed a speed restriction

9. Coincidence?

before one coming from the FAA. The decision came about after a routine flight test from the airport in Burbank. The purpose of the flight was to determine what would happen if the hydraulic boost system was activated during a maximum dive speed test. Apparently, the test didn't go well. As a result, Lockheed advised all Electra operators to limit the plane's speed until the company's engineers could develop a permanent fix. The solution consisted of attaching wing reinforcements between the inboard and outboard engine nacelles. Lockheed management made it clear to customers that there was no connection between the flight test work and earlier Electra crashes.

Within weeks of the FAA's decision to lower the Electra's speed, Lockheed came up with a theory known as whirl mode. It was suspected as the probable cause of the Electra disasters. It can occur when a sudden jolt, such as air turbulence, disrupts a plane's engines, much like outboard engines of an Electra. In less than a minute, the resulting vibration can weaken the engine mounts and transfer vibration into the entire wing. The airframe structure can then flex, the wing fails and breaks completely free of the fuselage.

A spinning propeller is no different than a gyroscope, both of them remaining in the same rotating direction until subjected to an outside force. This could be either turbulence or the abrupt maneuvering of its plane. A propeller reacts the same way that a disturbed gyroscope does. When its rotation results in a wobbling vibration, it's considered to be whirl mode. Stiffening the support holding a propeller in place could dampen that unwanted vibration. But if the support proved too weak to carry the load of a propeller, the damping could prove meaningless. Whirl mode is nothing new. It's a form of vibration inherent with all rotating machinery, anything such as drill bits, fan motors, and even the drive shafts of automobiles. Also present in every airplane, air turbulence passing over airframe surfaces can result in a flutter condition.

The government awarded a type certificate to Lockheed Aircraft Corporation for the Electra on August 22, 1958. Cautious before issuing any new type certificate, it requested that Lockheed make a number of changes to the airframe. Those same changes were also required from other manufacturers making turbine-powered planes, in some cases still on their drawing boards. Upon making those changes, the Electra supposedly complied with all the latest requirements. However, an unsuspected loophole had not been addressed.

Even though the Electra wing had been approved by the government for being "flutter resistant," a sizable external force could trigger its onset. The only sources powerful enough to provide such a force were the plane's control surfaces or propellers driven by its engines. The control surfaces were eliminated as a cause because they weren't capable of producing enough force to initiate failure of the wings. It meant the culprit had to be the actions of one or more propellers. It became necessary to determine exactly what type of propeller behavior would result in flutter. Testing conducted at the Lockheed plant indicated that wobbling propellers, driven by engines mounted in weakened nacelles, could create uncontrollable oscillations of its wings.

Whirl mode has little to do with the Electra's overall strength. Instead, the stiffness of its nacelle structure is what actually increased its strength. Stiffness is a force that prevents flutter, rather than increasing it. It can strengthen a nacelle's stiffness following a sudden jolt from turbulence or abrupt maneuvering. The engine began this process by wobbling on its mounts. When it started to wobble, so did its propeller, its rotation now disturbed. The wobbling motion is transferred to the wing structure, causing it to flex, soon leading to complete destruction of the plane's airframe.

In short order, the CAB investigators were convinced that whirl mode had destroyed the Electra's wing structure. Its failure was traced to undetected damage inside of an outboard engine nacelle. It weakened the entire wing. When the propeller began to wobble, likely due to the weakened engine mounts, disintegration of the rest of the plane followed, exactly what caused the Texas and Iowa crashes.

A question arose: Was the Electra's original wing structure too weak? The structural engineer at Lockheed, who designed the original wing, suggested that it should have a far stronger support structure. Lockheed management overruled him because it would reduce the plane's cruising speed and its airline customers wouldn't accept such a big speed reduction.[9]

Here's what a CAB report said about the cause of the Braniff International Airways Flight 542 Electra crash on September 29, 1959: "The Board determines that the probable cause of this accident was structural failure of the left wing resulting from forces generated by undampened propeller whirl mode."[10]

It is little known that the Electra had barely passed the government's flutter-resistant standards during its original certification in 1958. In order to pass, Lockheed reduced the amount of fuel being

9. Coincidence?

carried via tankage in the outboard sections of its wings. The government engineers concluded that much of this fuel would be consumed while taxiing for takeoff. Although legal at the time, it was a strange way to circumvent some of the early regulations.[11]

Much of the aircraft manufacturing industry operates like a club. Engineers move from one company to another, as do their fellow workers. The aircraft certification practice at an employer, such as Lockheed, can easily find its way to another manufacturer such as Boeing. One reason why the 737 MAX crashes happened in 2018 and 2019 was due to an unmonitored type of certification process.

When the FAA came into existence during 1967, representatives from a manufacturer were stationed at the plant to assure that its planes met federal aviation safety standards. To select qualified representatives, the FAA worked from a list of employees provided by the manufacturers. They were called designees. A problem soon came up: the manufacturers were also employers who issued paychecks to the designees. Aware of this oversight, the FAA changed the way designees were selected. Called Organization Designation Authorization (ODA), the latest process enabled a manufacturer to select its own employees to approve design work with concurrence of the FAA.[12] By 2009, the FAA turned over most of its inspection authority to Boeing Commercial Airplanes and other major aircraft manufacturers. During 2018 the lobbyists at Boeing made sure that a few paragraphs buried in the FAA Reauthorization Act of 2018 ceded even more authority to its company and the other manufacturers.

As an example of how ODA works inside a testing laboratory, an engineer working for a manufacturer might conduct the test of a system or component undergoing government certification. Meanwhile, a fellow employee, assigned to the lab as a "representative" of the FAA, would ensure that the test complied with federal regulations. An FAA employee never got involved in this process.

At the plant in Burbank, following the series of Electra crashes and avoiding a grounding of all its planes, Lockheed assigned one of them to a special test. It had previously been used for the Electra's original FAA certification testing in 1958. This time, its crew was charged with finding a cause of the accidents. Upon completing one of those flights, its pilot noticed that fuel was dripping from under the right wing. A close inspection revealed that some of the rivets fastened to the wing were either loose or missing. The rivets tied together ribs and cross members in each wing. In addition, and likely dangerous, a metal beam attached to one of its nacelles appeared to have buckled.

The CAB investigators were notified about this issue. Out of the 41 planes it inspected, 39 were found having cracked wing-clip rivets. Surprisingly, both the CAB investigators and Lockheed engineers didn't express much concern. About 3,000 of those rivets had been installed in each Electra, but the inspectors found only seven sheared ones in each plane they inspected. The investigators initially thought if they were left uncorrected, it could lead to serious weakening of the wing structure. However, after further evaluation, the discovery of sheared rivets was abandoned as a likely cause of the crashes.[13]

When it involved assuring the airworthiness of Electra's for the airlines, part of Lockheed's proposed solution was to reinforce the wing sections between its inboard and outboard nacelles that also enclosed its engines. None of this was encouraging news for executives and board members at Lockheed. At this point, there was no doubt that weakness of the Electra's engine mounts resulted in extreme vibration of the nacelles. In turn, this caused the wings to flex, the planes rendered uncontrollable before crashing. There was no doubt this is what caused those earlier crashes.

In short order, Lockheed accepted responsibility for all defects. It went on to spend a fortune funding its so-called Lockheed Electra Action Program. Nicknamed LEAP for lack of a better name, it called for modifying the wings of every Electra in existence, whether it was flying passengers at the airlines or moving along an assembly line at the factory in Burbank.[14]

The modifications involved tightening the engine nacelle structure and adding a series of rugged structural supports surrounding the engines and their gearboxes. Cowlings encircling the nacelles were modified to reduce vibration levels. The overall strength of the wings was increased using heavy gauge metal planking fitted to both its upper and lower surfaces. Not stopping there, the wing's internal bracing was strengthened with more planking. Altogether, the modifications ended up adding 1,400 pounds to the empty weight of each plane. The airlines were only required to fly their planes to the Burbank airport to modify them. It would take three weeks to complete each series of modifications. Lockheed was wise to modify them free of charge. Of course, it had been the company's fault that so many innocent people were killed..

An unanswered question was not answered for the benefit of

9. Coincidence?

At exactly 2:04 p.m. on a sunny afternoon on September 1, 2021, a memorial was unveiled to honor 78 people aboard Flight 529 and the first responders from the community who helped at the crash site. The event took place at a park across from where the Constellation had crashed (courtesy Mary Brown at Clarendon Hills Historical Society).

airlines that were flying these planes. Based on its accident history, the FAA had pulled back the Electra's original type certificate until every LEAP modification was inspected. Some executives at the airlines worried, thinking that the FAA might not approve the modified planes. Fortunately for the airlines, all of them were later "recertified" by the FAA.

On February 5, 1961, after each plane was modified after going through LEAP, the FAA lifted its earlier flight restriction. Although Lockheed's reputation for integrity had been recognized throughout the aviation industry, the same wasn't true with the traveling public. In spite of an expensive global advertising campaign, fully paid for by Lockheed, there was little interest from frequent air travelers to fly aboard the planes. Most of them bought tickets to travel aboard faster jets. As a result, no further orders were received at Lockheed for the Electra, its last order arriving at the executive offices in Burbank on February 26, 1960.

In a strange way, Lockheed Aircraft Corporation traveled a similar

17 Days and 17 Miles Apart

path to that of TWA, except the manufacturer was nearing bankruptcy due to the Electra crisis. TWA, its longtime and best customer for Constellations, decided to help the corporation with owner Howard Hughes ordering a fleet of 40 new Electras. It was a surprising move because the ill-fated planes had been involved in several fatal accidents. In addition, recognizing a financial setback Lockheed was facing, Hughes pondered whether its stock might be purchased at a bargain price.[15]

Not interested in annoying a sales prospect like Hughes, the executives at Lockheed sided with TWA's opinion about the crash of Flight 529. When it came time to improve the safety of the Constellations still in service, their executives lost all interest. They were far more interested in selling Electras to anyone wishing to buy them. Of course, one of those people happened to be Howard Hughes, as few other airlines had expressed any interest in the planes. As a longtime aviator, he had flown Electras on several occasions and liked them. The handful of accidents didn't seem to keep him on the ground. He took advantage of an opportunity to buy the 40 planes at a reduced price, working with Lockheed board chairman Bob Gross to close a deal. As chairman, Gross had every reason to believe that a large order from TWA, authorized by Hughes, would become a routine matter. After all, Hughes had been a personal friend for many years. In addition, TWA was Lockheed's most important non-military customer. But Hughes wanted something else in return. He was willing to buy the Electras if Lockheed would assist him with TWA's own financing problems. Jack Real, Hughes' longtime confidant, mutual friend of Gross, and the top executive over the LEAP program in Burbank, was aware of this unfolding: "His long-term financing had fallen out of bed, and he asked me to get Lockheed to take the lead role to bring the New York bankers together to finance TWA's new fleet of jets and turboprops."[16]

Not everyone at Lockheed was pleased with the endless maneuvering typical of Hughes' behavior. A member of the manufacturer's board of directors opposed selling Electras to TWA. A concern over this opinion caused Hughes to become angry. As a result, he was more committed than ever to move ahead with a deal to buy those planes. Gross and his marketing team had jumped at any opportunity to bring in more orders, the company suffering huge financial losses from the Electra accidents.

By itself, the LEAP modification work was extremely costly, requiring the wings of each Electra to be disassembled and modified. In

9. Coincidence?

essence, major sections of each plane were completely rebuilt—like it should have been done before its initial certification.

During the summer months of 1961, Lockheed moved five newly built Electras off its final assembly line. Hughes decided to buy three of them, possibly for personal transportation. Not sure exactly which ones to buy, he decided to take all of them. He also demanded that Lockheed guard the planes around the clock to isolate their cabins from germs.[17] Gross kept out of sight, having learned years before that disagreeing with Hughes would prove futile. It could lead to him cancelling the entire Electra order.

The banks remained disenchanted with his strange way of doing business. The funding he hoped to get from lenders in New York evaporated when the deal to buy the additional Electras was brought up. It became clear that TWA would never add an Electra to its fleet. Along with other bad news, his proposed deal to buy a controlling interest in Lockheed Aircraft Corporation stock also went nowhere.

Bob Gross's face revealed the stress he endured during the Electra manufacturing and financial crisis. On September 3, 1961, he died of cancer in a Santa Monica hospital. He was 64 years old. Ironically, his death occurred three days after Flight 529 crashed near Clarendon Hills.[18]

While working at the O'Hare crash site, the investigation of Flight 706 was interrupted by a spate of other aircraft accidents occurring elsewhere. The CAB was forced to pull some of its employees away from Chicago. Although annoyed by this happening, some employees working at the FAA didn't blame them. Instead, they realized that the lack of sufficient manpower was another example of a woefully understaffed agency. It was being forced to spread itself too thin. The aftermath of Flight 706 and other fatal accidents would hopefully result in long-needed Congressional funding to increase the number of accident investigators on its payroll.

The Flight 706 investigation was conducted under the supervision of structures chief John Leak, the same CAB employee who led the Flight 529 investigation. It proved interesting because the Constellation and Electra crashes did not result from structural failure. Instead, failures of their flight control systems in both the planes were caused by mechanics at their airlines ignoring important assembly procedures. If their hydraulic boost systems were simpler to understand, operate and service, or maybe being completely omitted by Lockheed, it might have been possible to prevent both of these crashes.

17 Days and 17 Miles Apart

When it came time for the CAB to publicly announce why Flight 529 had crashed, only a single reason was mentioned in its accident investigation report. An unidentified mechanic working in a TWA hangar had forgotten to install a vitally important part. The undisclosed cause was just as important. A system that moved the elevator control surface, consisting of cables and pulleys, was the same as in other Constellations. However, if a separate hydraulic boost assembly, or another cable leading to its cockpit, had been installed, it was possible that the crash could have been avoided. To save Lockheed and its airline customers much money, the manufacturer didn't want to redesign the existing system. It wasn't until flight control design work for the Electra got underway that engineers paid more attention to the design of elevator control systems.

In the Electra, a hydraulic boost system moved the elevator, the design making use of duplicate cables hooked to control wheels in the cockpit. Systems for its other control surfaces were not duplicated. Lockheed's engineering management was well aware of the Constellation's elevator control shortcomings, but didn't want to cause the crash of an Electra because of elevator failure. In the winter 1961 issue of *Field Service Digest*, a comprehensive series of two product support newsletters published by Lockheed, the company's attention to system redundancy for the Electra was discussed in detail:

> Unlike the rudder and aileron controls, the elevators have two independent cable systems, each of which is connected through control rods and bellcranks to each of the control columns. Since the dual controls in the flight station are interconnected by a control rod, it follows that a failure in any part of the elevator control system forward of the boosters in the aft fuselage, would still leave the elevators operable by either or both pilots.[19]

Lockheed made it clear that the Electra's aileron control system differed from one that moved its elevator:

> The aileron control system differs from the elevator system. The aileron cables consist of a single pair of steel cables routed from the control columns to the right side of the aircraft below the floor. The aileron slack absorbers have single cable terminals in each end in lieu of the dual fittings on the elevator cable units.[20]

Considering the amount of time and effort that Lockheed spent designing a failsafe system to move the Electra's elevator, one might wonder why it didn't do the same for the Constellation. As a corporation,

9. Coincidence?

STATE OF ILLINOIS
HOUSE OF REPRESENTATIVES
102ND GENERAL ASSEMBLY

HOUSE JOINT RESOLUTION NO. 45
OFFERED BY REPRESENTATIVES DEANNE M. MAZZOCHI

WHEREAS, On September 1, 1961, just after two in the morning, Trans World Airlines Flight 529 took off from Midway Airport bound for Las Vegas, Los Angeles, and San Francisco; and

WHEREAS, Five minutes into the flight, a two-inch long bolt snapped in the plane's elevator assembly, which caused the plane to crash in what is today Willowbrook, Illinois; and

WHEREAS, TWA Flight 529 crashed into an open field and immediately burst into flames, leaving behind a debris field of 200 by 1,100 feet; and

WHEREAS, 73 passengers, four of whom were from the Chicago land area, and five crew members were all killed on impact, making the crash of TWA Flight 529 the deadliest single plane crash at the time; and

WHEREAS, The four Chicago area victims were a pharmacist from Evanston who was on his way to visit his parents in Los Angeles, a nurse from MacNeal Hospital in Berwyn departing for a vacation in San Francisco, and two servicemen returning to duty in California; and

WHEREAS, September 1 of 2021 will mark the 60 year anniversary of this tragedy; therefore, be it

RESOLVED, BY THE HOUSE OF REPRESENTATIVES OF THE ONE HUNDRED SECOND GENERAL ASSEMBLY OF THE STATE OF ILLINOIS, THE SENATE CONCURRING HEREIN, that we declare September 1, 2021 as Trans World Airlines Flight 529 Memorial Day in the State of Illinois; and be it further

RESOLVED, That we remember and mourn those we lost on that tragic day in 1961 and extend our sincere condolences to their families and friends.

ADOPTED BY THE HOUSE OF REPRESENTATIVES ON MAY 29, 2021.

CONCURRED IN BY THE SENATE ON APRIL 9, 2022.

JOHN W. HOLLMAN
CLERK OF THE HOUSE

EMANUEL "CHRIS" WELCH
SPEAKER OF THE HOUSE

TIM ANDERSON
SECRETARY OF THE SENATE

DON HARMON
PRESIDENT OF THE SENATE

While dedicating the memorial, Representative Deanne Mazzochi from the State of Illinois House of Representatives declared September 1, 2021, would now be known as Trans World Airlines Flight 529 Memorial Day in the State of Illinois (courtesy Mary Brown at Clarendon Hills Historical Society).

17 Days and 17 Miles Apart

Lockheed agreed that its flight control systems were complicated. In another issue of the *Field Service Digest* during 1961, the complexity of the Electra's various systems was described in detail:

> Flight controls have become correspondently more complex. A control system on a modern air transport can contain any number of bewildering arrays of special devices which range through bob weights, static balance weights, spring tabs in various forms, hydraulic boosters, spoilers, spring cartridges, flying tabs, and so on. The Electra has its fair share of the above devices.[21]

The company's rationale for publicizing this degree of complexity was prompted by its perception of mechanic skill levels at the airlines: "Necessary or not, these complications are hard to justify to someone, such as an airline mechanic, who may not possess the knowledge and appreciation of an aerodynamicist or an experienced pilot."[22]

TWA and Northwest Airlines appeared to have plenty in common, mainly because both their ill-fated planes were designed and built by Lockheed. Each airline was a top-rated air carrier, but some of their maintenance practices were considered to be hit-and-miss in the aviation industry.

Sifting through the remains of Flight 706, the CAB investigators discovered that its rudder and elevator hydraulic boost controls were struck in an "engaged" position. However, the hydraulic boost assembly for controlling its ailerons was found disengaged. The cables routed from it to control wheels in the cockpit were designed to move through a series of pulleys. The cable and pulley arrangement had formed what Lockheed called a closed loop. Connected to the captain's controls, one of the cables remained under tension whenever the right wing moved down. A cable connected to the copilot controls also stayed under tension whenever the left wing went down.

Searching through the crash site near O'Hare, the investigators came across a broken control wheel apparently used by the captain. Its handle was positioned at a 90-degree angle, meaning he probably attempted to lower the wing on the left side to get one on the right back up. The investigators wondered if Flight 706 had crashed because part of its hydraulic boost system failed. If true, it would have prevented the pilot from moving the aileron on the right side.

All control cable connections were tested and found to be working properly—except for a threaded connector attached to one of the

9. Coincidence?

cables. The cable, along with its connector, had been designed to absorb a certain amount of tension. An examination conducted by the National Bureau of Standards, assisted by CAB and FBI investigators, verified that safety wire had not been installed to hold part of the connector in place. To validate this theory, a series of tests were conducted using a vibration source to simulate normal flight conditions. When the cable fully unscrewed, the aileron (and likely the entire plane) moved into a steep right wing-down position.[23]

Unknown until well along in their investigations, both the Electra and Constellation had crashed because their mechanics failed to attach parts of essential hardware to operate the flight controls. It was strictly human error.

Shortly before Flight 706 began its turn in the air after takeoff, the connector in question snapped apart. It became impossible to prevent a crash because the plane was flying too low over the ground. Two months earlier, when the boost assembly was replaced, its cable connector was left unscrewed. Safety wire was not securing it. However, a duplicate cable connector was found in rubble at the crash site, shielded from flames and soot. A single piece of safety wire had prevented it from loosening, but the other failed connector had no such protection.

It seemed unlikely that the Electra pilots could have applied more opposing aileron pressure to bring the right wing up. Worsening the unmanageable condition, other recovery techniques using rudder, asymmetrical power, or even the aileron trim tabs might have been effective overcoming the steepening bank. However, doing so would require more altitude to guarantee a successful recovery. Simply put, Flight 706 crashed because it ran out of enough altitude.

From June 27 to July 11 during 1961 was an especially bad stretch of time. The pilots who flew this particular plane wrote up at least eight aileron control problems. They were handed over to the Northwest maintenance department for action. Some of them reported a sluggish feel of the boost system and unusually erratic operation. Others asked that the plane be flight-tested.[24]

Flight 706 had made 29 passenger flights from July 11 until the day of its crash. During that time period, thousands of passengers had flown aboard a plane with a defective aileron control system. Its earlier problems far from resolved, a Northwest maintenance manager decided to replace the aileron boost assembly with a new one. It couldn't be determined who made a decision to remove and replace the assembly. Anyone from a group of almost two-dozen mechanics, crew chiefs, and managers could have been involved, but no one was talking.

In the Northwest hangar, an unknown member of the night shift removed the assembly on July 11. The mechanic performing this work later testified that he didn't follow the instructions provided in a maintenance manual for the Electra.[25] During removal of the assembly, he sniped off the safety wire from a connector that relieved tension on a cable.

Three shifts of mechanics eventually got involved in removing and replacing the boost assembly. None of them had consulted the Electra maintenance manual before undertaking the task. Correct procedures were not followed. Proper rigging and control of cable tension were not accomplished, even though the manual stipulated that both were required.

One of the mechanics didn't bother to tighten the cable tension. Nor did he replace the safety wire. Nobody bothered to inspect the completed work. Instead, the mechanic signed off his own work in the plane's logbook as being "completed." During the early morning hours on July 12, the Electra was pulled from its hangar and prepared for a test flight.[26]

The training of mechanics assigned to maintain the fleet of new Electras at Northwest was sporadic at best. The mechanics who removed and replaced the boost assembly did not get any formal training. Its missing safety wire and unscrewing of the connector disturbed the CAB investigators. It reminded them of a similar mistake that brought down Flight 529 seventeen days earlier. Sloppy maintenance practices were also in use at TWA. Testimony at a hearing for Flight 706 revealed that formal mechanic training was weak, little of it relevant to the Electra's flight control system.

In its accident investigation report, the CAB addressed a nonchalant attitude of the Northwest maintenance crews:

> The aircraft logs recording the corrective actions taken indicate that little effort was made to analyze the cause of these discrepancies and to correct them. This type of operation reflects a casual attitude on the part of maintenance personnel toward a potentially hazardous condition, which was also evident in the replacement of the boost assembly.[27]

The CAB leadership had plenty to say about the airline's inadequate supervision:

9. Coincidence?

The amount of supervision devoted to this aileron booster assembly change fell considerably short of meeting the safety minimums desired and expected in a task of this nature. Although the offices of the foreman and the lead inspector were physically located adjacent to each other, there was a decided lack of coordination between maintenance supervisors and the inspection department. Although the inspection department was a part of the aileron boost unit being changed, it failed to attach sufficient importance to it.[28]

According to a Flight 706 accident investigation report prepared by the CAB, the probable cause came across as clear, if not shocking: "The Board determines that the probable cause of this accident was a mechanical failure in the aileron primary control system due to an improper replacement of the aileron boost assembly, resulting in a loss of lateral control of the aircraft at an altitude too low to effect recovery."[29]

Both the CAB and pilot union had conducted painstaking investigations of the Flight 706 accident. They came to similar conclusions. The Air Line Pilots Association issued an investigative report on June 7, 1962. It pointed out how the loss of proper maintenance oversight contributed to the crash. Here's what the Air Line Pilots Association union reported:

> A review of statements and testimony of the personnel involved in this aileron boost package change indicates that three shifts were involved. Shift II and III removed the old package and shift I released the plane for a test hop. Testimony indicates that the forward end of both primary aileron control cable slack absorbers were unsafetied and loosened. The testimony also indicated that these slack absorbers were not tightened up or re-safetied. Proper rigging and aileron control tension checks were not accomplished although the Lockheed maintenance manual prescribes these.[30]

To fully understand Flight 706's complex flight control system, here's more technical detail from the ALPA report:

> The pilot's cable (for right aileron up) was found with the forward flex cable still threaded through the guide hole in the pulley bracket with the slack absorber and aft flex cable still attached. The Lockled connector to the length of flex cable was intact, complete with collar and properly safetied. The flex-cable stainless-steel male left-hand threaded connector attaching into the forward cadmium plated brass terminal block of the shock absorber was found unsafetied and backed out, showing 5 to 7 threads for an engagement. There was no evidence of any safety wire being installed on this connection. The aft connector of the slack absorber showed shielding of the brass terminal block from fire and soot by the safety wire. No shielding could be found on the unsaftied connector or brass terminal.[31]

17 Days and 17 Miles Apart

No lawsuits were filed against the federal government over the Electra fiasco. Nor was there a massive public outcry over the lack of action from members of Congress. For years, the governmental body had treated the CAB much like an unwanted stepchild, so this wasn't a surprise. Both the TWA and Northwest crashes were clearly a responsibility of their respective airlines, and Lockheed Aircraft Corporation as the builder of the planes.

The relatives and family members of people who died in the crash of Flight 706 waited for any acknowledgment from the lawyers at Lockheed. Running out of patience, they contacted their own lawyers, many of them eager to represent them in courtroom proceedings. By spring 1962, lawsuits totaling $55 million had been filed against Lockheed and engine maker Allison, the latter having designed and manufactured the plane's turboprop engines. Because the airlines had knowingly flown airliners having defective parts, and known to have questionable maintenance practices, Braniff International Airways and Northwest Airlines were pulled into the litigation proceedings. Amazingly, TWA and Lockheed escaped all of it.

"The testimony indicates that all inspection personnel concerned believed that responsibility for a follow up inspector notice rested upon line maintenance and not upon the Inspection Department. At the public hearing there appeared to be differences of opinion on the part of the carrier's maintenance and inspection personnel in their interpretation of the previously mentioned interoffice memorandum of June 21, 1957. These differences concerned whether it was the responsibility of line maintenance supervisors to give notice, or the Inspection Department to follow up, to insure that the aileron boost change was properly inspected upon completion."[32]

As it was for investigators attempting to pin down personnel responsible for causing TWA Flight 529 to crash, the internal decision-making at Northwest Airlines was somewhat similar. Nobody wanted to assume responsibility for Flight 706 crashing. Lawyers retained by the next of kin were fully aware of this confusion during trial proceedings for awarding damages to their clients.

The airlines slowly eliminated most of their Electra passenger service, some of the planes being modified with large cargo doors. They went on to transport shipments of freight over decades to come.

A key question still remained unanswered from officials at Lockheed: Was the original wing of the Electra too weak? A designer at the

9. Coincidence?

company already offered an answer after designing the Electra's wing structure for FAA certification. The management at Lockheed soon overruled what he wanted to improve.

From the $25 million the company spent on its LEAP modification program, most of that money went into strengthening its weak wings. It was proof that the original wing design, and not whirl mode by itself, was responsible for the Electra's series of fatal accidents.

Lockheed continued to face engineering and quality control challenges before and during the LEAP program. Newly hired workers assigned to its production line weren't careful while assembling the modified wing sections. Some Lockheed managers were upset because the planes undergoing modification happened to come from their most valuable customers—a double whammy for the troubled manufacturer.

Eastern Airlines employees found a rivet gun, screws, a small vacuum cleaner, and a paper cup stowed in the wing tanks of its two Electras during an inspection while undergoing modification. American Airlines employees found bolts missing from various parts of its Electras. Even Western Airlines reported finding trash in the fuel tank of a wing.

Lockheed couldn't provide a reason for why this had happened: "We had no excuse, no alibi, no extenuating circumstances, to fall back on. We just assumed our inspection checks were pretty good and we found out they were a long way from being as good as they should have been."[33]

The crash of TWA Flight 529 taught everyone a bitter lesson. The Constellation had lost all pitch control while flying 2,000 feet in the air. Its pilots managed to control the plane for a few minutes using aileron, rudder, and engine controls. They somehow kept the plane in the air, searching for a safe place to make a crash landing. Unfortunately, lacking sufficient control, the plane dropped rapidly, impacted an empty field, broke apart, and burst into flames. Everyone aboard died from the impact, suffocation, or flames. Airplanes are fabricated mostly from thin metal material that breaks into pieces on impact and catches fire. Few people can survive such a catastrophe.

As a final thought, Craig Hagstrom, an adult son of the Flight 706 captain, developed his own theories about what happened after its aileron control system failed. At the time of the accident, he was 13 years old. Over many years, he offered several kinds of opinions, some significantly different from those reported in CAB and ALPA accident investigation reports. In particular, he disagreed about the angle of the plane's right wing, reported by investigators to be almost vertical when the plane hit the ground. Although not a pilot, but well versed in aviation matters, Hagstrom offered this and other theories to anyone willing to listen or comment.[34]

The reason why Flight 529 crashed didn't satisfy everyone. Many years later, after TWA Flight 800 crashed into the ocean near Long Island, defective wire insulation as a cause is disputed to this day. Even more shocking, the loss of three jetliners that impacted the World Trade Center and Pentagon during 2001 caused some observers to doubt how it happened and disputed the way it was reported in the media. When it came to Flight 706, its final moments in the air could also be questioned. More than sixty years after its crash, accident reports prepared by the CAB and ALPA offer credible information. The people who had been involved in its investigation and preparation of its aircraft investigation reports are no longer available to support or dispute the conclusions. Taking this into account, it seems pointless to question anything other than what was originally reported at the time of the crashes.

Closing out the investigation at Clarendon Hills, it became clear that Lockheed had no interest in assisting the government or even people who lost family members in Flight 529. Lacking sufficient manpower, Lockheed continued to ignore requests for redesigning its flight control systems. Perhaps the requests were ignored because its airline customers were busy phasing out Constellations and replacing them with Electras. The officials at Lockheed continued to rely on those marketing efforts.

There was widespread concern that the Electra program might be cancelled due to its lackluster reputation with the traveling public. Without paying travelers at the nation's airlines, a weak market for the planes continued to exist. The Electra ended up becoming the last propeller-driven airliner that Lockheed would manufacture. The company's next major project was the three-engine L-1011 TriStar jetliner. It also proved unsuccessful as a product line and became the last airliner of any type Lockheed would design and manufacture.

Lockheed discontinued the production of Electras until all current orders for the planes were filled. Its executives became convinced that a sales saturation point had finally been reached. Most passengers traveling aboard the nation's airlines preferred doing so aboard jetliners and not in turboprop-powered planes. Similar to what happened with

9. Coincidence?

A Northwest Airlines Lockheed L-188 Electra prepares to depart Midway Airport in Chicago. At O'Hare International Airport on September 17, 1961, a similar Electra crashed on takeoff, killing 37 people aboard (courtesy American Aviation Historical Society [AAHS-36283]).

elderly Constellations, the days for carrying passengers in an Electra were also numbered.

Both of the crashes that took place in Illinois had resulted from sloppy maintenance of their flight control components. Considering the multitude of other problems affecting both the Constellation and Electra programs, it might have been smarter to do what other aircraft manufacturers suggested and have Lockheed keep its "power steering" systems out of their planes. It could save lives.

10

Aftermath

Among the 78 people who died in the crash of TWA Flight 529, about 22 of them weren't old enough to have celebrated their 20th birthday. Eleven were under the age of 10, while seven hadn't even enjoyed a fifth birthday. Most of them were traveling with their parents. These young lives were lost before they even reached adulthood. It's a big reason why the disaster turned out to be so tragic.

Both the Flight 529 and Flight 706 crashes were textbook examples of how the airlines and some aircraft manufacturers can unwittingly set their own rules, rather than follow rules mandated by the government. The aviation industry could bully a government agency and ignore its investigative findings. In some instances, it proved difficult for the Civil Aeronautics Board, that agency dissolved by Congress a few years after the crashes in 1961 were investigated by it. The aviation industry could bring the agency and many others to their knees. It wouldn't be the first or last time that such events happened.

Officials at the National Transportation Safety Board, an independent U.S. government agency founded in 1967, is responsible for investigating all types of transportation accidents. Over time, it ran into several similar problems, as did the CAB. However, as an independent agency, one might think it would not have an axe to grind with other agencies or corporations. Its primary role is to make the public aware of oncoming investigations, offer recommendations to prevent future accidents, and avoid undue influence from outsiders that could sway its official findings. The NTSB is well aware that the FAA, along with thousands of suppliers to the aviation industry, can attempt to exercise control over accident investigations of transportation equipment or parts that are used to manufacture such products. They prefer to publicize causes more to their liking than established facts coming from the government. When it came to the Flight 529 crash, six years prior to the

10. Aftermath

NTSB being established, this is what happened. Trans World Airlines, Lockheed Aircraft Corporation, and even leaders of the Federal Aviation Agency, had offered conflicting conclusions—they weren't the same as probable cause statements coming from the Civil Aeronautics Board.

During September 2022, several former leaders of the NTSB published an editorial in *Aviation Week & Space Technology*. It described several instances where aircraft manufacturers and the FAA attempted to lead its investigations astray.[1]

When a Boeing 767 crashed in Thailand, the NTSB identified movement of the jet's engine thrust reverser as a cause of the crash. Both manufacturer Boeing and the FAA said it would be impossible. However, the NTSB had made the correct judgment. In 1996, TWA became a victim of the most publicized airline crash in the nation's history. On July 17, 1996, a Boeing 747–100 jetliner, owned and operated by TWA as Flight 800, crashed into the ocean 12 minutes after taking off from John F. Kennedy International Airport in New York. Its destination was Paris. All 230 people aboard the plane perished.[2] The NTSB investigators later determined that chafed electrical wires caused an explosion in a nearly empty center wing fuel tank and the plane exploded. Boeing initially said that the explosion could not have happened. Even though it did, the manufacturer was convinced that the plane would not crash. The NTSB's investigation was correct. The 747 exploded, broke up while still in the air, and shattered into many large pieces.

During more recent years, fatal crashes of two Boeing 737 MAX jetliners, each operated by different foreign airlines, required serious changes of the plane's design. Looking further back in time, Lockheed might have incorporated some of those changes in the design of its own airliners. At least the Boeing accidents resulted in widespread public scrutiny that revealed the company's obscure engineering and manufacturing practices. From the result of a Congressional hearing, Congress required a complete overhaul of the FAA's aircraft certification regulations. Boeing initially assumed no financial or other responsibility for design defects that caused the two fatal accidents. Instead, it blamed the crashes on poorly trained or inept pilots being at their controls. During the 1960s, Lockheed publicly acknowledged complete responsibility for a series of major design flaws in the Electra turboprop airliner. The manufacturer ended up modifying every plane at its own expense.

As a longtime commercial aircraft manufacturer, Boeing decided to avoid expensive certification roadblocks, while staffers at the FAA weren't paying enough attention to what they were doing. The company was using its own inspection teams. Boeing engineers had designed a special avionic control system and installed it in each 737 MAX. It was something that even Boeing's own pilots didn't fully understand. Some of them weren't even aware of its existence. It was called MCAS, short for Maneuvering Characteristics Augmentation System. The only purpose for incorporating the feature in the plane was to save Boeing's airline customers millions of dollars by eliminating any need for expensive transition training in flight simulators. This was the stated purpose even though MCAS-equipped jetliners already killed several hundred MAX passengers and crewmembers. The rationale behind the ill-conceived MCAS system was strictly to satisfy Boeing's longtime airline customers. Executives at those airlines had convinced the executives at Boeing they wanted to fly MAX jetliners the same way they flew earlier model 737s. They didn't want to pour money into extra pilot training to operate Boeing's latest model jetliners.[3]

There's a little-known connection between the MAX series of jetliners and what happened more than 60 years earlier at other manufacturers. Some of the airliners designed and manufactured by Lockheed had crashed because their flight control systems had malfunctioned. The government's certification process had allowed the engineers at Lockheed to take advantage of serious shortcuts—a similar flawed process that later brought down MAX jetliners at Boeing.

Whether part of a Constellation or Electra, the flight control systems developed by Lockheed lacked sufficient approval from the FAA. It would have required significant modification of those systems to correct all their faults.

Although TWA was no longer managed under the tight control of Howard Hughes, the lack of safe practices continued to haunt TWA's maintenance operations. Thirty-five years after Flight 529 crashed in Illinois, European bound Flight 800 was a tired plane, having spent thousands of hours in the air. Throughout the inside of its airframe were countless mechanical and electrical defects needing attention, although this wasn't unusual for an aging jetliner.

Following a difficult four-year investigation of the Flight 800 crash, the NTSB released an accident investigation report with a probable cause on August 23, 2000. It had been a difficult investigation to conduct because of conflicting opinions. An explosion of flammable fuel

10. Aftermath

and air vapor in the plane's center fuel tank resulted in an explosion causing the fuselage to snap into large sections. But there was something more: electric arcing produced by chafed wiring is what began the chain of deadly events.[4]

In common with similar problems that existed in early model Constellations, portions of the 747 electric power system consisted of worn wiring, some never replaced during the plane's routine maintenance visits in TWA hangars. A review of Flight 800's maintenance records revealed that fuel had been leaking from its wing tanks throughout the preceding two years. At least two dozen logbook entries disclosed the existence of serious problems with its fuel systems. Considering the 747's age, the number of hours it flew over many years, and a large number of discrepancies needing repair, the plane should have been grounded long before attempting its final flight to Paris.

Something else was strange. The ages of the Flight 529 Constellation and Flight 800 Boeing 747 were about the same at the time they crashed. TWA continued to purchase new airliners, troubleshooting and repairing them as necessary, and then flying the planes in passenger service for as long as possible. The Constellation had been in the air for over 15 years and the 747 for more than 23 years. TWA went on to operate both of these planes, and many others in the TWA fleet, for as long as possible.

After many years operating as a major international airline, TWA was not in the best financial shape during the early 1990s. Saddled with an extreme amount of debt, it had been forced to sell its profitable European routes in order to survive. With little cash on hand to continue operating, TWA filed for bankruptcy during both 1992 and 1995. It had never fully recovered from a financial loss resulting from Flight 800 crashing. In January 2001, TWA made a third and final trip to the bankruptcy court. American Airlines ended up acquiring the company's assets and routes. Reorganized as a smaller domestic air carrier, TWA continued flying along a reduced number of routes until July 1, 2003, when it went out of business forever.

While investigating the Flight 529 crash, investigators from the Civil Aeronautics Board stayed with information they uncovered and avoided unrelated issues brought to their attention. It was clear that a TWA mechanic had made a deadly mistake while assembling the plane's elevator control linkage. When the CAB publicized this cause to the public, TWA, Lockheed, and even the FAA disagreed with its

17 Days and 17 Miles Apart

conclusion. The CAB investigators also recommended that the FAA require Lockheed to modify the Constellation's hydraulic boost system. Doing so would assure foolproof operation of the system, enabling the pilots to safely disengage it during an emergency and avoid an accident. Lockheed wasn't interested and the FAA didn't believe that a design change such as this was warranted. The response fueled a cavalcade of distortions, myths, and errors from within the aviation industry.

During a criminal trial a suspect is tried, convicted, and sometimes sent to jail. When it came time to uncover responsibilities for the Flight 529 and Flight 706 crashes, no one in the aviation industry was found guilty, jailed, or even fined. Other than a limited number of lawsuits resulting from the loss of Flight 706, nothing had been paid to families of the Flight 529 victims for financial, emotional, or physical damage that TWA had been responsible for.

If similar crashes would have occurred in today's highly litigated world, there's little doubt that a stream of lawsuits would follow with huge financial awards made to those families. During a more placid era in the early 1960s, commercial aviation was still in its infancy while it ushered in the beginning of its jet age. Many of the latest airliners were equipped with complicated and sometimes unreliable systems. The airlines were staffed with mechanics, many of them not understanding how the new systems functioned. Mishaps and accidents could be expected. It was the price to pay with a new generation of passengers who traveled frequently for business meetings and vacations.

All of the Constellation and Electra airliners built by Lockheed had been equipped with hydraulically boosted flight controls. The two airline crashes in Illinois, only 17 miles apart, were blamed on two distracted mechanics at their airlines. Over at TWA, one of the mechanics forgot to install a pin. At Northwest Airlines, another mechanic forgot to install inches of safety wire. In both cases, the missing hardware had disabled critical parts of their flight control systems. The captain flying the Constellation lost control after the elevator jammed. Meanwhile, the captain of the Electra encountered a jammed aileron. These were differently designed flight control systems, but the frightening results turned out to be nearly identical. The passengers in both of these airliners would likely be alive if the systems were never installed, or if safe maintenance practices had been used by maintenance employees.

Much like the MCAS systems installed in today's Boeing 737 MAX jetliners, pushing innovation to achieve a higher level of technological

10. Aftermath

achievement carries a hidden price. Innocent people can die in direct proportion to how today's galloping technology sometimes moves too far ahead of modern civilization.

Howard Hughes, the nation's troubled billionaire aviator, owned TWA at the time Flight 529 had crashed. Holding the majority of its stock, he had a major hand at the airline to ignore the CAB investigators and refused to implement the agency's recommendations. In common with the actions of other major corporations in America, it was a longstanding practice to avoid expensive lawsuits and stop unwanted publicity. Outside corporate offices at the airlines, and not important to much of the public, were lives of the family members who had died in crashes of its planes. The crash of TWA Flight 800 took the lives of 230 people on their way to meetings, schools, or vacations in France. The magnitude of such a loss caused TWA to drop out of sight as a leading airline. But the accident also brought together a group of surviving family members. Having a common interest in what had caused the crash, they decided to erect a memorial to memorialize each of its victims.

Known to many people as the TWA Flight 800 International Memorial occupies a two-acre parcel of land in Smith Point County Park in Shirley, New York.[5] A dedication ceremony at the site took place on July 14, 2002. A group, known as the Families of TWA Flight 800 Association, had raised money needed to construct a memorial. It features landscaped grounds with the flags of different countries stretched along a curved granite wall. The flags represent the 13 countries on which its victims resided. Their names are engraved on a side of the wall. An illustration on the wall's other side depicts a wave releasing 230 seagulls, each of the birds representing a victim. In July 2006, a black granite statue of a 10-foot-high lighthouse was added to the display. It was mounted above a tomb that contains personal belongings of the victims. Harry Edward Seaman, whose cousin died in the crash, designed the lighthouse. George Pataki, the governor of New York State at the time, dedicated the memorial.

Another memorial exists in San Diego, California. On September 25, 1978, a Pacific Southwest Airlines Boeing 727–234 crashed in a residential neighborhood of San Diego.[6] A Cessna 172 had hit the airliner from underneath. All 135 people aboard the jetliner and two in the Cessna died as did seven people on the ground. Similar to what caused the people in New York to get involved as a group, people in San Diego banded together to construct a memorial listing the names of all

On September 25, 1978, a Pacific Southwest Airlines Boeing 727-214 jetliner crashed in a residential neighborhood of San Diego. A Cessna 172 had hit the airliner. All 135 people aboard the jet and two in the Cessna were killed, as were 7 others on the ground. Displayed in Balboa Park is a memorial plaque placed there by members of the San Diego Aerospace Museum (author's collection).

10. Aftermath

its victims. Permanently displayed in Balboa Park is a memorial plaque placed there by the San Diego Aerospace Museum.

Twenty-four years after a McDonnell Douglas MD-83 jetliner crashed near the coast in central California, a Hueneme Beach Sundial Memorial now commemorates the 88 passengers and crewmembers who lost their lives on January 31, 2000.[7] They had been flying aboard Alaska Airlines Flight 261 as it neared Anacapa Island. The memorial features a 36-foot diameter concrete plaza furnished with a curving sand wall, and a seating area with a raised sundial at its center. The design work and funding was donated. Not surprising, Alaska Airlines had no interest in publicizing any details associated with the accident. The crash was caused by the failure of a vertical stabilizer mechanism along with widespread incompetence of the airline's mechanic staff. The memorial serves to keep alive the memories of those passengers and crewmembers dying on that day.

Today, the memorials in New York, California, and other places around the world exist for visitors and surviving family members to offer respect. Equally important, they serve to educate younger people about such disasters and how they can be prevented.

Seventy-eight innocent passengers and crewmembers died when Flight 529 slammed into the unyielding ground. In today's world, people under the age of 60 may have little or no remembrance of that day. Even younger couples, who may have purchased homes in neighborhoods not far from the crash site, may have no idea what happened a half century ago on an isolated stretch of land not far from Clarendon Hills Road.

During the early morning hours of September 1, 1961, volunteers at the crash site helped recovered the bodies of victims, assisted the investigators, and stopped the spread of flames resulting from thousands of gallons of burning fuel. The first responders and their children living in and around Clarendon Hills considered placing a memorial near the site.

Even though it had been almost sixty years since Flight 529 completed its final journey over the area, a memorial had never been erected at the actual site of the crash. In 2021, the time had come to remedy this oversight. The location of the crash site isn't far from Clarendon Hills Road. Across that street on its east side sits Prairie Trail Park, a seven-acre public recreational facility owned by the Village of Willowbrook. Situated on a portion of its well-maintained grass lawn, a permanent memorial was erected that lists each passenger and crewmember dying in the crash. Unveiling the memorial for public viewing was planned during a ceremony on September 1, 2021, the same date that the plane crashed. Although the crash actually happened at 2:04 a.m., it was decided to schedule the dedication during the afternoon at 2:04 p.m. instead.

The Flight 529 memorial would attract local residents, government officials, and the media. The event conveyed a deep concern for the victims, especially from the residents and first responders living near the crash site at the time. This was true even though they had no connection to the people who died in the crash. It took the combined interest and effort of a dedicated group of people from local communities to make the event happen.

The Clarendon Hills Historical Society was contacted by Sue Berglund from nearby Willowbrook concerning the disappearance of a

In a Northwest Airlines hangar, a Lockheed L-188 Electra likely undergoing periodic engine and airframe maintenance (author's collection).

10. Aftermath

small white cross at the crash site. Its loss inspired her to move ahead with an idea to build a permanent memorial. Unfortunately, there wasn't enough money to purchase land at the crash site for a permanent memorial. In spite of this shortcoming, the project got a firm start on April 8, 2021, when Keith Yearman, an associate professor of geography at the College of DuPage, expressed interest in the crash of Flight 529. He contacted Berglund, who in turn notified Jan Cummings, a vice president of the historical society, to decide how to proceed with the project. Mary Brown, a director at the society, joined them to plan a 60th anniversary event to honor every victim of the crash. However, the group wasn't sure how to get the ball rolling. In an email to the author, Yearman wrote: "I had no connection to the crash. It was just the right thing to do. Hopefully the memorial provides solace to some of the families."[8]

Brown, a longtime resident of the Clarendon Hills community, joined Berglund and other residents to organize a committee to construct and later dedicate the memorial. In 1961, Brown's father had served as the first village manager for Clarendon Hills. A volunteer with the local fire department, he had been at the site of the crash soon after the plane went down. Brown recalled: "The Clarendon Hills Fire Department arrived just fifteen minutes after the plane crashed. The looters were already there. My father, as one of the first responders, couldn't believe they would show up so quickly and take items from body parts."[9]

Berglund contacted Bill Remkus, the owner of Hinsdale Animal Cemetery in Willowbrook. As a child, he lived a short distance from the crash site. Both his father and brother were at the site of the crash during the early morning hours. Remkus joined other members of the committee and donated stone to construct the memorial. He and his wife also provided engravings to identify the names of all the victims and first responders in the community who had been at the crash site that morning.

Willowbrook was helpful by making public land available to construct the memorial, occupying only a small portion at the corner of the park. As for the actual crash site, an overgrown section of land still existed a hundred feet from the memorial. Brown had this to say: "That land really has been left alone all those years. It's considered sacred ground."[10]

The local fire and police departments also got involved with the dedication ceremony. They helped get the word out. As a child, Roger

Heidenreich remembered the crash, having grown up not far from it. His uncle had been the chief of the small Clarendon Heights Fire Department. Heidenreich kept a copy of a letter his uncle sent to TWA asking that his department be reimbursed for $873.47 to pay for its loss of firefighting equipment. The airline refused to pay for it. Instead, it mailed him a check for $150, labeling the amount as a "donation."

Mary Brown remembered how TWA failed to offer her town's volunteer fire department enough money to cover its costs for fighting the fire: "The fire department was basically housed in a garage at the time and all volunteer. The money they were asking for was greatly needed. TWA certainly didn't step up to the plate after the crash."[11]

Compared to other memorials acknowledging people who died in airline accidents, this one was different. There was no money available to proceed so the town needed to raise it from people living in the community. Even though the victims lived in other states and had no relationship to Willowbrook or Clarendon Hills, the local residents moved ahead with the memorial project.

Once the project gained momentum, members of the committee contacted local newspapers and television stations to announce the upcoming memorial dedication. Ben Bradley, a longtime reporter at WGN-9 in Chicago, responded. He was eager to conduct interviews of people who had lived near the crash site. Although he followed other aviation happenings in Illinois, he had never heard about the crash of Flight 529.

In Prairie Trail Park, not far from the crash site, a ceremony was arranged to begin at exactly 2:04 p.m. on September 1, 2021. A number of local officials were in attendance to offer speeches, followed by a dedication of the memorial. A representative from the Illinois state capitol presented the committee members with a signed resolution declaring *September 1, 2021, Trans World Airlines Flight 529 Memorial Day in the State of Illinois*.[12] The event was broadcast on a WGN-9 newscast that evening and made available to view online.[13]

Although they couldn't attend the ceremony dedication in person due to the distance, some family members of the victims later visited the memorial. For them, it represented a way to memorialize the lives of people lost and provide hope to educate future generations about what happened on that peaceful strip of farmland so long ago.

Jerry Broz and his wife, owning the cornfield where the plane crashed, decided to not build anything on that land. It would serve for

10. Aftermath

generations in the future as a remembrance of the victims who died there. However, over the years to come, title to the land likely changed hands, followed by houses being built around the site of the crash. To this day, land where the TWA Lockheed Constellation had dug into the cornfield still remains vacant. It would be difficult for people viewing the memorial to also visit the actual crash site. It is now surrounded by newer homes. This is why the Village of Willowbrook located the memorial across a street in its city-owned park.[14]

As a child, Elmer Maves also lived near

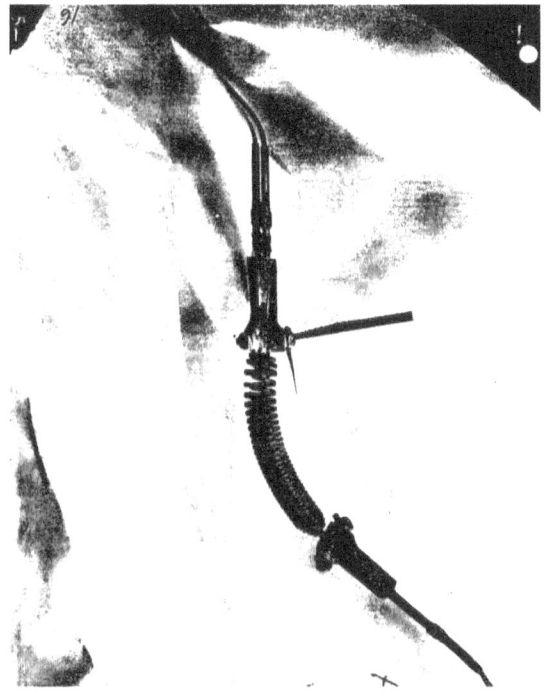

A photograph taken at the crash site of Flight 706 shows an unscrewed connector with its spring unraveled. The connector failed to operate an aileron hydraulic boost cylinder, leading to the crash of Northwest Airlines Flight 706 (public document, Civil Aeronautics Board report, September 17, 1961).

the crash site. Still awake during the early morning hours just before the crash, he witnessed the plane descend from high in the sky and fly low over his house. He visited the site of the crash many times over time, finding small pieces of the plane's airframe, some of them pushed up from under moist soil in the area. Maves and his brother, both teenagers at the time, ended up collecting hundreds of pieces of parts over the years. Following Maves' death in July 2021, Keith Yearman, a member of the memorial committee, fondly remembered the man. Prior to his death, Maves offered him hundreds of those pieces. Lacking enough space to store them at home, Yearman donated all of the pieces to the Clarendon Hills Historical Society.[15] The author was fortunate to have been provided some of them, courtesy of Mary Brown at the historical society.[16] One of them appeared to be part of a metal tray commonly used to serve Swanson frozen dinners. The word "Swanson" was still visible on the piece.

Most family members and friends of the victims went on to enjoy meaningful lives and careers. But there also exists a group of people who still recall the terrible night of September 1. For them, the thought of a family member dying, and in some cases several children, still makes this crash difficult to accept. Social media became a way for many of these people to get together to share memories and experiences.

A popular Facebook site called *TWA Flight 529*, administered by Cari Dobbs, receives credit for starting and overseeing an online meeting place. Bob Aiken, a passenger aboard Flight 529, who died in the crash that night, was an uncle and her father's oldest brother. Dobbs started the popular page on December 23, 2011. In her own words, here is what caused her to offer it:

> Reading the articles about the plane crashing shortly after takeoff, the names of all the lives lost, the families affected and the personal stories about some of the passengers really made it personal for me. I wanted to do something to keep their memories alive, to make sure these people weren't forgotten. They were brothers, sisters, fathers, mothers, grandparents, aunts, uncles and children. All of them lost due to the failure of a bolt on an airplane. These people left behind families, friends, neighbors and colleagues, and many of them were young, with the whole world ahead of them. That is why I created this webpage to honor them all, and to share their stories.[17]

Other people, mentioned on her page, included Flight 529 captain James Hedrick Sanders. As a commander of the flight, he was expected to transport 73 innocent people of all races and ages to their destinations safely and on time. He was surely confident that he could handle any inflight emergency. But during his final flight that night, this challenge became insurmountable.

During World War II, Vicki Ekmark's father had been a member of a B-17 bomber crew that flew bombing missions over targets throughout Europe. Sanders happened to be his pilot. Here is what Ekmark contributed:

> The captain of the plane that night was James Sanders. I know of him because he was the captain of the B-17 my father flew on during World War

10. Aftermath

II. The crew was one of the original cadre of men who went to England to fly bombing missions over Europe. The crew flew 25 missions and never crashed or was shot down, which was almost unheard of. Captain Sanders was an amazing pilot.[18]

Another contributor happened to be a high school friend of one of the four young women traveling to California to start new lives there. Her loss had a lifelong impact on him: "She wrote me a letter the day before departure that arrived three days after the crash. That letter is one of my most precious keepsakes. The letter arrived a week before I departed for my sophomore year in college. That school year was crushing. To this day, I re-read her beautiful letter as close to September 1st as I can."

A contributor posted about spending time with her grandparents, both of them dying in the crash: "They were on the flight to Los Angeles to visit my family. This tragedy impacted the rest of our lives. The first time I saw my father cry, I was six years old and didn't understand the situation. I simply wanted to hug and comfort him."

Still another Facebook contributor still remains haunted by the crash, her facing the loss of seven adults and children: "This event haunts me still. And I wasn't even alive when it happened. It took my father's brother, his wife, and all five of their children. They had been in Washington, D.C., visiting our family."

Another contributor, the son of a U.S. Army sergeant, was too young to have spent much time with his 22-year-old father before boarding the final flight. He remembered him in another post: "My dad died in that plane crash. I was seven months old at that time. My mom and dad were high school sweethearts, she was the prom queen and he was her escort—they married, had me, and he was gone. When military officers come to your home it's never good news. She was a 21-year-old widow. His death messed up our family pretty good and long term."

Not to be forgotten, residents, firefighters and volunteers from nearby communities continue to be bothered by the horror they witnessed that day. One of them offered a livid memory of the crash site: "I saw a small flash and the plane came straight down very close to where I was driving. I have been haunted by what I saw. I wandered around and tried to hear a sound. I naively thought I could help. I walked down and under trees and branches and saw terrible things. There was complete silence."

One of the volunteer firefighters still wants to forget what he saw that morning: "I was only 21 years old working for the summer highway department and called up to put up barricades at the crash site. The smells are still with me today what I saw and experienced that morning. I have tried to forget this but it is impossible."

Following an accident that resulted in the deaths of so many people, it was a common practice at major airlines to offer the next of kin some level of compensation. At TWA this didn't happen. Another contributor, who had lost her uncle and his entire family in the crash, commented about TWA in an October 31, 2021, post: "I have a letter from the attorney who handled the estate of my uncle, aunt, and five cousins. The letter states that TWA was offering a sum of $22,500. This may have been for funeral expenses."

In the letter, the family's attorney didn't recommend filing a lawsuit against TWA. The chance of winning was considered unlikely. He recommended taking the cash offer, which they did. Other than providing free airline tickets to attend the funerals of loved ones, only a small amount of money was offered for burial arrangements. To avoid the possibility of a lawsuit getting filed against the airline, the condolences were offered via letter, but not in person. TWA, Lockheed, and Howard Hughes continued to assume no responsibility for the crash.

The people and organizations that attempted to derail the investigation of Flight 529 are no longer alive. As a major corporation, TWA died a slow death decades ago. Lockheed faced an even worse dilemma. In 1976 it became embroiled in a major scandal. Its top executives were caught making illegal under-the-table financial payoffs to the leaders of other countries. Much of it was done during the heyday of the Electra program, convincing the leaders to purchase airliners and military planes from Lockheed. The criminals were caught, and to everyone's surprise, happened to be senior executives at Lockheed Aircraft Corporation in Burbank.

Chairman Daniel J. Haughton, along with former president and vice chairman A. Carl Kotchian, were forced to resign on February 13, 1976.[19] Both of these executives were lucky to have avoided prison sentences. During their reign at the company, Lockheed offered a series of questionable overseas payments as far back as the late 1950s. Most of them were made after 1969 when its financial health began crumbling due to steep losses associated with its failed Electra airliner program. At the time, every member of Lockheed's board of directors was likely aware of the illegal practice. They could have stopped it. Instead, they

10. Aftermath

did nothing, even though Lockheed recently received a government bailout of $250 million. The money was intended to keep it in business as a valuable defense contractor. It was well known that it was on the verge of filing for bankruptcy.

What morphed into a major corporate scandal in the United States and countries throughout the world resulted in passage of the Foreign Corrupt Practices Act on December 19, 1977. The act was intended to prohibit the bribery of foreign officials should they express interest in purchasing American-made products such as aircraft.[20]

Tens of thousands of employees working in Lockheed factories and offices had no idea what was happening. They included many longtime engineers who continued to design its latest military aircraft products. Kelly Johnson, principal inventor of the first Constellation during the early 1940s, was reported to have become so sick of these revelations that he was about to end his longtime career at the company and retire.[21]

The executives at Lockheed got involved with the illegal activity in order to bring in more aircraft business that it sorely needed. Failing at selling its commercial airliners against established competition, the board of directors attempted to shift the corporation's positioning to concentrate more on defense contracting. On March 15, 1995, Martin Marietta Corporation, an established manufacturer of missiles, rockets, and spacecraft, merged with Lockheed, the latter company ending its longtime reputation as one of America's top military aircraft manufacturers. It continued to design, manufacture and support aircraft, missiles, and satellites for defense equipment customers. The combined company became known as Lockheed Martin Corporation, soon leaving California and relocating to North Bethesda in Maryland.

It became clear that Martin had engineered a smart acquisition, but it didn't turn out that way later on. It had gained title to everything that Lockheed owned, including the aircraft undergoing design and fabrication, but also furniture, vehicles, buildings, and 320 acres of prime real estate spread across the airport in Burbank. During World War II, at least 94,000 people had been employed in its many buildings to create and manufacture the nation's highest performance warplanes. In the 1990s, Lockheed Martin transferred much of the work from Burbank to its other facilities around the country, none of the work remaining in California. Deserted buildings on the Burbank airport looked like they belonged to an abandoned ghost town. What had been left behind was a massive plume of groundwater, poisoned by solvents such as trichloroethylene (TCE) and hexavalent chromium known as Cr(VI). These and other solvents had contributed to groundwater contamination existing under much of the abandoned Lockheed property.

Lockheed Martin Corporation was successful in transferring Lockheed's projects, technology, and engineers to other places, but it left behind the deadly pollution. All older buildings scattered around the plant site were demolished by 1998, but they left an unwanted legacy for the corporation.

In 1996, a year after Martin acquired the company, thousands of local residents, previously living near the former Lockheed site, decided to sue the corporation. They had learned that Martin was forced to pay $66 million in secret settlement payments to 1,375 other residents in the area—$30 million of it going to former employees who were suffering from illnesses caused by years of working in Lockheed buildings. In 2002, facing years of expensive litigation, Lockheed Martin Corporation was forced to pay $1.25 million to settle outstanding claims filed by the residents. But it wasn't enough. The corporation was also required to pay at least $265 million to clean up contaminated drinking water supplies lurking beneath the former Lockheed property.[22]

Dozens of abandoned buildings, already leveled by an army of bulldozers, were replaced with shopping centers, parking lots and dozens of stores and businesses.

The failed Electra program likely contributed to a financial downturn that eventually brought the company down. However, Lockheed Martin didn't know about every detail before the merger. Chemical solvents resulting from more than a half century of aircraft production at the company had soaked into the soil. Environmental regulations required that the ground be excavated, an expensive process. The developed site viewed by today's visitors is no longer identified as Lockheed or Lockheed Martin Corporation. Other than the businesses located there, much of the site was turned into a parking lot to accommodate more than 6,000 automobiles driven by people flying in and out of nearby Hollywood Burbank Airport.

The battle over Howard Hughes' attempt to regain control of Trans World Airlines would be seen and heard in the nation's courtrooms for years to come. On May 3, 1965, Hughes was forced to sell his entire stake in the airline for more than $546 million. After moving to Las

10. Aftermath

Vegas, he invested in a large number of properties along its famed Strip. For the first time in decades, Nevada found itself obsessed by someone with an interest other than gambling.[23] He bought those properties with proceeds he received by selling his shares in TWA. Hughes went on a spending spree shortly after moving to the gambling mecca, astounding everyone who lived or worked in the desert city. He immediately took over the top floor of the Desert Inn. Within a short time after arriving in town, he bought the entire Desert Inn property where he lived. Purchasing the Sands, Castaways, and Frontier hotels came next, followed by the North Las Vegas Air Terminal, television station KLAS, Alamo Airways, and a 510-acre ranch situated on barren land outside of metropolitan Las Vegas.

On April 5, 1976, at the age of 70, Howard Hughes died aboard a chartered business jet flying him from Aculpulco, Mexico, to Houston,

Land adjacent to the Flight 529 crash site is for sale to anyone who doesn't mind living near a graveyard for 78 people. In this recent photograph, note the proximity of each proposed home site below an overgrown area above where the Constellation crashed (courtesy Mary Brown at Clarendon Hills Historical Society).

17 Days and 17 Miles Apart

Texas. He planned to check into a hospital to seek treatment for kidney failure. It would be the end of an amazing era, but one that family members of the 78 victims of Flight 529 paid little attention to. Today, more than 63 years after an otherwise enjoyable Labor Day weekend, memories of those victims still fill the minds of people who remember that day. It will never be forgotten.

TWA Flight 529 crashed into a tranquil agricultural field populated by nearby farmers and several dozen homes. For more than half a century, local real estate developers showed no interest in building houses there. They were aware that 78 people had died on its undeveloped land, now looking the same as it had years before the crash. Although the land was considered to be sacred by owner Jerry Broz and his wife, a number of homes were later built around it. However, real estate speculators in future years could change everything. A current example of a developer doing business in Illinois is a company called Solux Homes.

Chapter Notes

Preface

1. Aircraft Accident Report, *Loss of Control on Approach, Colgan Air, Inc. Operating as Continental Connection Flight 3407 Bombardier DHC-8-400, N200WQ, Clarence Center, New York, February 12, 2009* (Washington, D.C.: National Transportation Safety Board, NTSB/AAR-10/01).

2. Aircraft Accident Report, *American Airlines, Inc. DC-10-10, N110AA, Chicago, O'Hare International Airport, Chicago, Illinois, May 25, 1979* (Washington, D.C.: National Transportation Safety Board, NTSB-AAR-79-17).

3. Helen Massy-Beresford and Sean Broderick, "ICAD Study Examines Degradation of Airline Pilot Manual Flying Skills," *Aviation Week & Space Technology*, November 27–December 10, 2023.

Introduction

1. Throughout my career at companies owned by Howard Hughes, I had the pleasure of knowing engineers and managers who had worked directly for him. I began as a technical representative at the Hughes Tool Company, Aircraft Division, and later rose to a management position. Whether or not I worked directly for Mr. Hughes is a question I've often been asked. Although I did have a key role developing an attack helicopter for the U.S. Army, and worked indirectly for him, I never met Howard Hughes in person.

2. The AH-64 Apache helicopter precisely fits its role in a battlefield setting. Between 1984 and 1997, Hughes, McDonnell Douglas, and today Boeing produced 937 AH-64A helicopters for the U.S. Army and military services of other countries. The aircraft became so popular that Boeing started remanufacturing an earlier model AH-64D helicopter. In addition to the U.S. Army, the military forces of 11 other nations have ordered the AH-64D.

3. The talented man described in the introduction of this book was the late Carl Secrest. More than anyone working with my relatively small team, Carl had an incredible understanding of just about everything causing Lockheed Constellations to function properly, or if they didn't, how to fix them.

Chapter 1

1. Howard Hughes made sure that TWA advertised in every major newspaper in the United States, as well as in other countries. During 1958, strongly publicizing the airline's coast-to-coast Sky Club Coach service, this advertisement appeared in many of those newspapers.

2. TWA's easy payment plan was mentioned in many advertisements.

3. "78 Die in Crash of TWA Airliner," *Pittsburgh Post-Gazette*, September 2, 1961, page 1.

4. Obituary, Robert Marshall Aiken, *Washington Post*, September 2, 1961.

5. *St. Petersburg Times*, September 2, 1961, page 3.

Notes—Chapter 2

6. Many TWA newspaper advertisements had been targeted toward the parents of young children.
7. Associated Press, "Families ... Dreams ... Hopes ... 78 Lost," *The Milwaukee Sentinel*, September 2, 1961, page 2.
8. During the 1940s, TWA prided itself on initiating regular passenger service to Paris and other cities in Europe.
9. Jack Frye served as both the president of TWA and a Constellation captain for some of its coast-to-coast passenger flights. He had a mostly pleasant relationship with airline owner Howard Hughes—until getting fired by him.
10. Aircraft Accident Report, *Trans World Airlines, Inc., Lockheed Constellation, Model 049, N86511, Midway Airport, Chicago, Illinois, September 1, 1961* (Civil Aeronautics Board, adopted December 11, 1962), page 2.
11. Ibid.
12. Louis Barr, "The Lockheed Constellation; A History Part II," *American Aviation Historical Society Journal*, Spring 1984, page 53.
13. Accident Report, Trans World Airlines Flight 529, page 2.
14. "Former City Resident and Family Among 78 Dead in Airliner Crash," *New Britain Herald*, September 2, 1961.
15. "Jobseekers Were Aboard," United Press International, September 2, 1961, page 1.
16. *St. Petersburg Times*, page 3.
17. "Disaster Wipes Out Family of 7," *Pittsburgh Post-Gazette*, September 2, 1961.
18. Ibid.
19. Obituary, "Victim Is Fiance of N. Chili Girl," *Democrat and Chronicle*, September 2, 1961, page 1.
20. Associated Press, "Families ... Dreams ... Hopes ..."
21. Stu Butler, "Hinsdale, Il. Plane Crash, Sept. 1961," GenDisasters.com.
22. "Carefree Vacationers Wiped Out in Air Crash," *The Portsmouth Herald*, September 2, 1961.

Chapter 2

1. *Chicago Area Guide*, Midway International Airport article, date unknown.
2. Aircraft Accident Report, *Trans World Airlines, Inc., Lockheed Constellation, Model 049, N86511, Midway Airport, Chicago, Illinois, September 1, 1961* (Civil Aeronautics Board, adopted December 11, 1962), page 2.
3. Mike Ellis, "Clarendon Hills Part I: Reliving the 1961 TWA Airliner Crash," *Hinsdale Magazine*, April 2015.
4. Ibid.
5. Ibid.
6. Ibid.
7. Ibid.
8. "CAB Inquiry Seeks Cause of CHI Crash," *Skyliner* (TWA newsletter), September 18, 1961, page 1.
9. Ibid.
10. Ibid.
11. Stu Butler, "Hinsdale, Il. Plane Crash, Sept. 1961," GenDisasters.com.
12. Ibid.
13. Vicki Ekmark, "Rum Boogie Crew Members: The Pilot," *96th Bomb Group Newsletter*, February 2018.
14. Ibid.
15. The FAA defined Instrument Flight Rules as rules and regulations established by the FAA to govern flight under conditions in which flight by outside visual reference is not safe.
16. A so-called phugoid oscillation is characterized by a nearly constant angle of attack while changing airspeed and altitude. This situation took several minutes to settle down.
17. National Broadcasting Company (NBC), "Flight 529 Crash," live television broadcast, September 1, 1961.
18. Aircraft Investigation Report, *Transcontinental and Western Air, Inc.— Reading, PA, July 11, 1946* (Washington, D.C.: Civil Aeronautics Board, SA-120).
19. Charles Barton, "Howard Hughes and His Flying Boat," Aero Publishers, Inc., Fallbrook, California, 1982, page 199.
20. Louis Barr, "The Lockheed Constellation, A History, Part 1," *American*

Notes—Chapters 3 and 4

Aviation Historical Society Journal, Winter 1983, page 199.

21. *Ibid.*

22. Airworthiness Directives (ADs) are legally enforceable regulations issued by the FAA (or another government agency) to correct an unsafe condition in an aircraft, involving an engine, propeller or other airborne appliance.

23. In her Facebook post, former university student Susan Stephens described this incident to the readers.

24. Edward Betts, "The Original Connies, Part III," *American Aviation Historical Society Journal*, Winter 1991, page 304.

Chapter 3

1. Many communities such as Hinsdale were only a few miles from where TWA Flight 529 had crashed.

2. "Carefree Vacationers Wiped Out in Air Crash," *The Portsmouth Herald*, September 2, 1961, page 2.

3. *Ibid.*

4. Rudolph Unger, "After 30 Years, Few Traces of Air Crash," *Chicago Tribune*, September 3, 1991, page 3.

5. *Ibid.*

6. *Ibid.*

7. "78 Die in Crash of TWA Plane," *Pittsburgh Post-Gazette*, September 2, 1961.

8. Staff Report, "Clarendon Heights Volunteers First Firefighters to Arrive on Scene of Air Crash Disaster," *Volunteer Firefighter*, September and October 1961.

9. *Ibid.*, page 14.

10. *Ibid.*, page 15.

11. It wasn't until April 1, 1967, that a newly formed Department of Transportation (DOT) Board began operations. The CAB's longstanding accident investigation function was transferred to the National Transportation Safety Board (NTSB), another new agency. From that point forward, the FAA and CAB no longer had responsibility for airline crash investigations.

12. A voting trust is simply a written agreement describing how the responsibilities of a shareholder (such as Howard Hughes) would be transferred to a different trustee. In this case, that trustee happened to be a major financial organization in New York City.

13. Aircraft Accident Report, *Trans World Airlines, Inc., Lockheed 1049A, N 69020, and United Air Lines, Inc., Douglas DC-7, N 63240, Grand Canyon, Arizona, June 30, 1956* (Washington, D.C.: Civil Aeronautics Board, SA-320).

14. Robert Serling, "Howard Hughes' Airline," St. Martin's/Marek, New York, 1983, page 218.

15. Donald L. Barlett and James B. Steele, *Empire: The Life, Legend, and Madness of Howard Hughes*, W.W. Norton & Company, New York, 1979, page 623.

Chapter 4

1. Aircraft Investigation Report, *Pan American Airways, Willimantic, Connecticut, June 18, 1946* (Washington, D.C.: Civil Aeronautics Board, SA-118).

2. Aircraft Investigation Report, *Transcontinental and Western Air, Inc.— Reading, PA, July 11, 1946* (Washington, D.C.: Civil Aeronautics Board, SA-120).

3. Nobody working for TWA would accept responsibility for the crash of Flight 529 near Clarendon Hills in Illinois.

4. The FAA didn't mandate the installation of flight recorders in airliners until the mid–1960s.

5. "CAB Inquiry Seeks Cause of CHI Crash," *Skyliner* (TWA newsletter), September 18, 1961, page 1.

6. Aircraft Accident Report, *Trans World Airlines, Inc., Lockheed Constellation, Model 049, N86511, Midway Airport, Chicago, Illinois, September 1, 1961* (Washington, D.C.: Civil Aeronautics Board, adopted December 11, 1962), page 49.

7. *Ibid.*, page 4.

8. *Ibid.*, page 49.

9. Different types of stalls can affect a plane's stability and flight characteristics in different ways. Uncontrollable maneuvering witnessed by the crew of Flight 529 involved several types of stalls.

Notes—Chapter 5

A secondary stall occurs when a recovery attempt from a primary stall is too abrupt. An accelerated stall can occur at any airspeed. Assuming that a plane's elevator is fully functional, it's a simple matter for a pilot to ease back on a cockpit control wheel and recover. With Flight 529 this wasn't possible. The Constellation had lost all control of its elevator: there was nothing its crew could do to pull the plane out of a series of deadly stalls.

10. Maria Papageorgiou, "Life of FAA Administrator Najeeb Halaby," Federal Aviation Agency publication, date unknown.

11. Airworthiness Directive AD 64-07-04, issued by the Federal Aviation Agency on April 14, 1964, covered Model 049, 149, 649, 749, 749A, 1049-54, 1049C, 1049D, 1049E, 1049G and 1049H aircraft. It required an inspection of nuts, bolts and cotter pins installed in the parallelogram linkages of all Lockheed Constellations to ensure they were properly secured with safety wire.

12. "Missing Bolt May Be Clue to Crash," *Skyliner* (TWA newsletter), October 6, 1961.

13. Edward Betts, "The Original Connies, Part I," *American Aviation Historical Society Journal*, Summer 1991, page 117.

14. "Pilot's Flight Operating Instructions for Army Model C-69 Airplane," *Army Air Forces*, January 20, 1945, page 63.

15. *Ibid.*, page 2.

16. Accident Report, Trans World Airlines Flight 529, page 6.

17. Airworthiness Directive AD 61-24-04, issued by the Federal Aviation Agency on December 14, 1961, covered a special inspection of Model 049, 149, 649, 749 and 1049 series aircraft to determine if the horizontal stabilizer rear spar-to-fuselage attachments had cracked. If it could be damaged they were required to be repaired prior to any further flights.

18. Airworthiness Directive AD 61-19-03, issued by the Federal Aviation Agency on September 20, 1961, covered a special inspection of elevator control systems for Model 049, 149, 649, 749 and 1049 series aircraft. It would determine if bolts retaining the parallelogram arm linkage between the elevator boost valve and boost mechanism were properly secured with safety wire.

19. Lockheed R7V Constellations built for the U.S. Navy were designed specifically to transport military personnel and move disabled soldiers around to different hospitals.

20. Accident Report, Trans World Airlines Flight 529, page 11.

21. "Report No. G8047.5, Evaluation of Elevator Control System C/RC-121 Aircraft, July 13, 1961," Temco Overhaul and Aerosystems, crash report, page 9.

22. Accident Report, Trans World Airlines Flight 529, page 11.

23. *Ibid.*

Chapter 5

1. Aircraft Accident Report, *Trans World Airlines, Inc., Lockheed Constellation, Model 049, N86511, Midway Airport, Chicago, Illinois, September 1, 1961* (Civil Aeronautics Board, adopted December 11, 1962), page 8.

2. The executives and lawyers employed by TWA served under the direction of sole shareholder Howard Hughes.

3. Robert Serling, "Howard Hughes' Airline," St. Martin's/Marek, New York, 1983, page 319.

4. "Colossal Strip Tease Makes an Exciting Show at Kansas City," *Skyliner* (TWA newsletter), April 28, 1960, page 4.

5. "Howard Hughes' Airline...," page 319.

6. David Kent, email to author, March 11, 2019.

7. Accident Report, Trans World Airlines Flight 529, page 14.

8. "Missing Bolt May Be Clue to Crash," *Skyliner* (TWA newsletter) October 6, 1961.

9. Due to competition existing between the world's airlines, every effort was made to limit access to their flight and maintenance operations,

including access requested by government agencies.
10. Jerry Cosley, email to author, 2020.
11. Accident Report, Trans World Airlines Flight 529, page 13.
12. *Ibid.*, page 14.
13. Aircraft Accident Report, *Northwest Airlines, Inc., Lockheed Electra L-188C, N 137US, O'Hare International Airport, Chicago, Illinois, September 17, 1961* (Washington, D.C.: Civil Aeronautics Board, SA-364).
14. Accident Report, Trans World Airlines Flight 529, page 13.
15. Georg Kohne, et al., "Lufthansa Super Star," position paper prepared by Ralph M. Peterson, published January 18, 2019.
16. *Congressional Record* proceeding.
17. *Annual Report of the Civil Aeronautics Board*, 1960 Fiscal Year, page 1.
18. Donald J. Porter, Flight Failure: Investigating the Nuts and Bolts of Air Disasters and Aviation Safety, Prometheus Books, Guilford, CT, 2020, page 13.

Chapter 6

1. David B. Tinnin, "Just About Everybody vs. Howard Hughes," Doubleday & Company, Inc., Garden City, New York, 1973, page 11.
2. *Ibid.*, page 13.
3. *Ibid.*, page 18.
4. *Ibid.*, page 19.
5. Robert Serling, "Howard Hughes' Airline," St. Martins/Marek, New York, 1983, page 86.
6. Donald L. Barlett and James B. Steele, *Empire: The Life, Legend, and Madness of Howard Hughes*, W.W. Norton & Company, New York, 1979, page 216.
7. Tinnin, page 13.
8. Barlett, page 36.
9. *Ibid.*, pages 34–35.
10. *Ibid.*, page 107.
11. *Ibid.*, page 116.
12. *Ibid.*, page 106.
13. *Ibid.*, page 108.
14. *Ibid.*, page 126.
15. Charles Barton, "Howard Hughes and his Flying Boat," Aero Publishers, Inc., Fallbrook, California, 1982, page 148.
16. *Ibid.*, page 186.
17. Aircraft Accident Report, *Northwest Airlines, Inc., Lockheed Electra L-188C, N 137US, O'Hare International Airport, Chicago, Illinois, September 17, 1961* (Washington, D.C.: Civil Aeronautics Board, SA-364).
18. Barlett, page 127.
19. *Ibid.*, pages 136–138.
20. *Ibid.*, page 140.
21. *Ibid.*, page 142.
22. *Ibid.*, page 144.
23. According to an online post provided by the Mayo Clinic, an "obsessive-compulsive disorder (OCD) features a pattern of unwanted thoughts and fears known as obsessions. These obsessions and compulsions get in the way of daily activities and cause a lot of distress."
24. Tinnin, page 105.
25. Barlett, page 175.
26. *Ibid.*, page 143.
27. *Ibid.*, page 147.
28. Tinnin, page 26.
29. *Ibid.*, page 31.
30. *Ibid.*, page 37.
31. *Ibid.*, page 38.
32. *Ibid.*
33. Barlett, page 222.
34. Jack G. Real with Bill Yenne, *The Asylum of Howard Hughes*, Xlibris, 2003.
35. Tinnin, page 38.
36. *Ibid.*, page 50.
37. *Ibid.*
38. *Ibid.*
39. *Ibid.*, page 78.
40. Barlett, page 252.
41. *Ibid.*
42. *Ibid.*, page 253.
43. *Ibid.*, page 550.

Chapter 7

1. Aircraft Investigation Report, *Transcontinental & Western Air, Inc.— Cape May, New Jersey, May 11, 1947* (Washington, D.C.: Civil Aeronautics Board, SA-143).
2. *Ibid.*, page 4.
3. *Ibid.*, page 5.

Notes—Chapter 8

4. Airworthiness Directive AD 49-52-01, issued by the Federal Aviation Agency, superseding AD 49-22-01, affecting all Lockheed Model 49, 149, 649, and 749 aircraft, requiring inspection of the elevator booster system shift mechanism for a moisture condition, making it impossible to move the boost system shift lever.

5. Aircraft Investigation Report, *Transcontinental & Western, Inc.—Shannon, Erie, December 28, 1946* (Washington, D.C.: Civil Aeronautics Board, SA-138).

6. *Ibid.*, page 3.

7. *Ibid.*, page 5.

8. Document, lawsuit of *Alexander H. Pekelis vs. Transcontinental & Western Air, Inc.*, to recover compensation for death of a passenger resulting from the crash of a Lockheed Constellation in Ireland on December 28, 1946.

9. *Ibid.*, page 2.

10. Aircraft Investigation Report, *Transcontinental and Western Air, Inc.—Reading, PA, July 11, 1946* (Washington, D.C.: Civil Aeronautics Board, SA-120).

11. *Ibid.*, page 11.

12. *Ibid.*, page 10.

13. *Ibid.*, page 16.

14. *Ibid.*, page 19.

15. *Ibid.*, page 21.

16. *Ibid.*, page 25.

17. *Ibid.*, page 28.

18. Aircraft Investigation Report, *Trans World Airlines, Inc.—Near Cairo, Egypt, August 30, 1950* (Washington, D.C.: Civil Aeronautics Board, SA-220).

19. Accident of a Model 049 Constellation at Long Beach, California, airport on November 18, 1950. The same plane crashed during September 1961 near Clarendon Hills in Illinois. Aviation Safety Network, Flight Safety Foundation.

20. This type of lubrication, also known as oil dilution, is a method for temporarily decreasing the viscosity of lubricating oil to assist the starter of a reciprocating aircraft engine when an outside temperature is below freezing.

Chapter 8

1. Aircraft Accident Report, *American Airlines, Inc., Lockheed Electra, N 6101A, In The East River, La Guardia Airport, New York, February 3, 1959* (Washington, D.C.: Civil Aeronautics Board, 1-0038).

2. Aircraft Accident Report, *Northwest Airlines Lockheed Electra, N 121US, Near Cannelton, Indiana, March 17, 1960* (Washington, D.C.: Civil Aeronautics Board, SA-354).

3. To assure its passengers that the Electra fleet was safe after modifications at Lockheed and approved for flight by the FAA, many of the planes were renamed Electra IIs.

4. After reading about two fatal airline accidents within three weeks of each other in a similar geographical area, it was clear that many potential travelers decided to either stay home or use their automobiles to take trips.

5. "Pilot Lost Control of Plane in Chicago Disaster Killing 37," *The Minneapolis Star*, September 18, 1961, page 15B.

6. "Twin Cities Plane Crew United in Desire to Fly," *Pioneer Press*, page 137.

7. *Ibid.*

8. "Pilot Lost Control...," page 15B.

9. *Ibid.*

10. Known throughout the aviation industry as LEAP, an acronym for "leaping ahead," the catchy phrase had nothing to do with passenger comfort. Its sole purpose was to strengthen the weak wings of every Electra that Lockheed had designed or built incorrectly.

11. "Pilot Lost Control...," page 15B.

12. *Ibid.*

13. "List of Passengers Killed in Air Crash," *Minneapolis Tribune*, September 18, 1962, page 11.

14. *Ibid.*

15. *Ibid.*

16. Aircraft Accident Report, *Northwest Airlines, Inc., Lockheed Electra L-188C, N 137US, O'Hare International Airport, Chicago, Illinois, September 17, 1961* (Washington, D.C.: Civil Aeronautics Board, SA-364), page 7.

172

Notes—Chapter 9

17. "NWA Electra Crash Kills 37," *Pioneer Press*, September 18, 1961, page 2.

18. Aircraft Accident Report, Northwest Airlines Flight 706, page 17.

19. Aircraft Accident Report, *Trans World Airlines, Inc., Lockheed Constellation, Model 049, N86511, Midway Airport, Chicago, Illinois, September 1, 1961* (Civil Aeronautics Board, adopted December 11, 1962, page 13).

20. "Pilot Cries 'No Control' Before Electra Crash Tragedy," *Hourglass*, September 1961, page 2.

21. "37 Killed in NWA Electra Crash at Chicago Airport," *Minneapolis Morning Tribune*, September 18, 1961, page 1.

22. "I Saw It All; 4 Children, Wife Dead," *Pioneer Press*, September 2, 1961.

23. Aircraft Accident Report, *Eastern Airlines, Inc., Lockheed Electra L-188, N 5533, Logan International Airport, Boston, Massachusetts, October 4, 1960* (Washington, D.C.: Civil Aeronautics Board, 1-0043).

Chapter 9

1. Kenneth E. Wixey, "Lockheed Constellation," *Classic Civil Aircraft*, 1987, page 13.

2. *Ibid.*

3. The Constellation's Curtiss-Wright R-3350 piston engines seldom reached their planned 3,000-hour limit between Overhauls. Many of the engines barely reached 1,000 hours. They were sensitive to overheating and mechanical stresses that could result in premature engine replacement.

4. Airworthiness Directive AD 49-52-01, issued by the Federal Aviation Agency, superseding AD 49-22-01, affecting all Lockheed Model 049, 149, 649, and 749 aircraft, by requiring an inspection of the elevator booster system shift mechanism.

5. Charles Bartin, "Howard Hughes and His Flying Boat," Aero Publishers, Inc., Fallbrook, California, 1982, page 189.

6. Aircraft Accident Report, *Braniff Airways, Inc., Lockheed Electra N 9705C, Buffalo, Texas, September 29, 1959* (Washington, D.C.: Civil Aeronautics Board, 1-0060).

7. Aircraft Accident Report, *Northwest Airlines Lockheed Electra, N 121US, Near Cannelton, Indiana, March 17, 1960* (Washington, D.C.: Civil Aeronautics Board, SA-354).

8. Robert Serling, "The Electra Story: Aviation's Greatest Mystery," Bantam Books, New York, 1991, page 72.

9. *Ibid.*, page 149.

10. Aircraft Accident Report, "Braniff Airways, Inc...," page 26.

11. Serling, "The Electra Story...," page 149.

12. Donald J. Porter, "Flight Failure: Investigating the Nuts and Bolts of Air Disasters and Aviation Safety," Prometheus Books, Guilford, CT, 2020, page 13.

13. Although the engineers at Lockheed were investigating cracked metal clips in the Electra wings, the FAA was concerned with cracking of supports for the Constellation's horizontal stabilizer structure.

14. The engineers at Lockheed became overwhelmed in an attempt to improve the safety of the entire Electra fleet, LEAP being one of the programs occupying their time.

15. Robert Serling, "Howard Hughes' Airline," St. Martin's/Marek, New York, 1983, page 246.

16. Jack G. Real with Bill Yenne, "The Asylum of Howard Hughes," Xlibris, 2003, page 37.

17. Donald L. Barlett and James B. Steele, *Empire: The Life, Legend, and Madness of Howard Hughes*, W.W. Norton & Company, New York, 1979, page 260.

18. Gross, Robert Ellsworth, National Aviation Hall of Fame.

19. "Field Service Digest: Electra Flight Controls, Part One," *Lockheed Aircraft Corporation, California Division, November–December 1961*, Volume 8, Number 3, page 15.

20. "Field Service Digest: Electra Flight Controls, Part Two," *Lockheed Aircraft Corporation, California Division,*

Notes—Chapter 10

November–December 1961, Volume 8, Number 4, page 20.
21. "Field Service Digest: Electra Flights Controls, Part One," *Lockheed Aircraft Corporation, California Division*, November 1961, Volume 8, Number 3, page 3.
22. *Ibid.*, page 4.
23. Aircraft Accident Report, *Northwest Airlines, Inc., Lockheed Electra L-188C, N 137US, O'Hare International Airport, Chicago, Illinois, September 17, 1961* (Washington, D.C.: Civil Aeronautics Board, SA-364).
24. *Ibid.*, page 7.
25. *Ibid.*, page 8.
26. *Ibid.*, page 15.
27. *Ibid.*, page 32.
28. *Ibid.*, page 29.
29. *Ibid.*, page 32.
30. "O'Hare Accident Investigation Report," Air Line Pilots Association, June 7, 1962, page 14.
31. *Ibid.*, page 8.
32. Aircraft Accident Report, Northwest Airlines Flight 704, page 30.
33. Serling, "The Electra Story...," page 139.
34. Craig Hagstrom, "Help Researching 1961 Chicago Electra Crash," *Airliners.net*, undated.

Chapter 10

1. Jim Hall, Chris Hart, Deb Hersman, and Robert Sumwalt, "Safeguarding Space," *Aviation Week & Space Technology*, September 12–25, 2022, page 66.
2. Aircraft Accident Report, *In-Flight Breakup Over the Atlantic Ocean, Trans World Airlines Flight 800, Boeing 747-131, N93119 Near East Moriches, New York, July 17, 1996* (Washington, D.C.: National Transportation Safety Board, NTSB/AAR-00-03).
3. Donald J. Porter, "Flight Failure: Investigating the Nuts and Bolts of Air Disasters and Aviation Safety," Prometheus Books, Guilford, CT, 2020, page 13.
4. Aircraft Accident Report, "In-Flight Breakup ..."
5. Brian Kachejian, "TWA Flight 800 Memorial Stands in Tribute at Smith Points, NY," *Classic New York History*, 2003.
6. On September 25, 1978, a Pacific Southwest Airlines Boeing 727-234 crashed in a residential neighborhood of San Diego in California. A single-engine Cessna 172 hit the airliner, killing its 2 occupants. All 135 people aboard the jetliner died along with 7 people on the ground. The San Diego Aerospace Museum placed a memorial plaque honoring the victims in nearby Balboa Park.
7. Out of control, Alaska Airlines Flight 261, a McDonnell Douglas MD-83 jetliner, plunged into the Pacific Ocean not far from the coast in California. It had departed Puerto Vallarta in Mexico for the Seattle Tacoma International Airport. The accident was attributed to a loss of elevator pitch control. Excessively worn threads of a jackscrew was the cause, it designed to position the angle of the jet's horizontal stabilizer. A failure to adequately lubricate the threads of the jackscrew was blamed on poor maintenance practices at Alaska Airlines.
8. Keith Yearman, email to author, September 22, 2022.
9. Mary Brown became a major help to identify homes surrounding the crash site. Because a question arose as to whether the monument would be erected at the actual crash site or a city-owned park, her help clarifying this issue was appreciated.
10. The author exchanged email messages with Mary Brown, a lifelong resident of Clarendon Hills, beginning in late 2021. They concerned details about the crash site and how the crash affected the residents of her community.
11. Email from Mary Brown describing a lack of sufficient reimbursement from TWA for the local fire department to pay for equipment losses at the crash site.
12. Illinois General Assembly, House Joint Resolution H10045 for recognition by the state government of the Flight 529 crash.
13. Ben Bradley, "60 years after plane crash in suburbs, group working to honor victims of TWA Flight 529," wgntv.com, September 1, 2021.

Notes—Chapter 10

14. Unveiling of the Flight 529 monument attracted residents, government officials, newspapers, and a television station. The event conveyed deep interest on the part of residents and first responders who lived near the crash site, without having any connection to people who died in the crash.

15. Yearman email to author on September 22, 2022.

16. The Clarendon Hills Historical Society was founded by local members of the Friends of the Library in the community. It recognizes the importance of preserving history, whether good or bad that involved their village. Its slogan is "Preserving the Past for the Future."

17. Cari Dobbs, email to author on February 8, 2024.

18. Post on Facebook, March 4, 2017, from Vicki Ekmark concerning Captain Jim Sander's military flying experiences during World War II.

19. William H. Jones and John F. Berry, "Lockheed Paid $38 Million in Bribes Abroad," *Washington Post*, May 27, 1977.

20. More commonly known as FCPA, the Foreign Corrupt Practices Act is a United States Federal law that prohibits U.S. citizens and other entities from bribing foreign government officials that can benefit from mutual business interests.

21. Ben R. Rich and Leo Janos, *Skunk Works: A Personal Memoir of My Years at Lockheed*, Little, Brown, New York, 1994, page 10.

22. "San Fernando Valley (Area 1) Superfund Site: Burbank," U.S. Environmental Protection Agency (EPA), October 2018.

23. Laura Wolff Seanlaw, "Vegas's Revolutionary Recluse," *The Magazine of the National Endowment of the Humanities*, March/April 2010.

Bibliography

Aiken, Robert Marshall, *Washington Post*, September 2, 1961.
Aircraft Accident Report, *American Airlines, Inc. DC-10–10, N110AA, Chicago-O-Hare International Airport, Chicago, Illinois, May 25, 1979* (Washington, D.C.: National Transportation Safety Board, NTSB-AAR-79-17).
Aircraft Accident Report, *American Airlines, Inc., Lockheed Electra, N 6101A, In The East River, La Guardia Airport, New York, February 3, 1959* (Washington, D.C.: Civil Aeronautics Board, 1-0038).
Aircraft Accident Report, *Braniff Airways, Inc., Lockheed Electra N 9705C, Buffalo, Texas, September 29, 1959* (Washington, D.C.: Civil Aeronautics Board, 1-0060).
Aircraft Accident Report, *Eastern Airlines, Inc., Lockheed Electra L-188, N 5533, Logan International Airport, Boston, Massachusetts, October 4, 1960* (Washington, D.C.: Civil Aeronautics Board, 1-0043).
Aircraft Accident Report, *In-Flight Breakup Over The Atlantic Ocean, Trans World Airlines Flight 800, Boeing 747–131, N93119 Near East Moriches, New York, July 17, 1996* (Washington, D.C.: National Transportation Safety Board, NTSB/AAR-00-03).
Aircraft Accident Report, *Loss of Control on Approach, Colgan Air, Inc. Operating as Continental Connection Flight 3407 Bombardier DHC-8–400, N200WQ, Clarence Center, New York, February 12, 2009* (Washington, D.C.: National Transportation Safety Board, NTSB/AAR-10/01).
Aircraft Accident Report, *Northwest Airlines Lockheed Electra, N 121US, Near Cannelton, Indiana, March 17, 1960* (Washington, D.C.: Civil Aeronautics Board, SA-354).
Aircraft Accident Report, *Northwest Airlines, Inc., Lockheed Electra L-188C, N 137US, O'Hare International Airport, Chicago, Illinois, September 17, 1961* (Washington, D.C.: Civil Aeronautics Board, SA-364).
Aircraft Accident Report, *Trans World Airlines, Inc., Lockheed 1049A, N 69020, and United Air Lines, Inc., Douglas DC-7, N 63240, Grand Canyon, Arizona, June 30, 1956* (Washington, D.C.: Civil Aeronautics Board, SA-320).
Aircraft Accident Report, *Trans World Airlines, Inc., Lockheed Constellation, Model 049, N86511, Midway Airport, Chicago, Illinois, September 1, 1961* (Washington, D.C.: Civil Aeronautics Board, adopted December 11, 1962, SA-363).
Aircraft Investigation Report, *Pan American Airways, Willimantic, Connecticut, June 18, 1946* (Washington, D.C.: Civil Aeronautics Board, SA-118).
Aircraft Investigation Report, *Trans World Airlines, Inc.—Near Cairo, Egypt, August 30, 1950* (Washington, D.C.: Civil Aeronautics Board, SA-220).
Aircraft Investigation Report, *Transcontinental & Western Air, Inc.—Cape May, New Jersey, May 11, 1947* (Washington, D.C.: Civil Aeronautics Board, SA-143).
Aircraft Investigation Report, *Transcontinental & Western, Inc.—Shannon, Erie, December 28, 1946.* (Washington, D.C.: Civil Aeronautics Board, SA-138).

Bibliography

Aircraft Investigation Report, *Transcontinental and Western Air, Inc.—Reading, PA, July 11, 1946* (Washington, D.C.: Civil Aeronautics Board, SA-120).

Airworthiness Directive AD 49-52-01, issued by the Federal Aviation Agency, and superseding AD 49-22-01, regarding all Lockheed Model 49, 149, 649, and 749 aircraft, requiring an inspection of the elevator booster system shift mechanism.

Airworthiness Directive AD 61-19-03, issued by the Federal Aviation Agency on September 20, 1961, regarding the special inspection of Lockheed Constellation elevator control systems for all Model 049, 149, 649, 749 and 1049 series aircraft. It would determine if bolts in the parallelogram arm linkage between the elevator boost valve and boost mechanism were properly secured.

Airworthiness Directive AD 61-24-04, issued by the Federal Aviation Agency on December 14, 1961, covering a special inspection of Model 049, 149, 649, 749 and 1049 series aircraft to determine if their horizontal stabilizer rear spar-to-fuselage attachments had cracked. If found to be cracked they were to be repaired prior to further flight.

Airworthiness Directive AD 64-07-04, issued by the Federal Aviation Agency, on April 14, 1964, for Model 49, 149, 649, 749, 749A, 1049-54, 1049C, 1049D, 1049E, 1049G and 1049H aircraft, requiring an inspection of all nuts, bolts and cotter pins installed in the parallelogram linkages of all Lockheed Constellations to assure they are properly secured and safety wired.

Annual Report of the Civil Aeronautics Board, 1960 Fiscal Year.

Associated Press, "Families ... Dreams ... Hopes ... 78 Lost," *The Milwaukee Sentinel*, September 2, 1961.

Barlett, Donald L., and James B. Steele, *Empire: The Life, Legend, and Madness of Howard Hughes*, W.W. Norton & Company, New York, 1979.

Barr, Louis, "The Lockheed Constellation, A History, Part 1," *American Aviation Historical Society Journal*, Winter 1983.

Barr, Louis, "The Lockheed Constellation; A History, Part II," *American Aviation Historical Society Journal*, Spring 1984.

Bartin, Charles, "Howard Hughes and His Flying Boat," Aero Publishers, Fallbrook, California, 1982.

Betts, Edward, "The Original Connies, Part III," *American Aviation Historical Society Journal*, Winter 199.

Bradley, Ben, "60 Years After Plane Crash in Suburbs, Group Working to Honor Victims of TWA Flight 529," wgntv.com, September 1, 2021.

Butler, Stu, "Hinsdale, Il. Plane Crash, Sept. 1961," GenDisasters.com

"CAB Inquiry Seeks Cause of CHI Crash," *Skyliner* (newsletter), September 18, 1961.

"Carefree Vacationers Wiped Out in Air Crash," *The Portsmouth Herald*, September 2, 1961.

"Colossal Strip Tease Makes an Exciting Show at Kansas City," *Skyliner* (TWA newsletter), April 28, 1960.

"Disaster Wipes Out Family of 7," *Pittsburgh Post-Gazette*, September 2, 1961.

Ekmark, Vicki, "Rum Boogie Crew Members: The Pilot," *96th Bomb Group Newsletter*, February 2018.

Ellis, Mike, "Clarendon Hills Part I: Reliving the 1961 TWA Airliner Crash," *Hinsdale Magazine*, April 2015.

"Field Service Digest: Electra Flight Controls," *Lockheed Aircraft Corporation, California Division, November–December 1961*.

"Flight 529 Crash," *National Broadcasting Company*, archived broadcast, September 1, 1961.

"Former City Resident and Family Among 78 Dead in Airliner Crash," *New Britain Herald*, September 2, 1961.

Gross, Robert Ellsworth, National Aviation Hall of Fame.

Bibliography

Hall, Jim, and Chris Hart, Deb Hersman and Robert Sumwalt, "Safeguarding Space," *Aviation Week & Space Technology*, September 12–25, 2022.
"I Saw It All; 4 Children, Wife Dead," *Pioneer Press*, September 2, 1961.
Illinois General Assembly, House Joint Resolution, H10045, recognition of TWA Flight 529 crash.
"Jobseekers Were Aboard," United Press International, September 2, 1961.
Jones, William H., and John F. Berry, "Lockheed Paid $38 Million in Bribes Abroad," *Washington Post*, May 27, 1977.
Kachejian, Brian, "TWA Flight 800 Memorial Stands in Tribute at Smith Points, NY," *Classic New York History*, 2003.
Kohne, Georg, et al., "Lufthansa Super Star," position paper by Ralph M. Peterson, published January 18, 2019.
"List of Passengers Killed in Air Crash," *Minneapolis Tribune*, September 18, 1962.
Maguglin, Robert, "Howard Hughes His Accomplishments & Legacy," Sequoia Communications, Inc., Long Beach, California.
Massy-Beresford, Helen, and Sean Broderick, "ICAD Study Examines Degradation of Airline Pilot Manual Flying Skills," *Aviation Week & Space Technology*, November 27–December 10, 2023.
"Missing Bolt May Be Clue to Crash," *TWA Skyliner*, October 6, 1961.
"NWA Electra Crash Kills 37," *Pioneer Press*, September 18, 1961.
Obituary, "Victim Is Fiance of N. Chili Girl," *Democrat and Chronicle*, September 2, 1961.
O'Hare Accident Investigation Report, Air Line Pilots Association, June 7, 1962.
Papageorgiou, Maria, "FAA Administrator Najeeb Halaby," government published review, date unknown.
"Pilot Cries 'No Control' Before Electra Crash Tragedy," *Hourglass*, September 1961.
"Pilot Lost Control of Plane in Chicago Disaster Killing 37," *The Minneapolis Star*, September 18, 1961.
"Pilot's Flight Operating Instructions for Army Model C-69 Airplane," *Army Air Forces*, publication, January 20, 1945.
Porter, Donald J., "Flight Failure: Investigating the Nuts and Bolts of Air Disasters and Aviation Safety," Prometheus Books, Guilford, CT, 2020.
Real, Jack G., with Bill Yenne, "The Asylum of Howard Hughes," Xlibris, 2003.
"Report No. G8047.5, Evaluation of Elevator Control System C/RC-121 Aircraft, July 13, 1961," Temco Overhaul and Aerosystems.
Rich, Ben R., and Leo Janos, *Skunk Works: A Personal Memoir of My Years at Lockheed*, Little, Brown, New York, 1994.
"San Fernando Valley (Area I) Superfund Site: Burbank," U.S. Environmental Protection Agency (EPA), October 2018.
Serling, Robert, *The Electra Story: Aviation's Greatest Mystery*, Bantam Books, New York, 1991.
Serling, Robert, "Howard Hughes' Airline," St. Martins/Marek, New York, 1983.
"78 Die in Crash of TWA Plane," *Pittsburgh Post-Gazette*, September 2, 1961.
Staff Report, "Clarendon Heights Volunteers First Firefighters to Arrive on Scene of Air Crash Disaster," *Volunteer Firefighter*, September and October 1961.
"37 Killed in NWA Electra Crash at Chicago Airport," *Minneapolis Morning Tribune*, September 18, 1961.
Tinnin, David B., "Just About Everybody vs. Howard Hughes," Doubleday & Company, Inc., Garden City, New York, 1973.
Unger, Randolph, "After 30 Years, Few Traces of Air Crash That Killed 78," *Chicago Tribune*, September 3, 1991.
Wixey, Kenneth E., "Lockheed Constellation," *Classic Civil Aircraft*, 1987.
Wolff Seanlaw, Laura, "Vegas's Revolutionary Recluse," *Humanities, The Magazine of the National Endowment of the Humanities*, March/April 2010.

Index

Abilene, Texas 26
Acapulco, Mexico 165
Advanced Attack Helicopter (AAH) 6
AEC *see* Atomic Energy Commission
aerospace industry 19, 36
agricultural field 41–42, 117, 166
Aitken, Bill 73
Aiken, Robert "Bob" 12, 160
aileron controls. 5, 30, 37, 56, 84, 97, 121–122, 138, 140–141, 143, 152
Air Line Pilots Association 55, 143, 145–146
air pocket 34
air traffic control 2, 29, 49
air turbulence 34, 130–132
Airworthiness Directives, FAA 38, 62, 65–66, 128
Alamo Airways, Inc. 165
Alaska Airlines, Inc. 155
Allegheny County 20
Allison (engine supplier) 119, 144
ALPA *see* Air Line Pilots Association
American Airlines, Inc. 87, 92, 113, 145, 151
Anacapa Island 155
Anderson, Richard L. 116
Approved Type Certificate 16, 96, 129, 131
Arcadia California 118
Argonne National Laboratories 39
Army Air Corps, U.S. 26–27
Army Air Force, U.S. 84
ATC *see* air traffic control
Atlantic Ocean 11, 19, 69, 83, 94, 99
Atomic Energy Commission 39
Aviation Week & Space Technology 149
awards, military service 27

Balboa Beach 25
Balboa Park 154–155

bankruptcy 88, 91, 136, 151, 163
Barr, Louis 38
Bartram, John D. 20
Bensenville, Illinois 124
Berglund, Sue 157
Berklee School of Music 12
Berlin Wall 9
Berwyn, Illinois 24
Betts, Edward 38, 63
Beverly Hills 85
Bilski, Rosemary 117
Binghamton, New York 20
Black Hills Teachers College 25
Blumberg, Nathan J. (studio head) 110
Boca Raton 117
Boeing (manufacturer): (B-17) 26; (B-29) 34, 96; (377) 38; (727–234) 153; (737 MAX) 77, 133, 149–152; (747–100) 146, 149, 153; (767) 149
bomb shelters 9
Bombay, India 109
bombings 26, 48, 160–161
Bond, Ward (actor) 110
Boston 10, 12–15, 17–19, 22, 25, 33, 51, 125
Boyd, Alan 121
Bradley, Ben 158
Braniff International Airways, Inc. 130, 132, 144
Breech, Ernest R. 90
Brown, Mary 47, 152, 157–160
Broz, Jerry 41–42, 43–46, 158, 166
Buffalo, New York 1
Burbank, California 15, 61, 93, 95, 121, 126, 128, 131, 133–136, 162–163

CAA *see* Civil Aeronautics Administration
CAB *see* Civil Aeronautics Board
CAB Bureau of Safety 124

181

Index

CAB Engineering Division 124
CAB investigators 48, 52–56, 60–61, 65–66, 69, 71–74, 76–77, 91, 99, 100–101, 119, 121–125, 128, 132, 134, 137, 140–141, 151–152
CAB Witness Group 55
Cairo, Egypt 25, 109
California 5–6, 9–10, 12–13, 15, 18–19, 24–25, 27–28, 36, 53, 93, 107, 153, 155, 161, 163
Cannelton, Indiana 114
Castaways Hotel and Casino 165
certification practices, aviation 77, 133
Cessna Aircraft Company: Cessna 150 5; Cessna 172 153
Chamberlain, Edward North, Sr. 19
Chicago, Illinois 2, 10, 15, 18, 20–24, 30, 41, 48–49, 53, 63, 112–114, 116, 118–119, 121, 147, 158
Chicago Ridge 24
cigarette vending machines 24
Civil Aeronautics Administration 54–55, 75, 95–96, 108
Civil Aeronautics Board 2, 10, 53, 55, 77, 128–129, 148–149, 151
Civil Aviation Organization 4
Clarence Center, New York 1
Clarendon Heights Fire Department 121, 157–158
Clarendon Hills 2, 6, 15, 39, 47, 50, 52, 112, 120–121, 123, 137, 146, 155–158
Clarendon Hills Historical Society 36, 156–157
Clarendon Hills Road 40, 155, 159
clear air turbulence 34, 131
Clooney, George Timothy (actor) 9
coast-to-coast flights 10–11, 13–15, 79
codeshare 1
Colgan Air, Inc. 1
College of DuPage 157
Congress 77, 129, 137, 144, 148–149
congressional hearings 84, 129, 149
Continental Airlines, Inc. 1, 92
Continental Connection 1
Cook County 24
Cook County Morgue 124
Cook County Office of the Coroner 48
Cosley, Jerry 75
courtroom proceedings 69, 91, 104, 144, 164
Coutu, Joyce 118, 124
Cowen, Wesley 123
cross-country flights 15
Culver City plant 6, 82–85, 87

Cummings, Jan 157
Curtiss-Wright R-3350 engines 29, 31, 34, 55, 94, 96–97, 109–111

Delaware Bay 99, 100
Department of Commerce 54
Desert Inn Hotel & Casino 165
designee system 129, 133
Detroit, Michigan 10
The Dick Van Dyke Show 9
disagreement, FAA vs. CAB 71
DNA testing 48
Dobbs, Cari 160
Douglas Aircraft Company: (C-54) 118; (DC-3) 127; (DC-6) 38, 129; (DC-7) 10, 49
Duffy, Janice 118
Dunn, Raymond M. 70–72, 104
DuPage County 41
Dusak, Jack 73

East Boston 11
East Coast 10, 20, 22–24
East River 113
Eastern Air Lines, Inc. 125
Eckstein, Marion 118
Egypt 109, 112
Eisenhower, Pres. Dwight D. 54
Ekmark, Vicki 160
elevator control 7, 30–31, 33, 35, 37–38, 53–54, 56–57, 60, 62–65, 67–68, 70, 72–76, 84, 97–98, 100–102, 121, 123–125, 127–128, 136, 140, 151–152
Equitable Life Assurance Society 88–91
Erie, Pennsylvania 20
Ernest, George 47
Eureka, California 14
eyewitnesses, crash 124

FAA *see* Federal Aviation Administration (i.e., Federal Aviation Agency)
FAA Reauthorization Act of 2018 133
Families of TWA Flight 800 Association 153
FBI *see* Federal Bureau of Investigation
Federal Aviation Act of 1958 54
Federal Aviation Administration (FAA) 5, 24, 29, 37–38, 48, 54–55, 61–63, 65, 68, 70, 75–78, 90, 103–104, 114, 117, 121, 122, 128, 130–131, 133, 135, 137, 145, 148–152
Federal Aviation Agency (FAA) 48, 54, 62, 71, 93, 130, 149
Federal Bureau of Investigation 141

182

Index

Fidger, Nanette Gene 26, 28
Field Service Digest (Lockheed publication) 138, 140
firefighters 45–47, 161
first responders 45–46, 55, 121, 155–157
flight controls 30, 37, 56, 63–65, 99, 101, 121, 125, 127–128, 140–141, 152
Flight Engineers Association 55
flight manual, pilot 35, 64, 76
flight simulator 150
Florida 115–120
Florida Southern University 118
flying boat 37, 79, 83–84, 87, 129
Ford, John (Hollywood producer) 110
Ford Motor Company 90
Foreign Corrupt Practices Act 163
Fort Lauderdale 119
Fort Myers 117
Foss, Nancy 118
France 27, 93, 153
Freedom 7 (spacecraft) 9
Frontier Hotel (Las Vegas) 165
Frye, Jack 15
fueling at Midway 28–29
Fuller, Wayne 117

Gagarin, Yuri (cosmonaut) 9
Gander (Newfoundland) 15
General Dynamics Corporation 87
General Tire and Rubber Company 80
Geneva (Switzerland) 25
George, Charles C., Jr. 45
George Washington University 12
Gilliam, Frances Margaret 13
Golden State 12, 18
Good Samaritan Hospital 85
government bailout 163
Grand Canyon 49
Gross, Robert E. 80, 136–137
groundwater contamination 164

Hagstrom, Craig 145–146
Hagstrom, Ralph E. 116
Halaby, Najeeb E. 48, 54, 61–63, 75–76, 121, 130
Hamilton Standard propellers 31
Haughton, Daniel J. 162
Heidenreich, John 46
Heidenreich, Roger 157–158
Hibbard, Hall L. 37, 80
Hilton, Conrad "Nicky" 110
Hinsdale, Illinois 41
Hinsdale Animal Cemetery 157
Houston, Texas 81–82, 165

Hubley, Timothy 12
Hueneme Beach Sundial Memorial 155
Hughes, Howard Robard, Jr.: advertising obsession 81; arms-length relationships 79; avoiding taxes 81–82; board meetings 79; Culver City land purchase 82; D-2 airplane 83; deal maker 90; death 3, 165; as defense contractor 82; drill bits 81–82; drug addiction 86; Electra purchase plan 136; employee loyalty 81; flying boat flight 83; gaining TWA ownership 80; germs, fear of 137; H-1 Racer 79, 83; hearing loss 86; hospitalization after XF-11 crash 85; ignoring shareholders 80; loss of TWA ownership 90; management style 79; moviemaking fascination 80, 92; obsessive-compulsive disorder 86; oil boom 82; presentation, Senate committee 84; procrastination 87–88; real estate holdings 79; reclusive lifestyle 86; record setting flights 79; tool company earnings 88; TWA jet purchase crisis 87; TWA ownership 79; TWA stock decline 87; wartime government contracts 84; XF-11 accident 85
Hughes, Howard Robard, Sr. 82
Hughes Aircraft Company 6, 82–84, 87
Hughes Kaiser Corporation 83
Hughes Tool Company 6, 81–84, 88
human factors 50
hydraulic boost systems 5, 30, 35, 37, 56–57, 60–61, 63–64, 66, 68, 70, 75, 81, 84, 97–98, 100–101, 122, 125, 127–129, 131, 137–138, 140, 152

IBM computer systems 72
Idlewild Airport 10, 14, 18–19, 27; *see also* JFK International Airport
IFR *see* Instrument Flight Rules
Illinois 2, 6, 15, 20, 24, 114, 118, 147, 150, 152, 158, 166
India 109–110
Indiana 24, 114, 130
instrument flight plan 49
Instrument Flight Rules 29
Internal Revenue Service 81–82
Ireland 15, 102, 110–111, 115
Irving Trust Company 89

Jamaica Bay 18
jet transports 14, 87
JFK International Airport 18, 149
Johnson, Clarence L. "Kelly" 80, 163

183

Index

Kaiser, Henry J. 83
Kansas City 7, 64, 72, 81
Kansas City International Airport 64
Kennedy, Jacqueline B. 62
Kennedy, President John F. 9, 18, 62–63
Kent, David 73
Khrushchev, Nikita 9
KLAS-9 TV station 165
Kohne, Georg 76
Kotchian, A. Carl 162

Labor Day weekend 2, 14, 23, 42, 46, 166
LaGuardia Airport 15, 93, 113
Lake Forest, Illinois 118
Lake Michigan 30
Largo, Florida 117
Las Vegas 10, 12–13, 21, 23, 25, 27–28, 165
last rites 48, 121
lawsuits 3, 49, 71, 91, 103–104, 112, 144, 152–153, 162
Leak, John 123, 137
LEAP see Lockheed Electra Action Program
life insurance policies 23
Lockheed Aircraft Corporation 55, 61, 69, 71, 80, 94, 96, 113, 126, 130–131, 135, 137, 144, 149, 162–164
Lockheed acquisition by Martin
Lockheed Electra Action Program (LEAP) 117, 122, 125, 134–136, 144–145
Logan International Airport 10–12, 18
Long Beach Airport 111–112
Long Beach Harbor 83
Long Island 14, 18, 146
Looters, crash site 46, 55, 157
Los Angeles 5–6, 10, 13, 15, 19–20, 23–26, 82–83, 85, 110–111, 161
Los Angeles Country Club 85
Los Angeles International Airport 6, 10, 25–26, 110
Lufthansa (German Airline) 76

Madrid (Spain) 25, 27
Maloney, Richard 19
Manhattan Beach 25
Martin Marietta Corporation 163–164
Martin 202 129
Maryland 12, 163
Massachusetts 12
Maves, Elmer 159
Mayo Clinic 86

MCAS (Maneuvering Characteristics Augmentation System) 150, 152
McDonnell Douglas Corporation (MDC): DC-10 2; MD-83 155
McKenzie, Jeanette 117
memorial, Clarendon Hills 155–158
Mendota Heights 116–117
Mercury (Nevada) 12
Merrimack County 12
metallurgical analysis 73
Miami 114, 119
Mid-Continent International Airport see Kansas City International Airport
Midway Airport 10, 21–23, 25, 28, 30–31, 34–35, 39, 41, 54–55, 59, 73, 118, 120
Midway Hotel 53
Milford New Hampshire 12
Miller, Nolan 124
Milwaukee 118–119
Minneapolis 116–117
Minnetonka Beach 116
missions flown, wartime 26
Missouri 7, 64, 72, 81
Moffett Field 66
Monroe County 20
Montgomery Blair High School 12
Morocco 115
Muncie (Indiana) 24

National Broadcasting Company 36
National Bureau of Standards 141
National Guard 46
National Transportation Safety Board 74, 148–149, 150
Naval Reserve Officer's Training Corps 20
NBC see National Broadcasting Company
New Hampshire 12
New Jersey 1
New York City 14, 18–19, 49, 88, 94, 102, 109–110, 153
Newark 1
Newfoundland 15, 102
Newlin, James Laverly III 23, 25, 28–30
newspaper reporters 36, 45–47, 158
next-of-kin 3, 144, 162
North Bethesda 163
North Chili 20
North Las Vegas Air Terminal 165
Northern California 66
Northwest Airlines, Inc. 2, 5, 41, 114–117, 119, 122–124, 130, 140, 144, 152

184

Index

Northwest Flight 706 2–3, 5, 7, 84, 114–117, 119–121, 123–125, 137, 140–146, 148, 152
NTSB *see* National Transportation Safety Board
nuclear threat 9

Obama, Pres. Hussein Barack 9
ODA *see* Organization Designation Authorization
O'Hare International Airport 2, 22, 50, 76, 84, 112, 116, 118–122
Olson, Nancy Ann (actress) 110
Ontario International Airport 66
operator's manual 35, 64, 76, 102, 128, 142–143
Organization Designation Authorization (ODA) 78, 133
Orly Field 93

Pacific Ocean 85
Pacific Southwest Airlines, Inc. 153
Palo Alto 19
Pan American World Airways, Inc. 52
parallelogram linkage 57–58, 60–62, 65–66, 70, 74
Paris 15, 25, 27, 36, 93–94, 102, 149, 151
Pataki, George Elmer (New York governor) 153
payment arrangements 3, 11, 82, 88, 162, 164
Pearson, Barbara Jane 26, 28
Pekelis, Alexander Haim 103
Pennsylvania 19–20, 52
Pentagon, U.S. 146
Philadelphia 10
phugoid oscillations 33
Pittsburgh 10, 19–21, 23, 25
Pittsburgh International Airport 19
postwar years 34, 93, 102
power steering systems 127
Prairie Trail Park 155, 157–158
Pratt & Whitney engines 83–84, 113
Prestwick, Scotland 102
priests 48, 121

Quesada, Elwood Richard 54–55, 76, 130

Rabat, Morocco 115
Reading Airport 104–105
Real, Jack G. 89, 136
Redondo Beach 20, 25
remembrances, of victims 160–162

Remkus, Bill 157
Remkus, George 47
resolution, Flight 529 158
reverse thrust braking 98, 110
RKO Studios 80

sabotage 68, 121, 123
safety wire missing 5, 59 122–123, 125, 141–143, 152
Saint Petersburg 117
Salvation Army 19
San Diego 20, 24, 153
San Diego Aerospace Museum 155
San Fernando Valley 19
San Francisco 10, 19, 24, 112
San Francisco International Airport 10, 14, 112
San Joaquin Valley 66
Sanders, James H. 23, 25–31, 35, 160–161
Sands Hotel (Las Vegas) 165
Santa Monica 5, 26, 137
Savage, Harry 20
scavengers, crash site 55
Scranton, Pennsylvania 19
Seaman, Harry Edward 153
Securities and Exchange Commission 91
September 11, 2001, attack 146
Shannon Airport (Ireland) 11, 15, 102, 110–111, 115
Shepard, Alan Bartlett, Jr. (astronaut) 9
shift handle, elevator 30, 33, 56, 60–61, 64, 66–68, 70, 100–102
Shirley, New York 153
Silver Spring, Maryland 12
Sioux City 112
Skurcenski, Dr. Anton 19
Sky Club Coach 10–11, 13, 19, 22–23, 27–28, 51, 93
Skyliner (TWA newsletter) 63, 74
Smith Point County Park 153
smoking aboard airliners 24
social media 160
Solux Homes 166
South Saint Paul 117
Southern California 20, 66
Soviet Union 9
Space Race 9
Spain 27
stall condition 33, 61
Star of Dublin 112
Star of Paris 15, 93
Stephens, Susan 38

185

Index

Streator, Illinois 20
strike, airline pilot 51
Sturgis, South Dakota 25
submarines, wartime 83
Sudden Infant Death Syndrome 20
Sun, Monica 19
Sun Valley, California 13
Suncook, New Hampshire 12
Superior, Wisconsin 116
Swanson frozen dinners 160

Tampa, Florida 118–119
Tarrant, Dale 25, 28–31
taxpayers 77, 84, 129
Taylor, Elizabeth Rosemond (actress) 110
Technical Services Section, CAB 123–124
Texas panhandle 26
Thailand 149
Tillinghast, Charles C., Jr. 55, 72, 75
Topeka, Kansas 94
training flights, TWA 99–101, 104
Transcontinental and Western Air, Inc. 80
Trout, Frank 47
TWA Flight 529 2–3, 5, 7, 10, 12–15, 17, 18–27, 30–31, 33–39, 41, 49–50, 53–55, 58, 60–78, 81, 84, 90–91, 93, 98, 110, 112, 114–116, 120–121, 123–125, 128, 136–138, 142, 144–146, 148, 150–153, 155–158, 160, 162, 166
TWA Flight 529 (Facebook) 160
TWA Flight 800 International Memorial 153
Twin Cities 116
type certificates 96–97, 108, 129, 131, 135

United Air Lines, Inc. 49, 87, 92
U.S. Air Force 19, 25, 55, 66, 68, 113, 130
U.S. Army 6, 24, 94
U.S. currency 18
U.S. Navy 12, 14, 20, 62, 66–68
U.S. Post Office 48

Universal Studios 110
University of Minnesota 117
University of Pittsburgh 19
University of Rochester 20

Village of Willowbrook 155, 157–159
volunteers 46–47, 121, 155, 157, 161
voting trust 49, 89, 90–91

Wall Street 90
Walls, Carol 20
Warsaw Convention (international treaty) 103
Washington, D.C. 10, 53, 62, 126–129, 161
Waukegan, Illinois 118, 125
WAVES program *see* Women Accepted for Volunteer Emergency Service
weather 1, 15, 28, 41, 49, 54, 68, 87, 95, 102, 110–111, 113–115, 117
West Coast 12
West Palm Beach 117–118
West Side Story (movie) 9
Western Airlines, Inc. 25, 145
WGN-9 (Chicago TV station) 158
"willful misconduct" actions 104
Wisconsin 116
Wold-Chamberlain Field 116; *see also* Minneapolis-Saint Paul International Airport
Women Accepted for Volunteer Emergency Service 14
Woods, Estella 20
world oil glut 88
World Trade Center 146
World War II 10, 14–15, 19, 37, 51, 55–56, 62–63, 79, 93, 98, 118, 127, 160, 163
Wright Engine Division, Curtiss-Wright 94

XF-11 reconnaissance plane 84–87

Yale University 62
Yearman, Keith 157, 159